FIELDING'S
NEW YORK
AGENDA

The Buzz About Fielding

Fielding Worldwide

"The new Fielding guidebook style mirrors the style of the company's new publisher: irreverent, urbane, adventuresome and in search of the unique travel experience."

—San Diego Union Tribune

"Individualistic, entertaining, comprehensive."

—Consumers Digest

"Guidebooks with attitude."

—Dallas Morning News

"Full of author's tips and asides, the books seem more personal and more credible than many similarly encyclopedic tomes."

—Los Angeles Times

"At Fielding Worldwide, adventurous might well be the order of the day."

—Des Moines Register

"Biting travel guides give readers a fresh look."

—Houston Chronicle

"For over 30 years Fielding guides have been the standard of modern travel books."

—Observer Times

Fielding's Las Vegas Agenda

"A concise but detailed look at the capital of glitter and gambling."

—Atlanta Journal Constitution

Fielding's Los Angeles Agenda

"…contains much more than the standard travel guide. The lists of theatres, sports arenas and attractions are worth the book's price by itself."

—Baton Rouge Advocate

Fielding's New York Agenda

"Loaded with advice…puts the whole of the Big Apple in hand."

—Bon Appetit

Fielding's Guide to Worldwide Cruises

"One of the year's ten best books."

—Gourmet Magazine

"Perhaps the best single source for unbiased cruise information."

—The New York Times

"To be all things to all people is impossible, but this book pretty well does it."

—The New York Daily News

"You can trust them [Fielding] to tell the truth. It's fun—and very informative."

—New Orleans Times-Picayune

"The Bible. If scarcity is any indication of quality, then this book is superb."

—St. Petersburg Florida Times

Cruise Insider

"One of the best, most compact, yet interesting books about cruising today is the fact-filled Cruise Insider."

—John Clayton's Travel With a Difference

Fielding's The World's Most Dangerous Places

"Rarely does a travel guide turn out to be as irresistible as a John Grisham novel. But The World's Most Dangerous Places, a 1000-page tome for the truly adventurous traveler, manages to do just that."

—Arkansas Democrat-Gazette

"A travel guide that could be a real lifesaver. Practical tips for those seeking the road less traveled."

—Time Magazine

"The greatest derring do of this year's memoirs."

—Publishers Weekly

"Reads like a first-run adventure movie."

—Travel Books Worldwide

Fielding Titles

Fielding's Alaska Cruises and the Inside Passage
Fielding's America West
Fielding's Asia's Top Dive Sites
Fielding's Australia
Fielding's Bahamas
Fielding's Baja California
Fielding's Bermuda
Fielding's Best and Worst — The surprising results of the Plog Survey
Fielding's Birding Indonesia
Fielding's Borneo
Fielding's Budget Europe
Fielding's Caribbean
Fielding's Caribbean Cruises
Fielding's Caribbean on a Budget
Fielding's Diving Australia
Fielding's Diving Indonesia
Fielding's Eastern Caribbean
Fielding's England including Ireland, Scotland & Wales
Fielding's Europe
Fielding's Europe 50th Anniversary
Fielding's European Cruises
Fielding's Far East
Fielding's France
Fielding's France: Loire Valley, Burgundy & the Best of French Culture
Fielding's France: Normandy & Brittany
Fielding's France: Provence and the Mediterranean
Fielding's Freewheelin' USA
Fielding's Hawaii
Fielding's Hot Spots: Travel in Harm's Way
Fielding's Indiana Jones Adventure and Survival Guide™
Fielding's Italy
Fielding's Kenya's Best Hotels, Lodges and Homestays
Fielding's Las Vegas Agenda
Fielding's London Agenda
Fielding's Los Angeles Agenda
Fielding's Mexico
Fielding's New Orleans Agenda
Fielding's New York Agenda
Fielding's New Zealand
Fielding's Paradors, Pousadas and Charming Villages of Spain and Portugal
Fielding's Paris Agenda
Fielding's Portugal
Fielding's Rome Agenda
Fielding's San Diego Agenda
Fielding's Southeast Asia
Fielding's Southern California Theme Parks
Fielding's Southern Vietnam on Two Wheels
Fielding's Spain
Fielding's Surfing Australia
Fielding's Surfing Indonesia
Fielding's Sydney Agenda
Fielding's Thailand, Cambodia, Laos and Myanmar
Fielding's Travel Tools™
Fielding's Vietnam, including Cambodia and Laos
Fielding's Walt Disney World and Orlando Area Theme Parks
Fielding's Western Caribbean
Fielding's The World's Most Dangerous Places™
Fielding's Worldwide Cruises

FIELDING'S
NEW YORK
AGENDA

Nan Lyons

Fielding Worldwide, Inc.
308 South Catalina Avenue
Redondo Beach, California 90277 U.S.A.

Fielding's New York Agenda
Published by Fielding Worldwide, Inc.
Text Copyright ©1997 FWI
Maps, Icons & Illustrations Copyright ©1997 FWI
Photo Copyrights ©1997 to Individual Photographers

FIELDING WORLDWIDE INC.

PUBLISHER AND CEO	Robert Young Pelton
GENERAL MANAGER	John Guillebeaux
MARKETING DIRECTOR	Paul T. Snapp
OPERATIONS DIRECTOR	George Posanke
ELEC. PUBLISHING DIRECTOR	Larry E. Hart
PUBLIC RELATIONS DIRECTOR	Beverly Riess
ACCOUNT SERVICES MANAGER	Cindy Henrichon
PROJECT MANAGER	Chris Snyder
MANAGING EDITOR	Amanda K. Knoles

PRODUCTION

Martin Mancha   Ramses Reynoso
Craig South

COVER DESIGNED BY	Digital Artists, Inc.
COVER PHOTOGRAPHERS	Richard Elliot, Hiroyuko Matsumoto, Jon Ortner, Joseph Pobereskin (all Tony Stone Images)
INSIDE PHOTOS	Blackstar, Corel Photos, Jim Glab, New York Convention Visitors Bureau, New York State Division of Tourism, Westlight
CARTOONS	ClickART T/Maker, The New Yorker

Inquiries should be addressed to: Fielding Worldwide, Inc., 308 South Catalina Ave., Redondo Beach, California 90277 U.S.A., ☎ *(310) 372-4474*, Facsimile *(310) 376-8064*, 8:30 a.m.–5:30 p.m. Pacific Standard Time.
Website: http://www.fieldingtravel.com
e-mail: fielding@fieldingtravel.com

ISBN 1-56952-124-7

Printed in the United States of America

Letter from the Publisher

In 1946, Temple Fielding began the first of what would be a remarkable new series of well-written, highly personalized guidebooks for independent travelers. Temple's opinionated, witty, and oft-imitated books have now guided travelers for almost a half-century. More important to some was Fielding's humorous and direct method of steering travelers away from the dull and the insipid. Today, Fielding Travel Guides are still written by experienced travelers for experienced travelers. Our authors carry on Fielding's reputation for creating travel experiences that deliver insight with a sense of discovery and style.

Designed to save travelers time and money, Fielding's *New York Agenda* cuts to the chase, telling readers all they need to know to "do" the town. Whether you have a day or a week in New York, author Nan Lyons will take you straight to all the right places and off the beaten path.

The concept of independent travel has never been bigger. Our policy of *brutal honesty* and a highly personal point of view has never changed; it just seems the travel world has caught up with us.

Enjoy your New York adventure with Nan Lyons and Fielding.

RYP

Robert Young Pelton
Publisher and CEO
Fielding Worldwide, Inc.

ABOUT THE AUTHOR

Nan Lyons is best known as one of the authors, in collaboration with her late husband, Ivan, of the best-selling novel turned movie, *Someone Is Killing the Great Chefs of Europe*, and for travel articles in magazines such as *Bon Appetit*, *Travel & Leisure*, and *Food & Wine*.

Their nonfiction output includes *Imperial Hotel, A Century of Elegance at Tokyo's Imperial Hotel* and several guides to New York City. Nan Lyons is also the author of *Fielding's New York Agenda*, *Fielding's London Agenda*, *Fielding's New Orleans Agenda*, *Fielding's Paris Agenda*, and *Fielding's Sydney Agenda*.

ACKNOWLEDGEMENTS

For service above and beyond, I want to thank Avraham In-lender, Barbara Settanni, and most especially Janet Rodgers, and Tracy and Gary Fullup for being "godparents" who came through not only with tea and sympathy, but with shoeleather and love.

— Nan Lyons

A Word from the Author

The Agenda Series was designed to put the guide back into travel guides. Unlike other guides that are written by committee, I take full responsibility for the personal, candid and sometimes controversial opinions I have expressed in order to provide my readers with the quintessential New York experience.

Today, with travelers having just a few short days to spend on a trip, the only guide that is really useful is one that can distill the hundreds of choices that are available in New York into the very essence of the City.

If old friends were coming to town everything I would tell them is in this guide. Time is as valuable as money, and you need to know what you can afford to miss and what should be at the top of your agenda. My goal is to be selective, not provide you with endless details and historical minutia. The definition of the word "Agenda" is a list of business to be covered and that is my intention as well.

By exploring New York neighborhoods and listing a shopping and restaurant agenda for each, I have made it possible to construct a relaxed agenda for an afternoon or evening without having to leave the area. I also have suggested one, two, and three day agendas that cover most of what makes New York the most exciting, unique city in the world (I told you I was opinionated).

I am looking forward to putting my years of travel writing and globe-trotting at your disposal, so that at the end of your stay in New York, you'll leave knowing that you have taken away the very best it has to offer.

— **Nan Lyons**

Stars in the Agenda Guide's Eyes

Just a few words to fully explain the twinkle in our Agenda stars. Since this guide is geared to bring you only the very best a city has to offer, one might question why an additional rating system is necessary. The reason is that even with the "best" there is always finer tuning that might be done. However, this is in no way a competition between us and that adorably, chubby tire guy. So the agenda of the Agenda Stars is really to tell you how to go from best to superb.

★ ★ ★	**Superb**
★ ★	**Excellent**
★	**One of the Best**

The "Best Bite" restaurant choices have not been rated since they are just "drop-in" places as you visit the different neighborhoods of New York. If they're listed in "Best Bites" then of course they're the best.

I value your time too highly to cover every "down and dirty" choice that exists, and then bother to rate it. If it's in the guide, you can bet it has "star power."

— **Nan Lyons**

AGENDA HERE TODAY—GONE TOMORROW

In the words of Stephen Sondheim "Not a Day Goes By" without a restaurant closing, a new hotel opening, a store changing its address, or all of the above. Trying to keep up with the changes in New York is harder than diapering quadruplets. It's enough to drive any self-respecting travel writer to the nearest mental facility. And so gentle reader, have patience, if there were no changes in New York we'd all still be speaking Dutch.

TABLE OF CONTENTS

LIST OF MAPS

WHAT IS NEW YORK?

The magical view from the Statue of Liberty spans the Verrazano Bridge to the towers of Manhattan.

Visiting New York is like unpacking your first computer, you find yourself surrounded by lots of expensive pieces that don't seem to fit together. The parts make no sense. Nothing works unless it's hooked up to something else. That, in a nutshell, is New York.

This book is a user's manual to a complex piece of machinery (affectionately called the Big Apple) that generates more static electricity, has less memory, doesn't even try to be user-friendly, and is higher priced than any other place in the country. New York City can get away with it because there is nothing comparable.

The key to understanding New York is to first understand New Yorkers. The typical New Yorker is either Chinese, Jewish, Black, Italian, Dutch, Irish, Protestant, German or Ukrainian. In other words, like the unicorn, there is no such creature.

Nothing about New Yorkers is typical except their "attitude." New York Attitude, which hangs over the city like the moons of Jupiter during a solar eclipse, is based upon the concept of cash and carry. This is a city that moves to the beat of "time is money." In NYC, *everything* is money. It even costs money to stand still. Do you believe $16–$20 per hour to park your car in midtown?

Being a New Yorker is something that New Yorkers do better than anyone else. Whatever you want to say about them, they do their homework. It doesn't matter how little they earn or how much they spend: everyone is an expert. They know where to get the greatest hot dog in town, find the cheapest florist, which movie theater has the best sound system, and what bar is "hot."

It's hard being a New Yorker. On a daily basis, the city streets are littered with far more than old gum wrappers. After the exodus of the middle class to the outer boroughs and the suburbs, those remaining became unwitting characters in a 24-hour soap opera, "The Rich and the Homeless."

The truth is that a city with all the glitz of New York can't help casting a few shadows. Despite a social welfare program that's one of the country's most aggressive, the homeless are a sad fact of life today, an economic fallout you come upon everywhere from Paris or Rio to Hong Kong. Somehow New York is held accountable for problems no one else has yet solved.

But the quality of life that made New Yorkers shake their heads in despair just a few short years ago has given way to a new dedication by the Mayor's office to bring the city back to a kinder, gentler place. Even the "Chicken Littles" of the 80s are impressed by the drop in crime and the improvement in city hygiene. Once again the New York Phoenix has risen from its ashes.

The Bad News About New York

It's noisy.
It's expensive.
People are rude.
The weather is awful.
The streets are filthy.
The traffic is impossible.
It's not safe in the park at night.
Try to find a cab when you need one.

"So what else is new?" People have been saying those things for years and New York is still *the most visited city in the world*. I've used a "take no prisoners" approach that sidesteps the claptrap, the usual guidebook filler, the astroturf that tries to be all things to all travelers. I've sifted through the thousands of things that compete for your attention and your wallet to find those I consider the quintessential New York experience.

Street Smarts

New York City is comprised of five boroughs (independently governed local districts under the umbrella of the city government). The boroughs are Manhattan, the Bronx, Brooklyn, Queens, and Staten Island.

The streets are east/west horizontally, the avenues are north/south vertically. Most streets and avenues are numbered. The higher the number of the street, the further north. The higher the number of the avenue, the further west. All you have to do is "*think grid*."

Fifth Avenue divides midtown into east and west. Numbered Manhattan street addresses always include a designation for east or west. (There is a 25 *East* 57th Street and a 25 *West* 57th Street.)

While you'll hear people refer constantly to east and west, you won't hear many New Yorkers use north and south as reference points. Instead, they'll say "uptown" for north and "downtown" for south.

FYI: *Twenty blocks equal one mile.*

Drawing by Levin ©1993, The New Yorker Magazine, Inc.

AGENDA
PRIORITIES

The gilded statue of Prometheus has floated above Rockefeller Center's ice rink/cafe since the '30s.

No matter how sophisticated a traveler you are, it's easy to become overwhelmed by the abundance of "must-see" activities in New York. Part of the problem is that the city keeps changing. There's always something new to do. Just when you think you've covered all the bases, they go and slip in SoHo. Then, watch out! Here comes NoHo!

Make an agenda by selecting your most important priorities and noting the locations. Then read about the neighborhoods in which they're located. See if there are other things of interest to you nearby and estimate how much time you want to spend at each. The goal is to group priorities by neighborhood in order to avoid zig-zagging your way back and forth across the city.

A visit to New York is like being invited to an extravagant banquet prepared by the world's greatest chef. You pick up a plate and head eagerly for the buffet table. The question is, how to sample all those goodies without having to make a second trip? The answer is simple. You can't.

But that doesn't mean you have to go away hungry, either. It may take a turn or two around the table before you know what you really want. My suggestion is to be selective: AKA listening to me.

The Story Is In The Skyline

You don't rate your financial portfolio on the performance of a single stock. Similarly, you need to see New York in its proper perspective. That means seeing the skyline for all it's worth? ASAP. My favorite sites for viewing are:

Looking Up From

1. The deck of the Staten Island Ferry.
2. The promenade in Brooklyn Heights.
3. A window table at The River Cafe.

Looking Down From

4. Observation Deck atop the World Trade Center.
5. Observation Deck atop the Empire State Building.
6. A window table at Windows on the World.

The Top Three Sights

An elevator inside the Statue of Liberty carries visitors halfway up, then 168 steps lead to the remarkable view from her crown.

Statue of Liberty, The

Lower Manhattan • From Battery Park, take the Circle Line Statue of Liberty ferry leaving hourly between 9:30 a.m. and 3:30 p.m. $7 round trip; $5 children. (☎ 363-3200)

Every bit as corny as Kansas in August and as stirring as Kate Smith singing "God Bless America." If you had to symbolize the entire United States as well as New York, it would have to be Eiffel's other tower. There's a reason they didn't put Lady Liberty in Cleveland:

New York was the official port of entry through which millions of immigrants came seeking personal freedom. Restored for its centennial in 1986, the structure engineered by Gustave Eiffel and designed by sculptor Frederic Bartholdi makes for a once-in-a-lifetime experience. If you can, climb the steps to the crown for a quintessential view of New York's skyline.

The Empire State Building is an awe-inspiring sight.

Empire State Building, The

34th Street and Fifth Avenue. ☎ 736-3100. Open 9:30 a.m. to Midnight (last ticket sold 11:30 p.m.). Admission $4.50, children $2.25. But before you go in, stand across the street and look up.

For true New Yorkers this will always be the world's tallest building, at least in spirit. The World Trade Center's twin towers have all the warmth of a popsicle, and who cares about the Sears Tower in Chicago, anyway? The Empire State Building is a mere 204 ft. shorter than the Sears thing and a barely noticeable 127 ft. less than those boring Siamese monoliths. It's been a primary focal point of the New York skyline since it was completed in 1931. There's an open platform on the 86th floor (50 mile view on a clear day) and a closed observatory on the 102nd (up to 80-mile visibility). Open until midnight, the Empire State Building gives heightened meaning to the term "night cap."

If that's not enough of a thrill, then try the New York Skyride, the newest way to get breathtaking views of the city without leaving the ground. It's a motion-simulation that soars over the skyline, "crashes" into Wall Street and hurtles along with Coney Island's "Cyclone." It's located on the second floor.

Rockefeller Center

49th to 51st Streets and Fifth Avenue. You can wander through the public spaces on your own or take tours of both the General Electric Building and Radio City Music Hall. GE Tours, National Broadcasting Company, Monday thru Saturday, 9:30 a.m.–4:30 p.m., ☎ 664-7174. Radio City Music Hall tours, when not in use, Mon. thru Sun.
Admission $7.50, children $3.50 (☎ 632-4041).

Okay. We all know that the name "Rockefeller" is magical enough to make oysters and primitive art respectable. But give credit to "the

NEW YORK CITY

NEW YORK'S BEST VIEWS

The skyscrapers of Manhattan offer stunning panoramas of the bustling city and its surrounding waterways.

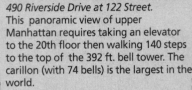

Riverside Church

490 Riverside Drive at 122 Street.
This panoramic view of upper Manhattan requires taking an elevator to the 20th floor then walking 140 steps to the top of the 392 ft. bell tower. The carillon (with 74 bells) is the largest in the world.

Empire State Building

350 Fifth Avenue.
Observation decks on the 86th floor offer thrilling views of the city. On a clear day you can see more than 80 miles.

World Trade Center

Chambers and Rector Streets.
An express elevator at Two World Trade Center zooms visitors to the 107th floor in 58 seconds for spectacular views from the observation deck or rooftop promenade. Windows on the World on the 107th floor at One World Trade Center may be the closest you get to dining in the clouds.

Staten Island Ferry/Statue of Liberty

Whitehall Street, South Ferry
At 50 cents, the ferry is still the best bargain in New York with incredible views of the harbor, Statue of Liberty, Ellis Island and Lower Manhattan. Lady Liberty is 305 ft. high. Visitors can climb 354 steps for the view from her crown.

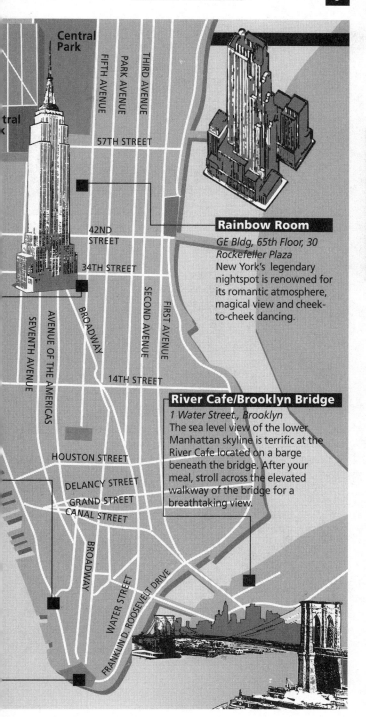

Central Park

FIFTH AVENUE

PARK AVENUE

THIRD AVENUE

57TH STREET

42ND STREET

34TH STREET

SECOND AVENUE

FIRST AVENUE

BROADWAY

AVENUE OF THE AMERICAS

SEVENTH AVENUE

14TH STREET

HOUSTON STREET

DELANCY STREET

GRAND STREET

CANAL STREET

BROADWAY

WATER STREET

FRANKLIN D. ROOSEVELT DRIVE

Rainbow Room

GE Bldg, 65th Floor, 30 Rockefeller Plaza
New York's legendary nightspot is renowned for its romantic atmosphere, magical view and cheek-to-cheek dancing.

River Cafe/Brooklyn Bridge

1 Water Street., Brooklyn
The sea level view of the lower Manhattan skyline is terrific at the River Cafe located on a barge beneath the bridge. After your meal, stroll across the elevated walkway of the bridge for a breathtaking view.

AGENDA PRIORITIES

Broadway at W. 44th Street is a theatergoer's paradise.

Postcard images spring to life at Rockefeller Center.

SoHo's unique stores are worth the trek.

The Chrysler building is an Art Deco classic.

Crowds line up early for Letterman show tapings.

Center" for the statue of Atlas, the statue of Prometheus above which
the nation's most famous Christmas tree is placed, Radio City Music
Hall, the G.E. Building, the Rainbow Room, the Channel Gardens,
and the skating rink. The ultimate city-within-a-city, the birthplace of
(nobody's perfect) THE MALL, Rockefeller Center is a unique urban
spectacle that has never lost its 20/20 vision since it opened in 1940.

Drawing by Richter; ©1994, The New Yorker Magazine, Inc.

The 21 Next Best

An Irreverent, but Alphabetical,
List of the Runners-Up

Brooklyn Bridge, The

A work of kinetic art that masquerades as a bridge. It was, for 20
years, the world's longest suspension bridge, a darkly beautiful Gothic
stone and steel symbol that opened the era of giant skyscrapers. It was
finished in 1883 at a cost of $25 million and 20 lives. Kenneth Clark,
the British historian, said, "All modern New York, heroic New York,
started with the Brooklyn Bridge." If the weather is good and your
shoes are comfortable, head down to City Hall and take a taxi across
the bridge to Cadman Plaza East near Prospect Street in Brooklyn.
Then walk back to Manhattan, as dazzling a mixed media event as
you're likely to find what with the water below, cars whizzing by, and
the spectacle of the huge overhead cables criss-crossing the sky.

Chinatown

There is something uniquely New York about Chinatown despite
everything the locals have done to retain their "Chineseness." The
streets are impossible to navigate, the shops daunting to enter, the
restaurants overwhelming in number. You can undoubtedly find
some of New York's best food down here if you know where you're

going and what you're ordering. Mulberry, Mott and Pell are the major streets. (See "Neighborhoods.")

Chrysler Building, The

405 Lexington Avenue, between 42nd and 43rd Streets.

An Art Deco masterpiece, its distinctive spire has been a shot of glitz in the skyline since 1930. For one brief shining moment, until completion of the Empire State, it was the tallest building in the world. Many consider it the female counterpart to the Empire State Building. A combination of geometric patterns, mirror-like stainless steel, gargoyles and auto icons (after all, it was built by Walter Chrysler) makes it a dazzling and unforgettable piece of New York. Be sure to go inside and see the richly-veined African marble lobby.

East Village

This is the perfect time to visit the most neurotic zip code in the book. The area has gone through the shock waves from its growing pains and has established itself as a force to be reckoned with—but you'd better get there before everyone becomes gentrified and discovers catalog shopping and shirts with alligators. (See "Neighborhoods.")

Fifth Avenue

Because it's there. (See "Neighborhoods.")

Stanford White's Washington Square Arch has been a Greenwich Village landmark since 1892.

Greenwich Village

Once upon a time, a hotbed for ideas. A magical kingdom where everyone had visions and translated them into books and paintings and plays. It can still be exhilarating to return to the scene of the shrine—if you avoid the weekend and the thundering hordes of pragmatic, humorless adolescents. (See "Neighborhoods.")

Guggenheim Museum

10071 Fifth Avenue (88-89th Streets), ☎ 423-3500. Wed. through Sun., 10 a.m.–6 p.m.; Fri.–Sat., 8 a.m.–10 p.m.; closed Thurs. Admission $8, children free.

The city's only Frank Lloyd Wright building is a glorious incongruity on sedate Fifth Avenue. The truth is, it would be incongruous anywhere on this planet. A crafty swirl of modernism, the question still is whether this form follows function. Does the building compete with the art for your attention? Or does the design of the building help you to better appreciate the art? "The Guggie" completed a zillion dollar renovation in '92, to add a ten story tower to the existing space, nearly doubling it.

Lincoln Center

Broadway and 65th Street.
Between you, me and Avery Fisher Hall, I don't consider this a sight to see, just a place to be. Why in the world would anyone go to Lincoln Center unless they had tickets to a performance or were headed for a stroll on the Upper West Side? I am not talking great architecture, splendid plazas or lovely cafes. But there are apparently enough people interested in early morning lobbies and empty theaters to support a tour program (☎ 875-5400) that charges an admission, which would be better spent toward the price of a ticket to the Metropolitan Opera House, the New York State Theater, Avery Fisher Hall, or the Vivian Beaumont Theater.

Lower East Side

Save this one for Sunday morning when it's jammed with bargain hunters. (Most stores close on Saturday anyway for the Jewish Sabbath.) The press of humanity sometimes offers a thrilling reminder of a vibrant street life long gone. (See "Neighborhoods.")

Madison Avenue

Once known primarily as the business address of the man in the grey flannel suit, upper Madison has become so continental, you don't expect to hear English spoken. (See "Neighborhoods.")

Metropolitan Museum of Art, The

Fifth Avenue and 82nd Street. ☎ *535-7710, Tues. through Thurs. 9:30 a.m.–5:15 p.m.; Fri. & Sat., 9:30 a.m.–8:45 p.m.; Sun. 9:30 a.m.–5:15 p.m. Closed Mon. Suggested admission, 12 & under free.*
Still the champ, the Met is bigger and better than ever. Its four block sprawling facade is a major sight in itself. On weekends, the area is transformed into the Big Apple version of a medieval square: there are musicians, jugglers and mimes at the foot of the massive staircase that leads up to the entrance and The Great Hall, one of the city's few interior landmarked spaces. The largest art museum in the Western Hemisphere, the Met houses more than paintings—it revives entire environments: the Temple of Dendur is one of the most stirring sights. But there's also the Great Armor Hall with mounted knights, a labyrinth of reconstructed Egyptian tombs, the astonishing Rockefeller collection of primitive art, and on and on and on.

Museum of Modern Art, The

11 West 53rd Street. ☎ *708-9480, Sat. through Tues. 11 a.m.–6 p.m.; Thurs. & Fri. 12-8:30 p.m. Closed Wed. Admission $8, children free.*
MOMA is one of the great city experiences. Its collection of modern art, daily film programs, and sculpture garden have been discussed as heatedly as back-fence gossip. While sometimes suspiciously less daring than its original collection, MOMA has courageously embraced industrial objects and even kitchenware as well as Dali, Degas and Duchamp. Don't make the mistake of thinking once you've seen one

museum, you've seen them all. MOMA and the Met are as different
as MGM and 20th Century Fox.

*The Museum of Modern Art (MOMA) is one of the great New York
experiences. Its collection of modern art, daily films and sculpture
garden shouldn't be missed.*

New York Stock Exchange

> *20 Broad Street (off Wall Street).* ☎ *656-5168. Third floor visitors gal-
> lery, 9:30 a.m.–4 p.m., Mon. through Fri. There are exhibits and a short
> film for the Gordon Gekko in all of us.*
>
> At last! A chance to visit your money. Still going strong despite an
> occasional "correction," some arrests, and a mean-spirited movie.
> The Exchange was founded in 1792 by 24 brokers who no longer
> wished to conduct business on street corners and in coffeehouses. As
> a vivid view of our system at work, it's a sight not to be missed.

Park Avenue

> Or, Shakespeare Was Wrong. What's in a name is what Park Avenue
> is all about. Granted, midtown Park has some real goodies, but Park
> above 60th Street isn't worth more than a moment of your time to see
> the big old buildings filled with big old money. (See "Neighbor-
> hoods.")

SoHo

> Nowadays, no more daring than a Julie Andrews movie, SoHo is
> SoWholesome and user-friendly that even accountants can have a
> good time among the loft dwellers. (See "Neighborhoods.")

South Street Seaport

> Proof positive that New Yorkers are no less susceptible to being
> malled to death if it's done with style. One of the city's most beautiful
> locations. (See Neighborhoods)

Staten Island Ferry

> ☎ *(718) 727-2508.*
>
> Ocean-going kitsch that's not to be missed. It's the best five mile, 25-
> minute, 50-cent ride (round trip) in the world. Although it is
> rumored that people actually live on Staten Island, all you have to do
> is turn around and come right back to Manhattan, surrendering your
> gripes about the city to the majestic skyline in front of you. The ferry

is located at the tip of Battery Park and runs every half hour between
6 a.m.–11:30 p.m., every hour other times.

Times Square

No self-respecting visitor should miss this bit of Americana, especially
now that it has been rescued from its tawdry past. Once the personi-
fication of urban blight, it has turned yet again, into a neon butterfly.
The historic old theatres that line the blocks between 6th and 8th avenues are being restored at a cost of over $18 million, to their former
glory, and even Disney is wishing upon all the new stars that are moving to the area. To date there is a mega huge Virgin Atlantic Mega-
store, Planet Hollywood, the sports world's The Official All Star Cafe,
and last but not least, Hansons, Times Square's very own Micro-
Brewery. Disney has decided to open one of its stores as well as participate in the square's renovations. Mickey's going to be on Broadway! Go at night when the signs are all lit up, hopefully on your way
to the theater. Stand on *42nd Street and Broadway* and look uptown.
That's where they stand to take the picture postcard views. Since the
transformation is still in progress, hold onto your purse or wallet
while you're looking. Things may have changed for the better but
New York is still New York.

Trump Tower

Fifth Avenue, between 56th and 57th Streets.
New York's most elegant monument to the city's nouveau riche. A
terraced glass tower that's no place like home except if the name on
your bankbook is Andrew Lloyd Webber. A truly luxurious residen-
tial/office building, Trump's civic triumph is in offering public spaces
that are worth every penny he spent on them. The atrium is a fantasy
of polished pink marble, gleaming brass, steep waterfalls and shops
overflowing with goodies for those terminally afflicted with conspicu-
ous consumption.

United Nations

United Nations Plaza, 42nd to 48th Streets and First Avenue. ☎ *963-
7713.*
*One hour tours are given daily every half-hour, Monday through Sunday,
from 9:15 a.m.–4:15 p.m. Admission $7, children $3.50. Children under
five are not permitted on the tour.*
There is a melancholy today about the UN: it has become more news-
worthy as a locale for demonstrations than as a battlefield for human
rights. Like the League of Nations, and the Pillsbury Bake-Off, it
somehow seemed more important at the time. Designed by an international team of architects, most notably Le Corbusier and Oscar
Niemeyer, the UN complex is purposely situated counter to the grid
pattern of New York's streets. It is very much international territory,
a forum for delegates from over 150 countries. (See "Neighborhoods.")

From the open rooftop promenade on the 110th floor of the World Trade Center, visitors get a spectacular view of the city.

World Trade Center

> *No. 2 World Trade Center Observation Deck.* ☎ *435-4170. Daily from 9:30 a.m. to 9:30 p.m.*
> Very big. The twin towers look like a huge number eleven. 110 floors. 1200 offices. 50,000 people working. 80,000 visitors daily. You don't come here for the view of the World Trade Center, but the view from it. Absolutely not to be missed. (See "Neighborhoods.")

AGENDA PRIORITIES

HOTELS

The First Entry In Your New York Agenda

The legendary Plaza Hotel has starred in more New York movies than Woody Allen. Donald Trump has restored it to all its glory.

Your Hotel

I am not, and never have been a member of the "who cares where you stay—how much time do you spend in your room anyway?" club. If some of you, like me, are official collectors of hotels as treasured travel memorabilia, then that's one of the reasons I have avoided including some obvious members of the chain gangs—despite the security blankets with which they make their beds—a truly New Yorkish hotel is at least as quintessential a city experience as being mugged.

Each of the hotels in this section has been stayed in, or at least visited and rooms inspected (with the exception of the Manhattan East properties where I visited two of the nine sites). I decided not to include a number of hotels for a variety of maddeningly idiosyncratic reasons ranging from too damn uppity (the otherwise brilliant Carlisle seems caught in a Kennedy-Camelot time-warp), too intense (the artsy Chelsea Hotel), too Leona for my taste (the Park Lane), too groupish (the well-located St. Moritz), too 42nd Street (Grand Hyatt—it's right atop Grand Central Station, for heaven's sake), and on and on. Simply, there are too many great hotels in New York to start out making compromises.

How to Select a Hotel

Our choices are based upon three golden rules:

1. When it's time to rest my weary bones, I think my weary bones deserve the best my money can buy.

2. Location, location, location. Since the easiest way to get around the city is on foot, stop and think about the pleasures of being able to walk back to your hotel after a business meeting. It's a lot simpler than dealing with traffic. Try not to stay on the Upper West Side if you plan to go to Wall Street on a daily basis. But no matter where you are, check out transport services, if any, offered by the hotel. (There are often complimentary limos to get you to that first appointment on time.)

3. The least expensive room in the best hotel is usually better than the most expensive room in a moderate hotel. A good hotel buys you a good concierge, sophisticated business systems, and many extra services and facilities that may even wind up saving you money.

HOTELS

AGENDA TIP

Assuming you've made the perfect choice, you should still take a peek at some other hotels when you're in town. I usually hotel hop for drinks or breakfast. Who knows: The next time you plan a trip, your first choice may be booked solid.

How to Make a Reservation

First, unless your travel agent can do better than the listed or "rack" rate, get yourself another travel agent. Or make calls yourself and ask about special deals and weekend or airline-sponsored packages. It's often possible to get a corporate rate just by asking for it. Many hotels cut rates by half on the weekend to fill rooms vacated by captains of industry. If you're attending a conference, there may be a discount even if you make your own reservation. And sometimes, you can get a special rate just by a little discreet bargaining.

If all else fails, you may want to try a hotel consolidator. You'll have to forgo your wish list but you can sometimes get an astonishing bargain: **Quick Book** (☎ *(800) 789-9887)*; **Express Reservations** (☎ *(800) 356-1123)*; **Room Exchange** (☎ *(800) 846-7000)*.

AGENDA TIP

Do not use the hotel's 800 number. Call direct.

The last thing you want to do is reach some telemarketing nerd in North Dakota who wouldn't know his arm from his armoire. The area code for Manhattan is 212. Add to the numbers in listings.

If you have preferences about type of bed, high floor vs. low floor, front views (noisy) or back (quiet), specific views, not wanting to be near elevators or service areas, whatever—let them know when making your reservation.

If you ask at this time, it's a request. If you wait until after you've arrived, it's a complaint. And why start off by complaining if you don't have to?

Try to get your requests in writing, although that doesn't mean they've been guaranteed. Then call the front desk a couple of days before you arrive. Ask them to check your reservation for your special requests.

Be sure you've guaranteed your time of arrival. No hotel is obliged to hold a reservation past the appointed hour. Therefore, you'll have to book with a credit card or a deposit. That's the only way you can rest assured.

That is, if you can forget about hotel service charges, parking fees, and a whopping 13.25% plus $2 per day room tax, a NY sales tax which is automatically added no matter what rate you've been quoted.

Call or fax the concierge as soon as you know which restaurants, shows, or exhibits you want to visit. Explain clearly that you will express your gratitude upon *arrival*. Then call back to make certain it's all been done or whether you need some alternates. The idea is to take care of this on home time, reserving precious travel time for travel.

The Top Agenda Hotel Choices

The Grand Hotel Experience	
The Four Seasons	$490–$630
The Waldorf Astoria	$290–$600
The Pierre	$375–$595
The New York Palace	$275–$450
The Plaza	$235–$650
The St. Regis	$425–$650
Essex House	$310–$500

The "Baby" Grands	
Hotel Plaza Athenee	$285–$590
Ritz Carlton	$305–$600
Hotel Elysee	$225–$825
The Mark	$325–$500
The Westbury	$285–$450
The Peninsula	$340–$700
SoHo Grand Hotel	$199–$949

The Eccentrics

The Algonquin	$245–$425
Morgans	$220–$475
The Royalton	$285–$400
The Wales	$165–$225
The Roger Smith	$195–$225

The Budget Best

The Gorham	$175–$195
The Franklin	$135–$145
Hotel Olcott	$95–$115
The Paramount	$180–$380
The Larchmont	$70–$90!!!
The Wyndham	$130–$210

The Suite Hotels

The Lowell	$295–$595
The Beverly	$149–$199
Manhattan East Suite Hotels	$119–$330

Bed and Breakfast

City Lights Bed & Breakfast Ltd.	$75–$350
New World Bed & Breakfast	$60–$200
Urban Ventures	$70–$320

Youth Hostel

Hostelling International, N.Y.	$22–$25

Algonquin, The   **$245–$425**   ★★

59 West 44th Street (Fifth & Sixth); 10036; ☎ *840-6800; FAX: 944-1449.*

The Algonquin is the best anachronism in town. It's a triumph of the human spirit that this hotel has survived in a city that too often thrives on dollars rather than sense. If you've ever marched to a different drummer, the drummer probably stayed at the Algonquin.

We all know about the Round Table, the witty darlings everyone loved in an age naive enough to worship literate people rather than beautiful ones, and that *The New Yorker* magazine was born there. The Algonquin is as literate as ever. Stepping into the lobby puts you center stage in something terribly British written by T.S. Eliot or Terrence Rattigan. The gracefully aging lobby armchairs are usually filled with actors and writers. There are even brass bells on each table to summon the butler. Oops: the waiter.

The rooms look as though they belong in a country inn rather than a few steps away from the Broadway theater. A few are a tight squeeze and can either be characterized as cozy or claustrophobic, depending on your commitment to the hotel. There are theatrical posters and English hunt prints everywhere. Liberty of London fabrics and brass beds complete the picture. 142 rooms. Credit cards: All major.

Hotel Beverly $149–$179   ★

125 E 50th Street (Lexington Avenue); 10022; ☎ *753-2700; FAX: 753-2700.*

The Beverly is one of the best buys in town. This small family-run hotel is right opposite the Waldorf so you can share its great East Side location without having to pawn Aunt Tillie's tiara. Huge junior and one-bedroom suites all have fully-equipped kitchenettes. How huge? You can bring the kids, and even Aunt Tillie. Accommodations here are bright, newly decorated, with armoires, and antique touches around the room. Especially welcome are the big sunny terraces in a few.

The lobby is as quiet as the public library but much prettier; a Chesterfield sofa here, a crystal chandelier there. Another bonus is a very savvy concierge who will try to perform small miracles on request. One guest needed a bandage for his horse's leg. Coming right up! 175 rooms, 25 suites. Credit cards: All major.

Hotel Elysee $225–$825   ★★★

60 East 54th Street (Madison & Park); 10022; ☎ *753-1066; FAX: 980-9278.*

This luxuriously snug little hotel in the east fifties is a place people tend to return to because of its dedication to charm, elegance and English country manor comfort. There's even a library to ease weary travelers' literary withdrawal. The rooms are wall to wall plush with real and semi-real antiques tossed about. The warm glow of peach is everywhere, except in the "drop dead" bathrooms that are carved from grey marble. The aroma of Caswell-Massey and money fills the air. To add even more jewels to the setting, continental breakfast, tea in the afternoon, and wine and cheese in the P.M. are included in the room rate.

The sumptuous Library is just the place to toast all your Madison Avenue shopping conquests at the end of the day.

Since 1926, the Elysee's highly personal style has catered to a very demanding trade that has included a number of big "B's": from the Barrymores, and Bankhead, to Peter "Jaws" Benchley, and Marlon Brando. It underwent a pricey renovation recently and turned from a Butterfly into a Peacock. 110 rooms. Credit cards: All major.

Essex House, The $310–$500   ★★★

160 Central Park South; 10019; ☎ *247-0300; FAX: 315-1839.*

The original Essex House, opened in 1931 was dedicated to the splendor of the Art Deco era into which it was born. In 1991 the Japanese Nikko hotel chain bought it and not only rebuilt it from front desk to mop closet, but they also restored it to its glorious Art Deco past.

The lobby has huge carved black marble columns and the marble floors have a mirror finish. Any minute you expect to see "you know who" and "you know who" gliding across the floor doing the Carioca. The look of money is everywhere especially in the rooms upstairs.

The splendor of the 30s has been left downstairs and the rooms upstairs are Louis XV at his very best. Rich fabrics, gorgeous furnishings and jewel-like colors. No two rooms are the same. This is grand-lux all the way. The x in Essex must stand for exceptional. 593 rooms. Credit cards: All major.

Four Seasons, The $490–$630   ★★★

57 East 57th Street; 10022; ☎ *758-5700; FAX: 758-5711.*
If Ayn Rand and Cecil B. DeMille had collaborated on a hotel, they would probably have come up with the Four Seasons. But I.M.Pei was the architect who finally got the job. Soaring into the clouds on 57th Street, the Four Seasons has the distinction of being the last grand hotel to be built in the city for the rest of the century. How's that for "significant."

The first thing one thinks of upon entering the 33 ft.-high grand foyer, with its onyx ceiling is—where is the Pharaoh buried? The hotel is dedicated to the spirit of the 30's but they must have meant Egypt in the 30's. Huge palms to the right of you, more palms to the left of you, and two massive columns to pass through before reaching the lobby proper. At any moment, trumpeters might appear to herald your approach.

The Four Seasons cost more than $360-million to build which averages out to about $1 million per room. Even though you don't have to be a bonafide millionaire to stay there (although at over $400 a room it would certainly help) you can be sure you'll live like one.

The rooms are sumptuous in decor and go on forever, big enough for partnership desks, deepset windows with cushioned seats to savor some of the best views in town. The colors are soft earth tones and the windows have electrically controlled drapes that can be operated from bedside. The luxuries just don't let up for a second! Fully stocked refrigerators, separate dressing rooms and Carrara marble bathrooms with sunken tubs and T.V. Until a Five Seasons comes along, this place will do nicely. 367 rooms. Credit cards: All major.

Franklin, The $135–$145   ★

164 East 87th Street; 10128; ☎ *369-1000; FAX: 369-8000.*
Illicit affair. Hideaway. Agoraphobia. All of these conditions will be creatively dealt with at the Franklin. However, Claustrophobia is definitely a no-no. This tiny, cutting edge, "in" inn is not for everyone. On the other hand it could be viewed as a completely unique New York experience. It just depends on how unique you're willing to get.

The feel of the Franklin is young. The staff looks as if they're on their way to a cub scout meeting. But most of them are dressed in black so nothing quite adds up here. The rooms are done in softly draped canopy beds and not much more. All are munchkin size and can only benefit from a lack of furniture. There's always one fresh red rose which either makes you feel Dracula will visit later or a representative from Hallmark.

We told you up front, this is not everyone's cup of cappuccino, but for the terminally trendy, this is the place to be. **46 rooms.** Credit cards: All major.

Gorham, The $175–$195 ★

136 West 55th Street (Sixth & Seventh Avenues); 10021; ☎ 245-1800; FAX: 582-8332.
One block from the Hilton and within sniffing distance of the Carnegie Deli is one of the city's best values. There is a fully-equipped kitchenette in almost every room, which is particularly handy for families. As a matter of fact, everything about the Gorham is handy: the location, a warm and helpful management, and some surprisingly large rooms. Most suites have kitchenettes as well as dining areas. From the small, marble lobby to the sleekly decorated accommodations, the Gorham has undergone a super-overhaul that upgraded everything to luxury status except the price. **170 rooms.** Credit cards: All major.

Larchmont Hotel $70–$90 ★

27 W. 11th Street (5th & 6th Avenues); 10011; ☎ 989-9333; FAX: 989-9496.
What a beautiful, calm, leafy street to have a small hotel tucked away. And a hotel that's downright CHEAP without being a threat to life and limb. The Larchmont must have been a wise Genie's gift to the tired traveler. It's the kind of place "My Sister Eileen" was looking for.

The Larchmont is very continental in style right down to the shared bathrooms and kitchen on each floor. If that is too catastrophic to contemplate then you are going to have to go back uptown and make friends with the "triple didget doosies" that make up the rest of the hotel scene. But at $90 for a small, charming double with rattan accents, and a cheerful staff to serve your complimentary continental breakfast, I'd think twice if I were you. **51 rooms.** Credit cards: All major.

Lowell, The $295–$495 ★★★

28 East 63rd Street (Madison & Park); 10021; ☎ 838-1400; FAX: 319-4230.
There's a small hotel (without a wishing well, but with just about everything else) that's lavish and sophisticated enough to look as though it might have been moved, lock, stock and high tea from London and dropped into NY's best zip code. Not so. Before the Lowell turned into a boutique beauty it was a mothy residential hotel that, in better days, had been home to Scott and Zelda, Dorothy Parker, Noel Coward, and Walter Lippman. Today it's considered one of the top choices for "hotel collectors."

The Lowell believes in the suite life: there are 44 of them and most have woodburning fireplaces, fine fabrics, Chinese porcelains, lacquered tables, books, fresh flowers and plants. Fully-equipped kitchenettes are stocked with snacks in the event you need a little something to keep body and soul together before having tea in the Pembroke Room, a traditionally English dining room with chintz tablecloths to the floor, draped windows, and the finest crystal and china. Let's face it, you've got to love them for having a lunch menu that offers both Beluga caviar and a Lowell Burger. 61 rooms. Credit cards: All major.

Manhattan East Suite Hotels $119–$330

505 East 75th Street; 10021; ☎ 465-3600; FAX: 465-3663.

Imagine that wealthy friends have offered you their apartment while you're in NY. The "home away from home" theory is what makes this group of properties one of the best options in town. Studio, one-, two- and even three-bedroom suites are available in top locations at the price you'd pay for a double room. Rates vary slightly depending upon location, but you'll find the same large rooms, fully-equipped kitchens, and comfortable furnishings that make the accommodations ideal for families and business travelers. Number of rooms varies. Credit cards: All major.

Surrey Hotel
20 East 76th Street (Madison Avenue); ☎ 288-3700; FAX: 628-1549.

Beekman Tower
3 Mitchell Place (49th & First); ☎ 355-7300; FAX: 753-9366.

Dumont Plaza
150 East 34th Street (Lexington Avenue); ☎ 481-7600; FAX: 889-8856.

Shelburne Murray Hill
303 Lexington Avenue (37th Street); ☎ 689-5200; FAX: 779-7068.

Lyden Gardens
215 East 64th Street (Second & Third); ☎ 355-1230; FAX: 758-7858.

Lyden House
320 East 53rd Street (First &Second); ☎ 888-6070; FAX: 935-7690.

Eastgate Tower
222 East 39th Street (Second & Third); ☎ 687-8000; FAX: 490-2634.

Plaza Fifty
155 East 50th Street (Third Avenue); ☎ 751-5710; FAX: 753-1468.

Southgate Tower
371 Seventh Avenue (31st Street); ☎ 563-1800; FAX: 643-8028.

Mark, The $325–$500

Madison Avenue (East 77th Street); 10021; ☎ 744-4300; FAX: 744-2749.

The Mark is one of the most amazing hotel success stories in the city. Located across the street from the famed (but frigid) Carlyle and charging almost as much for a deluxe accommodation, the Mark not only didn't shrink from such formidable competition but today is firmly ensconced as one of the best small European-style hotels we have.

Very low key but very elegant, this place hits the mark for service and privacy. It more than echoes the sedate feeling of its neighborhood and its regulars include Europeans, rock stars and LA types who like their privacy in very "cool" surroundings.

For the visiting C.E.O. crowd, the Mark has a shuttle that whisks them straight to Wall Street in the early A.M.

Upstairs most of the rooms are spacious, with a dash of Directoire for spice. The Piranesi prints on the walls are the real McCoy, imported fresh from London. The bathrooms are marble and filled with wall to wall amenities.

Even though the Mark is one of the places Madonna likes to play Truth or Dare, it is definitely still a discreet delight. 120 rooms, 64 suites. Credit cards: All major.

Morgans   **$220–$475**   ★ ★

237 Madison Avenue (37th Street); 10016; ☎ 686-0300; FAX: 779-8352.

Design, design, design! The minimalist lobby with its textured opalescent glass walls and stark leather furniture which echoed the cutting edge of the 80s has given way to a kinder, gentler 90s comfort. When it first opened its doors you either fell madly in love with Morgan's or else ran screaming for the nearest medieval tapestry. Andrée Putman, the hotel's original designer has given it a whole new "cozy" spin. Today chic takes a back seat to corduroy. The stark granite floors are now covered with a homey wool rug atop which are deep armchairs that encourage lobby lounging.

You want to talk exclusive, there isn't even a name outside to let you know you've arrived—the theory being, no doubt, that everyone who stays at Morgans has already arrived.

Rooms are in tones of ivory and taupe with a polyester be damned philosophy that's resulted in ultra-suede headboards down pillows, upholstered window seats and bird's eye maple wall units. But don't let all this warmth fool you. The walls are still adorned by the photographs of Robert Mapplethrop. Morgan's continues to "push the envelope." 83 rooms, 30 suites. Credit cards: All major.

Hotel Olcott   **$95–$115**   ★

27 West 72nd Street (Central Park West & Columbus); 10023; ☎ 877-4200; FAX: 580-0511.

One of the best bargains in town, the Olcott is on the Upper West Side—right down the street from the fabulous Dakota apartment house and the pulsatingly trendy Columbus Avenue. As a special bonus, Central Park is only a few steps away, and you can be at Lincoln Center in a hop, skip, and a jump. The rooms and suites are comfortable, if somewhat eclectically furnished, and the suites come equipped with full kitchens. Okay. But not with TV's. However, with the money you save, you can easily afford to rent one at a nominal charge from the management. 45 studios, 55 suites. Credit cards: Not accepted.

New York Palace, The   **$275–$450**   ★ ★ ★

455 Madison Avenue; 10021; ☎ 888-7000; FAX: 303-6000.

True to it's name, the New York Palace was built around the Villard House, the closest New York has ever come to having a palatial mansion where royalty could be entertained with pride. Villard who was no stranger to mega-buck dwellings commissioned Stanford White in 1882 to design his new residence. White, never one to miss an Italianate beat, built his version of a neo-Renaissance palazzo, right on Madison Avenue. Even after it ceased to be a private residence it was thought to be so heavenly that the New York Archdiocese bought it.

The mansion became the exquisite cornerstone for a hotel that was built by Leona Helmsley as part of her substantial empire. After the Helmsley bubble burst, the Sultan of Brunei (noted hotel rescuer; The Dorchester in London, The Beverly Hills Hotel in LA) acquired the Palace and has done a meticulous restoration of both the Villard House and the hotel tower that rises behind it. Today the property has been burnished to a new gleaming elegance. The public rooms are located in the Villard house and have been landmarked for their historic value as well as their beauty.

The entrance to the hotel is through the original carriage courtyard which leads to the lobby. At night tiny lights give it a magical appearance. The rooms upstairs, all 963 of them, have undergone a massive renovation to change them from "Leona Lethargic" to "Brocaded Brunei." Everything is lush and deeply carpeted. Pastels open the rooms to both the light and amazing views of the city. The marble baths only continue the level of luxury.

The latest Palace coup was persuading the most famous restaurateur in the city, Sirio Maccioni, to move his fabled Le Cirque into the Villard portion of the hotel. The negotiations for this gastronomic merger are said to have been more complex than the Louisiana Purchase. More news of this as the soup thickens. 887 rooms. Credit cards: All major.

Paramount Hotel $180–$380   ★ ★
235 West 46th Street; 10019; ☎ *764-5500; FAX: 354-5237.*
The Paramount may have nothing to do with that movie mill on the left coast but, it has all the wonderland glamour of Hollywood.

Yet another completely original offering from Ian Schrager, who brought us Morgan's and the Royalton Hotel. He created the Paramount to bridge the gap from the traditional hotel to a younger, 90's, interpretation. Not only has he brought his unique concept off with grand style and wit, but he's created a luxury atmosphere at K-Mart prices.

As with Morgan's, Schrager's first hotel experiment, Philippe Starck was called in to sign his usual playfully, stylish signature all over the place.

The Paramount is located right in the middle of the Theater district, which may account for the theatricality of its public spaces. The lobby has lush color, muted lighting and a curving gray staircase that would have made Ziegfeld gray with envy. It leads to a small plush mezzanine where tiny tables are covered with whatever snack du jour is "hot" now.

The rooms themselves are small but designed for comfort. It would seem a somewhat perilous decision, but the colors and fabrics are white and cream. Over the bed is a huge gilt-framed reproduction of "The Lacemaker" by Vermeer. She looks down protectively over the sleeping guests. Just one of Starck's witty touches. The bathrooms have inverted "ice cream cone"-shaped steel sinks and fixtures to make any alien creature feel right at home.

This place was created to be supremely "cool." 610 rooms. Credit cards: All major.

Peninsula, The   **$340–$700**   ★ ★ ★
700 5th Avenue (55th Street); 10019; ☎ *247-2200; FAX: 903-3949.*
The Peninsula group of Hong Kong decided to take a chapter from
"How the West Was Won" and opened the lush Art Nouveau flavored Peninsula Hotel on Fifth Avenue. The lobby has a crystal chandelier that would make the Phantom of the Opera green with envy.

Large guest rooms run to soft muted tones of grey and apricot with a
whiff of the romantic. Marble bathrooms are luxurious to the max,
some with 6-foot soaking tubs. To keep you in shape, there's a tri-
level health and fitness spa with everything from an indoor swimming
pool to outdoor sundecks. The roof top bar is at the top of everyone's
list because of the stunning views. 250 rooms. Credit cards: All major.

Pierre, The   **$375–$595**   ★ ★ ★
Fifth Avenue at 61st Street; 10021; ☎ *838-8000; FAX: 750-0541.*
Stepping into the lobby of the Pierre is like boarding a fabled luxury
liner. You can almost hear the gentle hum of a staff accustomed to
smooth sailing.

The brainchild of restaurateur Charles Pierre and an investment
group that included Otto Kahn, E. F. Hutton, and Walter Chrysler,
the Pierre opened in 1930 with the great Escoffier potting around in
the kitchen as guest chef.

The rooms upstairs are large, airy, and deep-down comfortable with
spectacular views of Central Park. The Suites are spectacularly opulent, big enough to have a gardener and a pool man. Sumptuous
bathrooms are definitely not part of the Pierre profile but the management apologizes for their size by stuffing them with amenities.

A favorite of the "tea for two" set is the Rotunda, an oval-shaped elegant space with floor to ceiling murals of courtly garden scenes. If you
look carefully the woman peeking out from behind the trellises bears
a striking resemblance to the late Jacqueline Onassis. At her request,
the artist altered the likeness, but she's still there if you look closely.
201 rooms. Credit cards: All major.

Plaza, The   **$235–$650**   ★ ★ ★
Fifth Avenue at 59th Street; 10019; ☎ *759-3000; FAX: (212) 546-5234.*
New York's grandest European-style hotel, the Plaza is where Frank
Lloyd Wright lived from 1953–59 during the construction of the
Guggenheim Museum. Small wonder. This hotel looks as good from
the outside as it does from within. Declared an official landmark, it
was built in 1907 along the lines of a French Renaissance chateau by
the same architect responsible for another NY landmark, the Dakota,
a famed apartment house on the Upper West Side. The Plaza, always
larger than life, was purchased by the King of "Larger than Life,"
Donald Trump for $390 million. He promised to "upgrade" it into
the most luxurious hotel in the world. Not that it's exactly been a Bed
and Breakfast. The Plaza underwent a complete restoration—the gold
leaf moldings glow from the ceilings, and both the Oak and Edwardian Rooms have been returned to their original splendor. Bedrooms
are filled with antiques, crystal chandeliers and bedside lamps that
light up when you touch them. If you're an aficionado of high ceilings, ask for a room on a lower floor.

Unfortunately the "The Donald" was no more committed to the Plaza than he was to Ivana. He just sold it (at a loss, I might add) to the family of Fahd the King of Saudi Arabia. Does that mean there will be camels parked out front? Stay tuned for the next Agenda bulletin. 807 rooms. Credit cards: All major.

Hotel Plaza Athénée $285–$590   ★ ★ ★

37 East 64th Street (Madison & Park); 10021; ☎ *734-9100; FAX: (212) 772-0958.*

A pocket of Right Bank elegance on an East Side tree-lined street. Like its Parisian counterpart, it reeks par excellence. Take three steps down to enter the lobby and from the moment you plant your tootsies on the gleaming black-and-white tiled floor, you inhale the sweet smell of success. Tapestry-covered walls and leather upholstered elevators help you rise to the occasion: rooms of uncommon comfort with king-size beds, plush velvets, lush brocades and sumptuous accessories (robes by Porthault) in pale pink marble bathrooms. Attention to detail is a way of life here. Each room has a small pantry and a fridge that's stocked with Evian water. Home turf to Fortune 500 CEO's as well as such enfants du paradis as Elizabeth Taylor, Joan Collins and Farrah Fawcett when in town. 160 rooms. Credit cards: All major.

Ritz-Carlton, The $305–$600   ★ ★ ★

112 Central Park South (Sixth & Seventh); 10019; ☎ *757-1900; FAX: 757-9620.*

The Ritz-Carlton is one of those rare hotels that is gracious and intimate without ever losing its cool. Above all, everything about the place is professional: it's not just luxurious, it's comfortable. It's not just comfortable, its warm and friendly. The staff and the service they offer every guest, from standard double to Penthouse suite, is impeccable. A $22-million renovation was recently completed to make the Ritz even more glorious than it was before. They also added the Ritz Carlton Club Floor and for the cost of breakfast for two in most N.Y. hotels, you can have complementary breakfast, light lunch, tea and nibblies in the afternoon and an open bar throughout the day. If you have a case of the terminal munchies, this is the option for you.

Soft pastel bedrooms are decked out in brocade covered walls, fine art, and a sprinkling of antiques. Rooms with views of Central Park are prime property for those who want a sight for their sore eyes. There is no better one to be had. 210 rooms. Credit cards: All major.

Roger Smith Hotel, The $195–$225   ★

501 Lexington Avenue (47th Street); 10017; ☎ *755-1400; FAX: 319-9130.*

When a sculptor/painter/guitarist, sees a down at the heels hotel on Lexington Avenue and decides to renovate it, what do you get: an art attack!

James Knowles and his wife Suzanne inherited the hotel, but neither one knew quite what to do with it. Knowles finally realized that he could not only transform the hotel into the gallery of his dreams, but he could also run a truly artistic establishment, "a hotel with an art bias."

Knowles did the bronze sculptures that frame the entrance. He also created the bronze insets in the front of the lobby desk.

The rooms themselves are works in progress with original art covering the walls on a rotating basis. Knowles combined antiques from the old hotel with an update for style and comfort. To quote the manager "The Roger Smith is to the visual arts what the Algonquin is to literature."

The Roger Smith is definitely my idea of art appreciation. 200 rooms. Credit cards: All major.

Royalton $285–$400 ★ ★

44 West 44th Street; 10036; ☎ 869-4400; FAX: 575-0012.
In the '80s there was restaurant as theater but in the '90s the stage was set for hotels in New York to take over and become the place for movers and shakers to be seen. Though the Royalton was completed in 1988, the extraordinary design of Philippe Starck was looking ahead to the millennium. The hotel was conceived as a huge mansion with the lobby making up the living room, game room, library, breakfast room, and dining room. One melting into the other.

The lobby is a full block long and filled with Starck's whimsical furniture and lighting fixtures. The front desk and other hotel services are concealed behind a floor-to-ceiling mahogany wall. Royal blue carpeting runs the entire length of the lobby and creates the feeling of a moving walkway.

Upstairs the halls are inky blue and dimly lit to add a touch of drama after an evening out.

Inside the rooms, the feeling is of an A-deck accommodation on the *SS MGM*—mahogany, velvets, deep tones and beds that go on forever.

The bathrooms match the bedrooms for luxury and most have deep circular tubs. They all have enough glass and stainless steel to make any surgeon ecstatic. The Royalton is the kind of hotel where a spy and a mogul can co-exist without a care. 205 rooms. Credit cards: All major.

St. Regis $425–$650 ★ ★ ★

2 East 55th Street (Fifth Avenue); 10022; ☎ 753-4500; FAX: 541-4736.
You've heard of Astor's pet horse. Well, this is Astor's pet hotel. When Col. John Jacob Astor opened the St. Regis in 1904, it was the tallest hotel in NYC. But that wasn't enough. He wanted it to be the city's most opulent.

The St. Regis, after being closed for three years during a top to bottom renovation, has returned in an even more opulent version. If anything, the rooms are more lavish than they were when old John Jacob was in charge.

The New St. Regis draws more on Old World splendor than new world posh for its character. Each floor has its own butler on call 24 hours a day. The rooms have silk wall coverings, 12 to 15 foot ceilings and warm rich colors. The bathrooms more than match the luxury of the rooms. Downstairs, the St. Regis' new look is strictly "old money." From the burnished brass and glass kiosk that shelters the

HOTELS

doorman to the famous Maxfield Parrish murals in the King Cole bar, which incidentally is: "The Birthplace of the Bloody Mary." 365 rooms. Credit cards: All major.

RED SNAPPER

A French bartender named Fernand Petiot brought the recipe with him to the St. Regis' King Cole bar in 1934. The original recipe called for half vodka and half tomato juice. Some say that Ernest Hemingway named it. St. Regis owner Vincent Astor disapproved of the name, since the word Bloody was considered British slang. And so, he renamed it the Red Snapper. Here's the recipe for the St. Regis bloody mary:

Red Snapper

1–1 1/2 oz. vodka

2 oz. tomato juice

1 dash lemon juice

2 dashes each salt, black pepper

cayenne pepper, 3 dashes

Worcestershire and lemon juice

to a shaker glass. Then add

ice, vodka, tomato juice.

Shake, pour into highball glass.

SoHo Grand Hotel   **$199–$949**   ★ ★

310 W. Broadway; 10013; ☎ 965-3000; FAX: 965-3141.

It had to happen. It was only a matter of time. An area as vibrant and mercurial as SoHo would finally have to come up with a signature hotel in which the Dealers and Wheelers could rest their weary but elegant bones at the end of their gallery-hopping day. Even the name of the hotel projects the playful, trendy philosophy of the neighborhood. The SoHo Grand is anything but. It is dedicated to "haute" minimalism at its very best.

The second floor lobby is a soaring space punctuated by a cast-iron and glass staircase suspended by cables from the mirrored ceiling. If that's not enough drama for you there are huge columns made of brick that reach up more than 16 feet. Above the front-desk there is an enormous clock that seems to remind everyone that the 21st century is happening today at the SoHo Grand. The two-story windows that overlook West Broadway are draped in chocolate-colored velvet to offset the austerity of the place, as is the plush furniture strewn around the vast expanse. Is this New York in the '90s or Berlin in the '30s? It's hard to tell.

The 369 rooms upstairs are small, comfortable and luxuriously efficient. The decor celebrates the local SoHo artists by using a desk that resembles a drafting table and night tables that echo sculptor's stands. The soft shades of gray and beige give the small, cleanly-designed rooms a feeling of space and order. The bathrooms are semi-institutional, but remember, we're talking minimalism and design, not heart-shaped tubs in the Poconos.

Aside from the gorgeous views from most of its rooms, the SoHo Grand's edge is that it's only an "art-beat" from Chinatown, the

Breakfast at Norma's at the Parker Meridian, 118 West 57th Street (between 6th and 7th Avenues); 001 212 708 7460. This midtown hotel serves wildly creative breakfasts till 3pm. For a more laid-back atmosphere, try Bubby's, 120 Hudson Street (at North Moore); 001 212 219 0666. This TriBeCa kitchen is where John Kennedy Jnr used to breakfast.

You can get chocolate chip cookies, cinnamon buns and delicious salads at the City Bakery, 3 West 18th Street (between 5th and 6th Avenues); 001 212 366 1414.

Lobster rolls at the Pearl Oyster Bar, 18 Cornelia Street (between Bleecker and West 4th); 001 212 691 8211. Tiny seafood restaurant that offers great value.

Cuban food at Cafe Habana, 17 Prince Street (at Elizabeth); 001 212 625 2001. Delicious food in simple tiled surroundings, popular with Nolita's poncho- and jeans-loving *jeunesse dorée*

Rooftop cocktails at the High Bar of the Gramercy Park Hotel, 2 Lexington Avenue (between 21st and 22nd); 001 800 221 4083. A favourite haunt of Sofia Coppola, this is where Humphrey Bogart married his first wife. Or try the glamorous bar at the Mercer Hotel, 99 Prince Street (at Mercer); 001 212 966 6060.

Prix fixe lunch at the elegant and reliable Gotham, 12 East 12th Street (between 5th Avenue and University Place); 001 212 620 4020. Or the quintessentially American Craft restaurant/bar, 43 East 19th Street (between Broadway and Park Avenue); 001 212 780 0880.

Cupcakes at the Magnolia Bakery, 401 Bleecker Street (at West 11th); 001 212 462 2572. West Village bakery whose divine cupcakes have been a cult favourite since they first appeared in *Sex and the City*. If you can't get to New York, try Hummingbird Bakery in London's Portobello Road; 020 7229 6446.

the jewellery box. They were unlo
and unworn, except by ancient To
do-gooders, librarians and geogra
teachers. No one my age gave them the tim
day. Very occasionally, someone deeply
fashionable (and most probably European)
would just about get away with wearing a
monstrous diamond-encrusted leaping leo
on an expensive lapel, but most brooch we
belonged to a bygone, more elegant era.

But, strangely, all this has now changed.
Brooches have come of age again. They're
enjoying a bling-bling renaissance, having
rediscovered by my generation.

"I've always loved them, darling," declar
Joan Collins when I asked how she rated th
"They perk everything up and add a bit of g
to a plain coat or jacket. Can't live without

We went out a few days ago on a girlie se
for trinkets. Joan had just finished doing a
junket promoting her latest novel, *Misfortu
Daughters,* and wanted some frivolous rewa

I've shopped with Joan before. She's deci
when it comes to shopping for clothes, a fas
mover and one of those rare women who
instinctively knows what will work best for
"Dress up" as opposed to "dress down" is h
maxim — something that she has managed
pull off successfully throughout her career.

There's no dithering about with Joan, nor
she only patronise expensive designers. "I l
most of my clothes in America where they'r
much cheaper," she confided, "but Zara is
sensational, and I always, always find stuff
I like to mix it all up. I never get rid of my
clothes; I keep everything because what go
around eventually comes around again."

"Brooches are 'in' at the moment, aren't t
I asked as we headed towards King's Road.

"They're back with a vengeance," she said
put two on the other day and had to ask Per
[her husband] if it was over-the-top. I thoug
might have looked like a Christmas tree."

"What did he say?"

Joan grinned. "Percy is the most adorable
husband in the world. He said I did, but the

South Street Seaport, Greenwich Village, and Wall Street. So who can argue with all that? 367 rooms. Credit cards: All major.

Waldorf-Astoria, The   **$290–$600**   ★ ★ ★

301 Park Avenue (49th & 50th Streets); 10022; ☎ *355-3000; FAX: 872-7272.*

When the Waldorf-Astoria opened in 1931, it was the largest hotel in the world, occupying an entire city block from Park Avenue down to Lexington. It had 2200 rooms and no two were alike. Today, after being designated a New York City Landmark, it was trimmed down to a dietetic 1380 units. Needless to say, the Waldorf is not the place to go for "continental intimacy."

Even the most jaded of travelers gets a big kick out of pulling up to the entrance of the Waldorf and seeing all those flags dancing in the wind. Suddenly, you feel like the most important person in the world. Inside, the lobby glows like a dazzling deco dream. It seems as though, at one time or another, everybody on the planet passed below the bas-relief ceiling. The lobby feels like an annex of the United Nations. In fact every U.S. president from Herbert Hoover on has occupied the Presidential Suite.

The Waldorf is such an institution that you almost forget there are rooms upstairs just for sleeping. Well, there are—and they're comfortable and bright and quiet. Try to reserve on the Park Avenue side for a city view that can put you into the picture postcard business. If you prefer your hotel experience to be a little more personal than staying over at the Pentagon, the Waldorf Towers is a better choice. A superplush hotel within the hotel, it has its own entrance and staff accustomed to catering to the whims of such diverse guests as Albert Einstein, Queen Elizabeth and Frank Sinatra. (Separate rooms, please!) 1692 rooms. Credit cards: All major.

Hotel Wales   **$165–$225**   ★ ★

1295 Madison Avenue; 10128; ☎ *876-6000; FAX: 860-7000.*

Upper Madison Avenue is New York at its calmest, its least crowded and its most "lets take time to smell the roses" mode. It's also the gateway to Museum Mile on Fifth. The Wales fits the graciousness of the neighborhood like a velvet glove.

If turn-of-the-century charm presses your buttons, the Wales is a perfect choice. The rooms have rich oak molding, fireplaces with carved mantles, and furniture which tends to be simple, but completely in character. Some of the rooms are more elaborate than others. The staff does a "wale" of a job keeping the hotel on its toes.

Sundays there are concerts in the beautifully restored ballroom which also serves as the place guests have their complementary breakfasts and tea. 86 rooms. Credit cards: All major.

Hotel Westbury   **$285–$450**   ★ ★ ★

69th Street and Madison Avenue; 10021; ☎ *535-2000; FAX: 535-5058.*

While all eyes have focused on the British invasion of Broadway, there's been a backstage takeover at some of the city's best hotels. That accounts for the Devonshire cream that appears regularly at tea in this Trusthouse Forte property. As elegant as the avenue on which

HOTELS

it's located, the Westbury has just enough stiff-upper-lip to make you check your Filofax to be certain you're in New York and not London.

You certainly can't tell from the lobby. It's all creamy and beige with tapestries on the wall and Queen Anne chairs to set the tone. The beautifully-carved oval ceiling and the balcony that discreetly over-hangs the room give you a good idea why the hotel was landmarked recently.

Upstairs the rooms and suites are fitted in chintz, florals, and Ralph Lauren plaids. Some may even have canopy beds but all are supremely comfortable. They each have their own lush, dramatic cachet—no two are the same. Just like the clientele. 235 rooms. Credit cards: All major.

Wyndham Hotel   **$130–$210**   ★ ★ ★

42 West 58th Street (Fifth & Sixth); 10019; ☎ *753-3500; FAX: 754-5638.*

Every once in a while you come upon something that has no relation to its time and place. It belongs frozen in the deja-vu of a wonderful past experience. That's probably the feeling most people have after they've stayed at the Wyndham. It doesn't conform to the present, to its snitzy location, or to the usual New York hotel experience. It is as personable and theatrical as its guest list past and present: Peter Usti-nov, James Clavell, Harold Pinter, Eva Marie Saint, Carol Burnett, the Cronins, the Oliviers and dozens of other show biz show-stoppers passing through town.

John and Suzanne Mados who lovingly keep the lamplight burning at the Wyndham have an office filled with more memorabilia than Sotheby's could auction in a week. Their famous guests are forever leaving behind belongings they know they can pick up on their next visit. The astonishing thing about the Wyndham, aside from who you see in the elevator, are the room rates. Here, in one of the most expensive neighborhoods in town, across the street from the Plaza yet, around the corner from Central Park South, just a stone's throw from Fifth, a luxuriously furnished suite with a kitchenette costs less than a single room at one of the Chain-Gangs.

And wait until you see these rooms. Some of them are the size of small tennis courts. Fabric on the walls matches the dramatically draped drapes. Beds are king-size. Parlors (yes, they have parlors here) often have fireplaces. The Wyndham is a wonderful hotel because the Mados' make it wonderful. Book as far in advance as possible. 201 rooms. Credit cards: All major.

Bed and Breakfasts

B&B's started in England years ago and are still a welcome fixture on the travel agenda. The theory is that people with extra rooms in their apart-ments offer visitors bed and breakfast at a price well under the going rate in hotels. Aside from the economics, many people like the idea of staying with a New York family. It's a great way to meet the locals, and there's almost always a spare umbrella in the closet or a little advice on how to navigate the city. All B&B's have been visited by the agencies and the hosts have been screened. Aside from single and double accommodations, you can rent studio, or one- and two-bedroom apartments from the agencies.

City Lights Bed & Breakfast Ltd.

P.O. Box 20355, Cherokee Station
New York, NY 10028
☎ *(212) 737-7049; FAX: 535-2755*

New World Bed & Breakfast

150 Fifth Ave., Suite 711
New York, NY 10011
☎ *(212) 675-5600; FAX: 675-6366*

Urban Ventures, Inc.

38 West 32nd St.
New York, NY 10001
☎ *(212) 594-5650; FAX: 947-9320*

All agencies urge you to reserve as far in advance as possible. If you cancel with notice, your deposit is refunded less a service charge. If you cancel without notice, one night's fee is charged.

Hostelling International, N.Y.

891 Amsterdam Avenue (103rd Street)
New York, NY 10025
☎ *(212) 932-2300*

The city's first youth hostel has accommodations for non-youths as well, even if you're older than George Burns. Five to a room in a largely Hispanic area near Columbia University.

"Location, location, location."

Drawing by Bruce Eric Kaplan; ©1994, The New Yorker Magazine, Inc.

HOTELS

AGENDA TRAVEL ADVISORY

Grand Central Terminal's historic fixtures are frequently unnoticed by the throngs of commuters who hurry through.

Getting To Midtown

From JFK
John F. Kennedy International Airport

The trip from JFK is the longest, most aggravating and most expensive 15 miles you're likely to travel outside of a Malaysian jungle. *No matter how you do it, or what you pay, it's going to take you about an hour*.

Taxi

There are usually uniformed taxi dispatchers to help you, although they often supply more heat than light. The important things to remember are that drivers are required by law to take you anyplace you want to go within the city limits; one flat fare of $30 pays for all passengers in the event you decide to share a cab, and you are required to pay tolls and a $.50 surcharge between 8 p.m. and 6 a.m. The official fare no matter what your driver tells you, from JFK to midtown is $30. (Tip 15 or 20 percent of the fare). Try to keep some perspective: getting into midtown is not as bad as being in a Turkish prison.

Express Buses

Carey Airport Express, *$13.50*, ☎ *(718) 632-0500, (800) 249-0909.*
Leaves for East and West 42nd Street every 30 minutes.

Minibuses

Depart from all JFK terminals. Make arrangements at Ground Transportation Counter.

Gray Line, *$16.50,* ☎ *(212) 315-3006, (800) 451-0455.*
Approximately 60 minutes to major midtown hotels.

Public Transportation

The best way to save money. Take the Q10 bus *(Green Bus Lines;* ☎ *(718) 995-4700)* or the Q3 bus *(NYC Transit Authority;* ☎ *(718) 330-1234)* to connect with the NYC subway system. Bus fare is $1.50 (exact change only). Subway fare is an additional $1.50. Takes forever. Figure on 1-1/2 to 2 hours.

Limousine

Make arrangements at Ground Transportation Counter.

From LGA
Laguardia Airport

If you can possibly book yourself into LaGuardia, do so. It's the most convenient, easiest to negotiate, airport in the city. If you grit your teeth, you can hop into a cab and be in midtown in 25 minutes. Meter should run about $20–$25 plus toll and tip. (See notes under JFK).

Express Buses

Carey Airport Express; *$9.50;* ☎ *(800) 284-0909.*
Leaves for East and West 42nd Street every 20–30 minutes. Travel time is approx 40 minutes.

Minibuses

Depart from all LGA terminals. Make arrangements at Ground Transportation Counter.

Gray Line; *$13.50;* ☎ *(212) 315-3006.*
Approx 45 minutes to major midtown hotels.

Ferry

DELTA Water Shuttle; *$30.00;* ☎ *(800) 543-3779.*
Operates mornings and late afternoons from LGA to Wall Street. The trip takes 25 minutes to midtown.

Public Transportation

Bargain basement. Take the Q-33 bus *(Triboro Coach;* ☎ *(718) 335-1000)* to connect with NYC subway system. Bus fare is $1.50 (exact change only). Subway fare is an additional $1.50. ETA: under an hour with good connections.

Limousine

Make arrangements at Ground Transportation Counter.

From NIA
Newark International Airport

Okay. So, it's in New Jersey. It's not as convenient as LGA but it's better than JFK. Red Alert to Dedicated Budgeteers: there is no "public" transportation from New Jersey into Manhattan. If you can afford to think about a taxi, which will run about $40.00 plus tolls and tip, you might as well have a cleaner, more comfortable ride in a limo. Travelling to Newark, the fare is calculated on the meter, plus $10 and tolls. And tip. (See notes under JFK.)

Express Buses

> *NJ Transit Express; $9;* ☎ *(201) 762-5100.*
> Leaves for Port Authority Bus Terminal every 15–30 minutes. Travel time is approx 30–45 minutes.
>
> *Olympia Trails Express Bus; $9;* ☎ *(212) 964-6233.*
> Leaves every 20 minutes for World Trade Center and Grand Central Station. Travel time same as above.

Minibus and Shared Ride

> Make arrangements at Ground Transportation Counter. Travel time is approx 55 minutes.
>
> *Gray Line; $18;* ☎ *(212) 757-6840.*
> Departs all NIA terminals to major midtown hotels.

Limousine

> Make arrangements at Ground Transportation Counter.

From Grand Central Station
> *42nd Street between Madison and Lexington Avenues;* ☎ *532-4900.*

If your luggage is heavy, get a porter. It's a hefty walk from the train platform to the street. Then, you're on your own unless you hire someone to get you a cab. This is not as silly as it sounds because you don't want to leave your luggage unattended on the street while hunting for a cab. A dollar for your new "press agent" will do the trick. If you're determined to take public transportation, check the transit maps carefully.

From Pennsylvania Station
> *33rd Street and Seventh Avenue,* ☎ *(800) 872-7245.*

Same rules apply as Grand Central, except it's somewhat easier (read: more organized) to get a cab.

From the Port Authority Bus Terminal
> *41st Street and Eighth Avenue;* ☎ *564-8484.*

This is rough turf. Hold onto your belongings tightly and get into a cab as quickly as possible. You may have better luck snaring a cab on the Ninth Avenue side. Do not linger here.

A WORD ABOUT CAR RENTAL

Don't.

Getting Around

You know the old joke.
Q: How do you get to Carnegie Hall?
A: Practice! Practice! Practice!

It says a lot more about New York than most people realize. Look at any bus or subway map and you'll find that getting to Carnegie Hall is a cinch. It's even within walking distance of many major hotels. The real joke is that no self-respecting New Yorker equates the phrase "getting somewhere" in terms of transportation.

© 1992, 1994 AL ROSS

GRIDLOCK

The best way to get around the city is to be outrageously wealthy and have a chauffeur-driven limousine, preferably with a phone, TV, and wet bar to while away the hours while trying to get across town. Otherwise, the choice is simple. Walk.

The numbered streets that run north to south are relatively short. Even without hiking boots, you'll be able to cover ten blocks in about fifteen minutes. The east to west avenue blocks are often significantly longer and it takes almost triple the time to get from Fifth to Sixth Avenue than it does from 59th to 60th Street. Here's what you'll need for hassle-free transportation around town:

1. A plan.

2. Comfortable shoes.

3. A collapsible umbrella.

Midtown Traffic Golden Rules

During the morning rush hour, it is more difficult going downtown. During the evening rush hour, it is more difficult going uptown.

It is *always* more difficult going across town(east/west) than going uptown or downtown.

The plan is an easy one to make. All you have to do is group activities by neighborhood so that you can walk from A to B to C. Use a map to be certain that A to B to C goes in the same direction as the traffic and you'll have the option of hopping onto a bus or into a taxi. Look at your map to locate a hotel or some major landmark near your final destination. That's the best way to find a taxi. As a last resort, head for the nearest subway stop. Nothing beats the subway for speed.

New York has more bus and subway stops than Hamblin had rats. Back in the days when city commissioners spent time doing things other than being indicted, somebody put together a real neat package to get people from here to there with breathtaking efficiency.

But let's face it, even though a few of those horror stories you've heard about the subways are true, there has been a noticeable drop in subway crime in the last few years. Still, the old adage about safety in numbers is one to heed and there are usually no problems at all during rush hour. Simply, there's no faster or easier way to get around the city.

How to Take the Subway

Subways run 24 hours. The peak rush periods are between 7:30–9:30 a.m. and 4:30–6:30 p.m. and should be avoided if possible. It's a good idea to stand in the designated "off-hours waiting areas." They are generally in sight of the token booth where someone is on duty. Travel in a middle car near the conductor, or in the first car near the driver. Do not ride in the last car, or an empty car, at any time. Do not stand at the edge of the platform.

Happily, in the last few years subway crime in New York has gone way down. By the same token that doesn't mean you're free to wear the family tiara during your trip. (And don't advertise that you're a tourist by draping cameras around your neck or displaying a convention badge on your pocket or lapel.)

You can usually change train lines without paying an additional fare. Check with the agent on duty in the token booth. You'll find subway stations well-marked, making line changes relatively easy. As a rule of thumb, it's more difficult going across town by subway than uptown or downtown.

Be certain your valuables are not easy pickings. A favorite trick is to grab a purse or wallet in that split second before the door closes, leaving the victim on the train while the thief exits safely along the platform. In all fairness, many New Yorkers ride the subways at all hours and experience no problems. And the aforementioned tips would apply to subway travel in any city in the world. But don't tempt fate. If you plan to travel after midnight, grit your teeth and take a cab.

Subway Fare: $1.50. Recently the Transit Authority introduced the MetroCard, which can be prepaid in any amount up to $80 at the subway token booth. Most riders prefer to prepay a card for ten rides at a time. The card makes hopping a train even more convenient. You just pass the card through the machine and it debits the $1.50 fare. You can use the Metro-Card on N.Y.C. buses as well. At the moment tokens are still being used if you prefer them but the T.A. is threatening to faze them out. Tokens can be purchased at the same booths that sell the MetroCard but the booths are not always open. If you plan to travel by subway and bus (the same token is accepted on buses), it's advisable to buy a few extras. Don't expect to be able to cash in your extras, however.

How to Take the Bus

As often as possible. In addition to being safer, cleaner and generally more aesthetically pleasing, you get to see the city while the world rolls by. Not all bus lines run 24 hours so be sure to check if you're planning to use the bus after midnight. Rush hour periods are the same as the subway.

Use some street smarts waiting for a bus during off hours. If you're alone, and it's dark, instead of standing in the bus stop, wait near an open store. While buses are relatively free from the kind of violence that stalks the subways, thieves will wait to grab a purse when the bus pulls into a stop and then exit quickly down the street. Buses permit you to transfer from one bus route to another without paying an extra fare. The bus system is wonderfully flexible, allowing you to go from uptown or downtown to east or west. Simply ask the driver for a transfer when you get on. However, if you already handed him a transfer from another bus as your fare, you can't get another one without paying extra.

Bus Fare: $1.50. Drivers do not make change nor do they accept bills. You must have $1.50 in exact change or else a subway token or the Metro Card.

How to Take a Taxi

Once upon a time, the cliché Manhattan cabby was a lovable, garrulous kind of lug with a heart of gold who was just waiting for you to step in and shout, "Follow that car!" or "Once around the park, driver." Forget it. The typical '90s cabby can sometimes be short-tempered and rude, or a recent arrival to this country who barely speaks English, and who knows New York about as well as you know Timbuktu. Occasionally, you'll come across one who smiles and says, "Thank you," but as a group, they should be approached with the same caution as a pool of snapping turtles.

By law, the driver is required to take you to any destination within the five boroughs. If you have a problem, simply note down the driver's I.D. number and ask for help at your hotel. If all else fails call the New York Taxi and Limousine Commission, ☎ *(212) 221-8294.*

Drawing by R. Chast; ©1983, The New Yorker Magazine, Inc.

Adding a 15% tip to the fare on the meter is the norm. Do not calculate your tip to include any tolls or the highway robberish $.50 surcharge that is legally added by most cabs after 8 p.m. For extra service in handling bags or being almost human, make it 20%. The fare on the meter starts with $2, then jumps 30 cents for each additional 1/5 mile. In heavy traffic you can go through cash faster than a trip to Vegas!

And then there are "gypsy" cabs. There are thousands of unlicensed, un-insured cabs who roam the streets officially unrecognized but in full view. These are the guys with the foam rubber dominoes, baby shoes or plastic saints hanging on the rear view mirror who may or may not have meters and charge whatever the traffic will bear. These caballeros have no visible I.D. and are likely to vanish into thin air should there be any trouble.

Our best advice is walk. Walk as much as possible.

AGENDA TRAVEL
ADVISORY

NEIGHBORHOODS

The cast iron Bow Bridge crosses The Lake at Central Park.

The magic of Manhattan lies in its infinite variety. Although the entire city is coated with a diamond-bright glitz, upon closer inspection one sees that the glowing facets of the city are its neighborhoods. There are dozens of Manhattans waiting to be discovered. It all depends upon what you want and how you define excitement.

Fifth Avenue

Everyone in New York becomes Irish for the St. Patrick's Day Parade down Fifth Avenue.

There is probably no one street in the world that stirs up images of an entire city the way Fifth Avenue does. Not even the Champs-Elysees, for all its splendor as the world's grandest boulevard, represents Paris more than Fifth Avenue symbolizes New York.

From its beginnings in **Washington Square Park**, Fifth Avenue was built heading north. Uptown. It was the address for America's best known millionaires from Astor to Vanderbilt. Today, Fifth Avenue epitomizes Manhattan more than any other thoroughfare. It's not only the spine of the city—it separates east from west—but it synthesizes the glitter and the gossip that makes New York hum. It's an address made famous by the Vanderbilts, **Rockefeller Center**, **St. Patrick's Cathedral**, the **Empire State**

HARLEM

Marcus
Garvey
Park

N

Upper
East Side

©FWI

Randall's
Island

St. Nicholas Ave.

W. 116th St

Central Park N

E. 110th St

E. 106th St

Ward's
Island

FDR DR

The
Reservoir

5th Ave
Madison Ave
Park Ave
Lexington Ave
3rd Ave
2nd Ave
1st Ave

E. 96th St

East River

UPPER

EAST SIDE

E. 86th St

Carl
Schurz
Park

Central
Park

E. 79th St

5th Ave
Madison Ave
Park Ave
Lexington Ave
3rd Ave
2nd Ave
1st Ave
York Ave
East End Ave

E. 72nd St

E. 68th St

E. 57th St

Roosevelt
Island

Queensboro Bridge

Central Park S

Sutton Pl

D   E   F   G

93 113 101 104 605 114 92 97 180 737 109 330 570 126 96 87 86 350 32 11 485 305 56 55 43 67 11 12 13 14 15 16 17

Museums

86	Center for African Art, 54 E 68 St	E16
87	Center for Inter-American Relations, 680 Park Av	E16
92	Cooper Hewitt Museum, Fifth Av & E 91 St	E14
93	El Museo del Barrio, 1230 5 Av	E13
96	Frick Collection, 1 E 70 St	E16
97	Guggenheim Museum, Fifth Av & E 89 St	E14
101	International Center of Photography, 5 Av & E 94 St	E14
104	Jewish Museum, Fifth Av & E 92 St	E14
109	Metropolitan Museum of Art, 5 Av & E 82 St	E15
113	Museum of the City of New York, Fifth Av & E 103 St	E13
114	National Academy of Design, 1083 Fifth Av	E14
126	Whitney Museum of American Art, E 75 St & Madison Av	E16

Foreign Currency Exchanges

| 737 | Chemical Bank, 126 E 86 St 410-2913 | E14 |

Places of Interest

32	Central Park Wildlife Conservation Center/Central Park Zoo, Central Park	E17
43	Gracie Mansion, East End Av & E 88 St	G14
55	Roosevelt Island	G17
56	Roosevelt Island Tramway	F17

Transportation Terminals

| 11 | Airlines Ticket Office, 1 E 59 St | E17 |

Hotel Accommodations

180	Franklin Hotel, 164 E 87 St	E14
305	Lyden Gardens Suite, 215 E 64 St	F17
330	Mark, 25 E 77 St	E15
350	Mayfair Hotel Baglioni, 610 Park Av	E17
485	Regency, 540 Park Av	E17
570	Surrey Suite, 20 E 76t St	E15
605	Wales, 1295 Madison Av	E14

Building, **Trump Tower**, some of the world's most fashionable department stores, and the Easter Parade.

The Famous "400"

The phrase denoting the "in" group came about when Mrs. Astor, in 1892, sent out 400 invitations to a ball she was giving in her Fifth Avenue mansion. It is reported that the figure 400 represented the number of people who could be accommodated.

Today, there are three separate "Fifth Avenues": midtown Fifth, lower Fifth, and upper Fifth. The fact that they are sufficiently unrelated and might as well be in three different cities is part of what makes New York so frustrating. And exciting. It's what makes New York, New York.

Midtown Fifth

This stretch of the avenue is twenty-four carat New York. Try starting at 63rd or 64th and Fifth and walk down from there. If you're into the wonderful world of incongruities, think about scheduling a stop at the recently-refurbished **Central Park Zoo** *at Fifth Avenue between 63rd and 64th Streets.* Indisputably the world's best address for an animal refuge, the original Zoo was more reminiscent of a rich man's indulgence than a wildlife environment, and was long overdue for a major overhaul. Today $35 million later the monkeys are in full swing in one of three "environments" that make the animals feel much more at home. There is a very modest admission charge.

Before you reach 59th Street, savor the feeling of upper Fifth: sedate, more secure than Leavenworth and Fort Knox combined—with Central

NEIGHBORHOODS

Park on one side and all that filthy rich real estate on the other. You'll note there are no shops on this stretch of the avenue. The first sign of commerce is the drop dead chic of the **Hotel Pierre** *on the corner of 61st Street*. Its tower is a recognized part of the skyline. (See Hotels).

The Fifth Avenue we all know and love begins at **Grand Army Plaza** and 59th Street, where a statue of Pomona, the goddess of abundance, graces the tiered pools of the **Pulitzer Memorial Fountain**. There's hardly a movie shot in New York that hasn't included this spot, from *Arthur* to *The Way We Were*. One of the reasons is the legendary **Plaza Hotel** (See Hotels), still making headlines since it was built in 1907 for the then incredible sum of $12-1/2 million and more recently when it was sold by Donald Trump for over $300 million. If you're not staying here, put the **Plaza** on your sight-seeing list.

Across from the **Plaza**, on the other side of the Plaza (Grand Army) is the white marble mumbo-jumbo of the **General Motors Building** whose singular architectural virtue is that it makes you appreciate the other build-ings in sight all the more, including the crackle-snap elegance of the Sherry-Netherland Hotel, the world's tallest apartment hotel when it opened in 1927.

One of the grandest dames among New York shops is the landmark **Bergdorf Goodman**, *at No. 745 between 57th and 58th streets*. (See Shop-ping)

AGENDA TIP

Bergdorf's has the best department store ladies room in town—with a great view of Central Park.

If you have children, grandchildren, godchildren or even just a Peter Pan complex, don't leave 58th Street without a stop at **F.A.O. Schwarz**, a bona fide branch of Santa's workshop Yopu can even dance on the piano keys Tom Hanks made famous in *Big*.

Heading toward 57th Street, it becomes clear why you're not in Kansas anymore, Toto. If Fifth is the avenue that epitomizes NYC, then 57th is the only street with enough panache to dare cross it. Broader in both size and scope than Fifth, 57th is the art gallery capital of the Western Hemisphere, the home of **Carnegie Hall**, the **Hard Rock Cafe**, and **Hermes**. Smack on the corner of 57th and Fifth is the store whose name has become as synony-mous with luxury and quality as it has with breakfast.

And it's only a few steps from ritzy **Tiffany** to glitzy **Trump Tower**, but they're light years apart in the same way old money is from new. There's an inbred, cultivated style to **Tiffany** that money can't buy. **Trump Tower**, on the other hand, is everything that money can buy. The polished pink mar-ble sleek of the atrium arcade with its multi-storied waterfall overflows suc-cess. You can have a snack at the foot of the waterfall to fortify yourself during a boutique break. Or, there's a very snappy little Italian Restaurant with good pastas and desserts. If part of your rest-stop includes a freshen up, you can thank Donald Trump for providing some of the classiest bath-rooms in town.

One of the things that makes New York so civilized is the **Doubleday Book Shop** directly across the avenue. It has four floors of books stocked by a buyer who really appreciates the printed word. You're likely to find celebs night-owling through the stacks here.

Once you go into **Steuben Glass** (glass slippers by order only), you'll understand why you hated drinking out of jelly jars. Cut glass and cut crystal are no better produced than at Steuben. This stuff is expensive, but worth every penny; however, butterfingers beware.

Given my druthers, I'd pass right by Gucci. But there are legions of out-of-work Hollywood producers who swear by Gucci loafers and obviously enough others willing to overpay on their social security to shop here. Your choice. If you've got money to burn, split your net worth between **Ferragamo** and the really classy (Read: no designer initials) leather goodies at **Bottega Veneta** on Madison Avenue.

Disney has brought Snow White, Cinderella, and of course that fun couple, Mickey and Minnie to 5th Avenue, in a charming setting fit for a prince. While the crass-cash-register driven, Warner Store is a blight on the corner of 57th Street, Disney has added a touch of whimsy to the Avenue.

DIAMOND MINING ON FIFTH

*For those who believe diamonds are a girl's best friend. Romancing the stones begins at **Van Cleef & Arpels**, crosses over to **Buccellati**, heads speedily toward **Harry Winston**, allows for as much time as you want at **Cartier's** and a minute to peek in at **Fortunoff's** before careening down to 47th Street and the diamond district. Take a deep breath and turn right on 47th, where movie buffs will recall Laurence Olivier was identified as a Nazi doctor in Marathon Man. If truth be told, they should award a doctorate in diamonds to anyone who can make it all the way from Fifth to Sixth on this monomaniacal block. There is likely to be no danger to your self-esteem or net worth if you know what you're doing. The bad news is that if you don't know how to buy a diamond, you probably shouldn't even be wearing one.*

The prime reason you'll be interested in 53rd Street is because it's the gateway to the **Museum of Modern Art** (See Museums, page 213) For devotees of twentieth-century art, MOMA is a must.

A pair of 1905 mansions on the corner of 52nd Street serve as home base for one of the world's great jewelers. Like **Tiffany's**, **Cartier's** is a gem of many facets. And that's despite the ho-hum "Les Musts" line developed to serve those whose trust funds are temporarily in limbo. The "real" Cartier's is as first-class as you can get (just ask anyone from Tokyo) and its good taste suits every palate if not every pocketbook.

When **St. Patrick's Roman Catholic Cathedral** (50th and 51st Street) opened in 1879, New Yorkers complained because it was too far "out of town" for them. The ground on which it stands was purchased originally as a cemetery—at the time the city did not extend above 42nd Street. It is today in the very heart of the metropolis, just opposite **Rockefeller Center** and **Saks Fifth Avenue**. Patterned after the cathedrals in Cologne and Rheims, it ranks eleventh among the world's largest churches.

St. Patrick's Cathedral at 50th & 51st on Fifth Avenue is patterned after the cathedrals in Cologne and Rheims.

Rockefeller Center *(50th and Fifth) (see Priorities, page 7)* is the unchallenged hub of the city and is to be seen as part of the Fifth Avenue experience or on its own. Be sure to tour the area, either as part of a group or on your own. Under no circumstances miss a chance to see the inside of **Radio City Music Hall** *(50th Street and 5th Avenue)*—either buy a ticket to a scheduled event or take a tour. It's the largest indoor theater in the world and houses an inner city for performers that is mind-boggling.

ROCKEFELLER CENTER: THE INSIDE STORY

There are:
388 elevators
48,758 office windows
65,000 people working
97,500 locks
100,000 telephones
175,000 daily visitors
240,000 daily population
(Only 60 U.S. cities exceed this total)

Saks Fifth Avenue, taking the entire blockfront on Fifth between 50th and 49th Streets, is the only thing to rival Rockefeller Center in its monumental salute to Capitalism. Saks isn't glitzy or trendy or particularly young at heart, but like an aging beauty it is still devoted to glamour. Okay, the glamour of yesteryear. Savvy New Yorkers know that when Saks has a sale, the markdowns are major and not to be missed.

The stretch down to 42nd Street is only mildly interesting and certainly not worth the trek unless you haven't seen Patience and Fortitude, the marble lions in front of the **New York Public Library** on 42nd Street.

Continue down Fifth. The only shopping of note is a branch of the **Metropolitan Museum's gift shop** on 40th Street and **Lord and Taylor's** department store at 39th Street. It is because of the **Empire State Building** (see Top sights, page 7) that this otherwise uninteresting area is on everyone's agenda.

Agenda Shopping/Midtown Fifth

A La Vieille Russie

781 Fifth Avenue; ☎ *752-1727, Mon.–Fri., 10 a.m.–5:30 p.m.; Sat., 11 a.m.–4 p.m.*

Right on the northeast corner of 59th Street is one of New York's most splendid delights. A la Vieille Race, a shop of impeccable taste and credentials, offering rare jewelry treasures from Czarist Russia, including the masterworks of Faberge.

Bergdorf Goodman

754 Fifth Avenue; ☎ *753-7300, Mon.–Sat., 10 a.m.–6 p.m.; Thurs., 10 a.m.–8 p.m.*

Mr. Bergdorf, a tailor who specialized in recutting men's suits to fit women (talk about being ahead of the times!), was bought out by Mr. Goodman in 1901. It took 27 years before the store moved to its present location, site of the old Cornelius Vanderbilt mansion. Today the Bergdorf name is still synonymous with being on the cutting edge of fashion. Very European in design, Bergdorf's buzzes with a cluster of tiny boutiques: Turnbull & Asser, Chanel, Fendi, Angela Cummings, and others—along with nooks and crannies jam–packed with the store's signature items. Bergdorf's knows their customers aren't afraid to take risks, so you're likely to come upon one-of-a-kind items here.

Bergdorf Goodman Men

745 Fifth Avenue; ☎ *753-7300, Mon.–Sat., 10 a.m.–6 p.m.; Thurs., 10 a.m.–8 p.m.*

The Bergdorf Man is as luxuriously outfitted as the Bergdorf Woman—definitely separate but equal. Suits by Brioni, shirts by Turnbull & Asser, ties by Humes and for riding to the hounds, the London Tack Shop. You can almost see the Ghost of Fred Astaire browsing through the ascots.

Tiffany and Company

727 Fifth Avenue; ☎ *755-8000, Mon.–Sat., 10 a.m.–5:30 p.m.*

There's more good taste within this building than the entire chocolate factory in Hershey, Pennsylvania. Not surprisingly, you will find that even relatively inexpensive items (key chains, pens, stationery) become instant treasures because of their provenance. Abraham Lincoln, Diamond Jim Brady, and Sarah Bernhardt all shopped here.

Warner Bros. Studio Store

1 East 57th Street; ☎ *754-0300, Mon.–Sat., 10 a.m.–7 p.m.; Sun., 10 a.m.–6 p.m.*

Looney Tunes on Fifth. Downstairs Bugs, Tweetie and Sylvester on mugs, ties, costume jewelry. Upstairs Bugs, Tweetie and Sylvester on plates, silverware, pots and dishtowels. Above that is a gallery for more affluent toon addicts. Framed single cell clips of your favorites can cost up to four figures and that's a lot of carrots, Doc.

Trump Tower

725 Fifth Avenue; ☎ *832-2000, Mon.–Sat., 10 a.m.–6 p.m.*

A Mall by any other name would be a lot cheaper. Some of the highlights are:

Saity—Indian Jewelry and crafts.

Galleria Cano—Pre Columbian art runs the gamut from $20 to $35,000.

Boehm—If you're in the market for breakable birds, they are world famous for their porcelain.

Aspreys—They have the most expensive bundles from Britain.

Ferragamo—Italian leather beauties that are smart enough to get you anywhere you want to go.

Urbani—Wall to wall delicacies from Italy including Black and White truffles, truffle oils, caviar and smoked salmon. YUM!

Henri Bendel

712 Fifth Avenue; ☎ *247-1100, Mon.–Sat., 10 a.m.–6 p.m.*

Think young, then think even younger. Bendel's has boutique-mania. They're all over the store filled with drop-dead fashions and accessories. They balance trendy and classy and come out with sybarite sizzle.

Coca Cola Fifth Avenue

711 Fifth Avenue; ☎ *418-9260, Mon.–Sat., 10 a.m.–6 p.m.; Sun., Noon–5 p.m.*

Yet another licensing gimmick store to hit 5th. If tee shirts, keychains, and posters go better with Coke, this is the place to be, but will the image of 5th Avenue survive (sob)?

Disney Store, The

711 5th Avenue; ☎ *702-0702, Mon.–Sat., 10 a.m.–8 p.m.; Sun., 11 a.m.–6 p.m.*

Mickey and Minnie in bronze over the door to welcome you and your charge cards. Yet another example of the "Malling" of 5th. The good news is that the store really has a bit of charm and the sales staff is referred to as the "cast."

Christian Dior

703 Fifth Avenue; ☎ *223-4646, Mon.–Sat., 10 a.m.–6 p.m.*

Three floors of Dior's. New to 5th Avenue but good old fashioned classic designs. A perfect antidote to theme store poisoning.

Bijan

699 Fifth Avenue; ☎ *758-7500, Mon.–Sat., 10 a.m.–6 p.m.*

Refugee from Rodeo Drive. Same men's fashions but no earthquakes.

Takashimaya

693 Fifth Avenue; ☎ *350-0100, Mon.–Sat., 10 a.m.–6 p.m.*

As architecturally elegant on the outside as the truly unique treasures to be found inside. Unlike its sprawling parent in Tokyo, the New York branch is a museum-like space to exhibit cut flowers as stunningly as it presents contemporary Asian art. Everything in the store has been selected for its excellence of design. Even the restaurant on the lower level, the Tea Box, is designed to transport the spirit to a calmer place. The Japanese Aesthetic carries over to the prices which are inscrutably, indescribably high.

Museum Company, The

673 Fifth Avenue; ☎ *758-0976, Mon.–Sat., 10 a.m.–6 p.m.; Sun., 11 a.m.–5 p.m.*

Reproductions of art from over 200 museums all over the world. Sculpture, jewelry, art make this a truly ageless gift shop. Even better than being able to wear Cleopatra's earrings, part of the profits go directly to the museums to increase their revenue.

Ferragamo

663 Fifth Avenue; ☎ *759-3822, Mon.–Sat., 10 a.m.–6 p.m.*

A whole store devoted to that luxurious Ferragamo look. Not just shoes but clothes and accessories. My Ferragamo runneth over.

Saks Fifth Avenue

611 Fifth Avenue; ☎ *753-4000, Mon.–Sat., 10 a.m.–6 p.m.; Thurs., 10 a.m.–8 p.m.; Sun., 11 a.m.–5 p.m.*

This was the place the boss's wife always shopped. A New York version of Harrods, where quality still counts. Chances are you are already familiar with Saks, but the main store, unlike its spinoffs in malls across the country, retains an aura of sophistication that would be difficult to duplicate elsewhere. Perhaps it's the setting—St. Patrick's on one side and Rockefeller Center across the street. Saks has worn well through the years and continues to attract millions of shoppers.

Agenda Best Bites/Midtown Fifth

Harry Cipriani

> *781 5th Avenue;* ☎ *753-5566.*
> *Cuisine: Northern Italian. Avg. $30–$60.*
> *Lunch: Noon–3 p.m.*
> *Dinner: 6–10:45 p.m.; Closed Sun.*
>
> They're a long way from their home in Venice where Harry's Bar is mythic, but they fit right in on Fifth. Very New York, air blown kisses, and a great view of the avenue. Great for a drink and a plate of something that ends in i. Just don't take it all too seriously. Credit Cards: All major.

Bergdorf Goodman   **$$**

> *754 5th Avenue;* ☎ *753-7300.*
> *Cuisine: International. Avg. $20–$40.*
> *Hours: Mon.–Sat., 10 a.m.–6 p.m.*
>
> Cafe on Five. A life-saver if you have a smoking charge card and you have to give it a rest. Bright, airy and wholesome, it gets you back to the battlefield with renewed vigor. Credit Cards: All major.

Trump Tower   **$**

> *725 Fifth Avenue;* ☎ *832-2000; The Med Grill,* ☎ *751-3276. Med Grill Cafe.*
> *Cuisine: Italian. Avg. $20 pp.*
> *Lunch: 11:30 a.m.–4 p.m. Closed Sun.*
>
> The Cafe is a relaxed self-service choice for super fresh sandwiches and a cappuccino on the run. The restaurant is for lingering over some well-prepared Mediterranean cuisine. Credit Cards: All major.

Aquavit

> *13 West 54th Street;* ☎ *307-7311.*
> *Cuisine: Scandinavian. Avg. $30–$60.*
> *Lunch: Noon–3 p.m.*
> *Dinner: 6–10 p.m.; Closed Sun.*
>
> Downstairs in the splendor of the two story dining room, the herring is served in an atmosphere of detached Scandinavian silence. You can almost hear the gravlox curing. But upstairs in the modestly priced cafe you can feast on open-faced sandwiches and other cold table delights with the relish of a Viking at a long-boat convention. Credit Cards: All major.

Tea Box Cafe at Takashimaya, The

> *693 5th Avenue;* ☎ *350-0100.*
> *Cuisine: Japanese. Tea Avg. $10.*
> *Hours: 11 a.m.–6 p.m.; Closed Sun.*
>
> Sushi cum Grosvenor Square and that's not all. Tiny exquisite sandwiches of smoked salmon, seared ginger steak, shrimp with lemongrass and surroundings to feed your aesthetic appetite as well. Thirty six different kinds of tea brings out the Mikado in all of us. Credit Cards: All major.

China Grill

60 West 53rd Street; ☎ *333-7788.*
Cuisine: Asian. Avg. $30–$45.
Lunch: 11:45 a.m.–3 p.m.
Dinner: 5:30–11 p.m.

Oriental high-tech cuisine that borrows the best from L.A. and Peking to create a super-elegant signature. If they've got mussels with black bean sauce on the menu, do not hesitate! Credit Cards: All major.

Saks Fifth Avenue

5th Avenue at 50th; ☎ *753-4000.*
Cuisine: American. Avg. $20.
Hours: All day, 10 a.m.–6 p.m. Closed Sun.

A department store restaurant with a wine list! Unheard of in N.Y. until Saks opened Cafe SFA on the 8th floor. Sandwiches with imagination, soups served with a flair and either a pink lemonade or a Bloody Mary, depending on how you looked in the three-way mirror in the try-on rooms. The views of the Spires of St. Patrick's Cathedral are spectacular. Credit Cards: All major.

American Festival Cafe

20 West 50th Street at Rockefeller Center; ☎ *246-6699.*
Cuisine: American. Avg. $35–$50.
Hours: 7:30 a.m.–midnight, Mon.–Fri.; 9 p.m.–midnight, Sat. & Sun.

What could be better than sitting back and watching the skaters in the Rockefeller Center Rink glide by as your fork almost reaches your mouth. Some people say the steaks being turned out by the kitchen are a 10, and of course, the figure eight's are flawless. Credit Cards: All major.

Lower Fifth Avenue

Once you leave the **Empire State Building**, Fifth becomes impossibly boring for quite a stretch. The avenue has narrowed, both physically and mentally. There are blocks that are downright tacky and you have better things to do with your time. The one exception is the "**Flatiron**" building on the corner of 23rd and Fifth. It marks the beginning of the **Flatiron District**. (See Neighborhoods page 104.)

This has become a particularly fertile stretch of Fifth. In the past few years the area around it has blossomed into the favorite turf for trendy new restaurants and even trendier designers. Today, lower Fifth is also a magnet for the shop-till-you-drop and brunch with the brunch-crowd.

The lower end of Fifth, below 14th Street, belongs more properly to **Greenwich Village**. If you're on Fifth looking down toward Stanford White's **Washington Arch**, **Chelsea** is to your right (West) and Gramercy Park is to your left (East).

Agenda Shopping/Lower Fifth

Daffy's

111 5th Avenue; ☎ *529-4477. Mon.–Sat., 10 a.m.–8 p.m.; Sun., Noon–7 p.m.*

Discount designer heaven for everyone. Well worth a quick look as you amble down the Avenue. Credit Cards: All major.

Emporio Armani

110 5th Avenue; ☎ *727-3240. Mon.–Sat., 11 a.m.–7 p.m.; Sun., 1–6 p.m.*
Always one of the hottest stores in town. Menswear from the master himself. Suit yourself and go! Credit Cards: All major.

Paul Smith

108 5th Avenue; ☎ *627-9770. Mon.–Sat., 11 a.m.–7 p.m.; Sun., Noon–6 p.m.*
For the CEO who likes his clothes veddy British, veddy now, and veddy expensive. Credit Cards: All major.

Barnes & Noble

105 5th Avenue; ☎ *807-0099. Mon.–Sat., 9 a.m.–8:30 p.m.; Sun., 11 a.m.–6:30 p.m.*
Two huge stores on opposite sides of 5th. One for textbooks and the other is their mega-sale annex. Book lovers can while away an entire week here. Credit Cards: All major.

Eileen Fisher

103 5th Avenue; ☎ *924-4777. Mon.–Sat., 11 a.m.–5 p.m.; Sun., Noon–7 p.m.*
Clothes that are soft and cool and natural and "right." Women love her casual elegance and style. Credit Cards: All major.

B. Shackman & Co.

85 5th Avenue; ☎ *989-5162. Mon.–Sat., 11 a.m.–6 p.m.; Sun., Noon–6 p.m.*
Since 1898, they've been selling favors and novelties that are wonderful for the child in all of us. Credit Cards: All major.

Agenda Best Bites/Lower Fifth

Eureka Joe $

168 5th Avenue; ☎ *741-7500.*
Cuisine: Lt. food. Avg. $10.
Hours: Mon.–Sat., 9 a.m.–8 p.m.; Sun., 10 a.m.–6 p.m.
More a Hosanna than a Eureka, this place serves coffee and sandwiches with the ambiance of your Aunt Sadie's living room. Overstuffed couches and chairs make this the best sit-down place on the Avenue. Credit Cards: Cash only.

City Bakery $

22 E. 17th Street; ☎ *366-1414.*
Cuisine: Lt. food. Avg. $10.
Hours: Mon.–Sat., 7:30 a.m.–6 p.m. Closed Sun.
A real find in a city where fresh usually describes your cab driver's retorts. At City Bakery every salad, every sandwich, every muffin seems just born. The tarts, cakes and pastries are among the best in town. Credit Cards: Cash only.

Chat'N'Chew   **$**
> *10 E 16th Street;* ☎ *243-1616.*
> *Cuisine: American. Avg. $15.*
> *Hours: 11:30 a.m.–11 p.m., 7 days.*
> Just your average, small town, folksy place plunked right off 5th,
> maybe you *are* still in Kansas, Toto. While the name may be a touch
> too much direction for some, the food requires only a hearty appetite
> and an appreciation for super home cooking. Credit Cards: All major.

Steak-Frites   **$$**
> *9 E 16th Street;* ☎ *463-7101.*
> *Cuisine: International.*
> *Lunch: Noon–5 p.m. Avg. $20.*
> *Dinner: 5 p.m.–midnight. Avg. $35.*
> The most uttered phrase in every bistro in Paris echoes in your ears as
> you cut into your meat. This place is jumping most of the time but
> you'll never see anyone from the Pritikin Institute here. Credit Cards: All
> major.

Mesa Grill   **$$$**
> *102 5th Avenue;* ☎ *807-7400.*
> *Cuisine: Tex-Mex/eclectic. Avg. $30–$45.*
> *Lunch: Noon–2 p.m.*
> *Dinner: 5:30–10:30 p.m.*
> A celeb chef who pots around with Tex-Mex has made this place hot-
> ter than a tamale. Bobby Flay, who also owns Bolo (See Flatiron Dis-
> trict page 110), has given the place and the plates a wild west look.
> Two stories high with an emphasis on industrial china. Flay's food is
> always innovative and the crowd is always "in". Credit Cards: All major.

Upper Fifth Avenue

It's above 59th Street that Fifth makes the transition from commercial
concourse to residential boulevard. With rare exception, the large apartment houses on Fifth are understated to the point of monotony.

What makes this section of Fifth a must for visitors is the liberal sprinkling of museums that's resulted in "**Museum Mile**," a grouping of ten cultural institutions between 82nd and 104th Streets:

El Museo del Barrio
> *1230 5th Avenue (104th Street).*

Museum of the City of New York, The
> *5th Avenue at 103rd Street.*

International Center of Photography
> *1130 5th Avenue (94th Street).*

Jewish Museum, The
> *1109 5th Avenue (92nd Street).*

Cooper-Hewitt Museum, The
> *2 East 91st Street.*

Guggenheim Museum
> *1071 5th Avenue (89th Street).*

Metropolitan Museum of Art, The
> *5th Avenue at 82nd Street.*

Frick Collection, The
> *1 East 70th Street.*

All of the above will be discussed in the Museum Agenda (page 207).

The upper end of Fifth is reached easily via Madison Avenue buses and taxis that are one block east of Fifth.

A crafty swirl of modernism, the Guggenheim Museum designed by Frank Lloyd Wright is as compelling as its art.

57th Street

The Street That Dares to Cross Fifth Avenue

If I had to select one street (not avenue) that best exemplifies New York, it would be 57th. From the grungy west end of it to the posh Sutton Place east end, it highlights all the intellectual, sometimes pretentious, sometimes Hollywood Theme Park, occasionally ugly and highly creative aspects of the city. After a walk on 57th you feel as though you've really been someplace. And you have.

Coliseum Books

    1771 Broadway (57th Street); ☎ *757-8381.*

NEIGHBORHOODS

For a large selection of discount and remaindered books as well as one of the best paperback sections in town.

Hard Rock Cafe

221 West 57th; ☎ *489-6565.*

Most likely has the wittiest canopy in town: half a Cadillac over the entrance. You'll also find the Hard Rock Store next store selling T-shirts and other instantly-forgettable memorabilia. People still line up for hours at a time, even though there's probably a Hard Rock opening somewhere in the world every four seconds. The food is terrific (one of the best B.L.T's in town) and the prices are modest by comparison to the bill you'll get from your M.D. to repair your damaged ear-drums.

Le Bar Bat

311 West 57th Street; ☎ *307-7228.*

Yet another theme bar, this one's ambiance would warm Bela Lugosi's heart (if there weren't a stake through it). The Bat population have deserted their belfry and hang upside down from the ceiling. If that weren't enough to raise your blood pressure, Vampire vamps line up to sample a Vietnamese menu. Dancing until the first rays of the sun.

Art Student's League

215 West 57th Street; ☎ *247-4510.*

Budding Rembrandts stop in to see what lectures are being given in town.

Brooklyn Diner USA

212 W 57th Street; ☎ *977-1957.*

The guy in the back, the one in the leather jacket, looks just like the Fonz. Relax, it's just a male model making the scene at this pale imitation of a real diner. Still, the outside looks good and the inside produces a pretty good burger and a fair malted. They also serve weird combo plates like Ziti, pancetta and scrambled eggs. What would the Fonz say?

Osborne Apartments, The

205 West 57th Street.

Has one of the most ornate stonework facades of any residential building. If you can, sneak a peek into the marble lobby.

Carnegie Hall

881 Seventh Avenue; ☎ *247-7800.*

Still the grandest concert hall in NY, especially after undergoing its recent facelift. The acoustics here are the closest you can get to Mt. Olympus. When originally built in 1891, the city's theatrical district was down around 34th Street and Carnegie was sandwiched into a residential area. Tchaikovsky was guest conductor during opening week ceremonies.

Uncle Sam's Umbrella Shop

161 West 57th Street; ☎ *247-7163.*

Will keep you singin' in the rain. They're all handmade from small folding jobs to huge doorman-sized varieties. Also canes and walking sticks.

Russian Tea Room, The

150 West 57th Street.

Neither Russian nor a tea room. In fact, it isn't even open now. Warner LeRoy has bought it and intends to re-invent it a-la- MGM Hold on to your Blinis! (SOB)

Planet Hollywood

140 West 57th Street; ☎ *333-7827.*

A much better way to show your support to Schwarzenegger and Willis is to see their movies. This place should have remained in outer space. Visually, just a tacky knock-off of the Hard Rock, the menu is definitely in the B picture category.

Stack's Rare Coins

123 West 57th Street; ☎ *582-2580.*

One place where they may take a wooden nickel. Numismatists throughout the world have been flipping over Stack's since 1858— which just about makes it the country's oldest coin collector since Pocahontas' piggy bank.

Sidney Janis Gallery

110 West 57th Street; ☎ *586-0110.*

European and American modern art.

Steinway Hall

109 West 57th Street; ☎ *246-1100.*

Even though it became the Manhattan Life Insurance Building, it still maintains an ornate showroom for the most famous concert piano in the world. The salesmen aren't above letting someone who looks serious run through "Chopsticks."

Jekyl and Hyde Club, The

1409 6th Avenue (57th Street); ☎ *541-9505.*

If you're in the mood for singing skeletons, talking masks, bleeding portraits, and more than 250 varieties of beer with your monster burger, you have arrived. Five floors of amusement park "thrills" with a menu to match. Be prepared to enter as Jekyl and exit as Hyde.

Motown Cafe

104 West 57th Street; ☎ *489-0097.*

Diana Ross may not wait on your table but the flavor of the Supremes is in the food as well as on the jukebox. There is wall-to-wall Motown memorabilia, crisp fried chicken, and sweet potato french fries. The Temptations themselves would be tempted by this top-of-the charts hit.

Allan Frumkin

50 West 57th Street; ☎ *757-6655.*

East and West Coast figurative artists.

Mangia

50 West 57th Street; ☎ *582-5414.*

A soaring space, super-modern with the most delectable salad bar I've ever seen. In the back, a grill section and in the front, coffee and fantasy pastries.

Rizzoli Bookstore

31 West 57th Street; ☎ *759-2424.*

As close as you'll get to Italian elegance without crossing a border. Perhaps the most sumptuous digs for a bookstore that you're likely to find. Aside from glossy foreign magazines and art books, there's always a sensitive collection of what's hot at the moment.

Tibor de Nagy

29 West 57th Street; ☎ *421-3780.*
Sculpture and nonobjective art.

Charivari Ltd.

16-18 West 57th Street; ☎ *333-4040.*
The sleekest, most downtown (in many ways) shop in this 14K gold chain.

9 West 57th Street

Because it's a great-looking building with a wonderful big fat red nine.

Sharper Image, The

4 West 57th Street; ☎ *265-2550.*
The catalog store to end all catalog stores. Everything is right there for instant gratification. Just get on line with the rest of the yuppies.

Corner of 57th Street and Fifth Avenue, The

Well worth a few moments. Stand in front of **Bergdorf's** and then cross over to **Tiffany's**. Look up and down the avenue. It doesn't get much more NY than this, except perhaps at night when it's not as crowded and the buildings are lit up. (Try not to hold the Warner Store against me. It may occupy the corner but not my heart.

Nike Town

10 E 57th Street; ☎ *946-2710.*
Where once stood the romantic, Parisian department store, Galeries Lafayette (which failed miserably in heartless N.Y.), there now stands a huge sporting goods emporium. 57th Street, once known for art, music, and the expansion of the intellect is now the home of the "state-of-the-art" sneaker. Talk about running amok!

Chanel

15 East 57th Street; ☎ *355-5050.*
Their new lavish 16-story Chanel building, with it's double staircase modeled on the one at Versailles serves "hot" Coco all year round. Karl Lagerfeld, having taken over helm and hem, serves up a dollop of drama along with the drop dead chic of that famous "little wool suit." Worth a visit just to inhale all that No. 5.

Burberry's

9 East 57th Street; ☎ *371-5010.*
Has the most beautiful bundles from Britain. In addition to the famous raincoat that defies the London fog, there are four floors of Burberry plaid for him and her. Luggage to match.

Hermes

11 East 57th Street; ☎ *751-3181.*
Yet another French connection, this time with some of the most expensive (and wonderful) leathers and perfumes in the world. (All those H's are for the hundreds and hundreds you can spend here.)

Wally Findlay Galleries

17 East 57th Street; ☎ *421-5390.*

European and American artists.

Pace Gallery

32 East 57th Street; ☎ *421-3292.*
Modern and contemporary. Adjoining galleries have prints and primitive art.

Victoria's Secret

34 East 57th Street; ☎ *758-5592.*
The place for anyone who loves giving or wearing luxurious lingerie and lounge clothes. The store itself is equally sumptuous and filled with good scents. Some designer undies for men as well.

Buccellati

46 East 57th Street; ☎ *308-2507.*
Extraordinary handcrafted silver upstairs, extraordinary jewels downstairs. Italian designs at their most sumptuous.

Holland & Holland

50 East 57th Street; ☎ *752-7755.*
The "colonies" branch of the famous London shop for hunters. This is the first time Tally-Ho has been heard on 57th Street.

Celine

51 East 57th Street; ☎ *486-9700.*
French from head to toe—shoes, bags, clothes. All Paris originals.

Hammer Galleries

51 East 57th Street; ☎ *644-4400.*
19th century and 20th century European and American artists.

Louis Vuitton

51 East 57th Street; ☎ *371-6111.*
The place to go for a double dose of LV's on everything from key chains to steamer trunks, although why anyone would want to use a perfect stranger's initials is beyond us.

Four Seasons Hotel

57 East 57th Street; ☎ *758-5700.*
See Hotels, page 24.

S.J. Shrubsole

104 East 57th Street; ☎ *753-8920.*
Marvelous antique British silver that would leave even Henry Higgins at a loss for words.

Hammacher Schlemmer

147 East 57th Street; ☎ *421-9000.*
Basically an entire department store for gadgets priced anywhere from a few dollars to a few thousand. Everything that's sold is tested by the Hammacher Schlemmer Institute so you can be sure your cuckoo clock is perfectly sane. Lots of games here, too.

Lillian Nassau

220 East 57th Street; ☎ *759-6062.*
The other big Tiffany collection on 57th Street, but this is Tiffany art glass from the past. Even if you're not a collector, it's worth a trip to see this technicolor wonderland.

Midtown

N/S - 59th Street to 34th Street
E/W - East River to the Hudson River

The midtown skyline includes the city's most famous skyscrapers: Empire State, Chrysler, GE, Lever House, and Seagram buildings.

Ever since Hollywood first used those opening shots of Manhattan skyscrapers and bustling crowds to set the scene for a movie about New York, everyone's image of the city has been midtown. Can you hear Gershwin on the sound track? You remember the scene: well-dressed people, all hurrying off to close a big deal with the most important person in the world or meet the love of their life on top of the **Empire State Building**.

Midtown Manhattan. Pure magic. The East Side shops are filled with fantasies that money can buy, and the West Side theaters with priceless dreams. The streets in-between form the grid for a board game named "Power."

What gives midtown its incredible energy is that everyone you see is actively pursuing a success story.

Midtown East

Madison Avenue

Most famous for being the business address of "The Man in the Gray Flannel Suit," midtown Madison is no longer inhabited solely by ad agency Type-A pre-cardiac patients. More pragmatic communicators, like **IBM** and **AT&T**, have settled in where CBS (now on Sixth Avenue), **Random House** (now on Third Avenue) and *Look* magazine (now a memory) once held court.

The **IBM Building** *(590 Madison Avenue, 56th to 57th Streets)* is a seriously modern green granite prism that looks to us as if it would have been much happier on some other block. What with Fifth Avenue's **Trump Tower** soaring above it, and the **Sony Building** across the street, it's difficult to see the forest for the trees. But what lovely trees there are: the street level IBM Atrium is a public space filled with leafy greens and flowers, tables and chairs, and a sculpture fountain. A kiosk sells light refreshments.

The former AT&T Building, Philip Johnson's huge temple to architectural excesses, **550 Madison** *(55th & 56th Street)* is now Sony's huge temple of consumer excess. Both sides of the building have a Sony store filled with the latest from the land of the lotus root. Between there's an atrium with chairs to lounge in and two snack shops. Even a theater ticket outlet.

AGENDA TIP

Just across the street, Checque Point USA (551 Madison) is where to have your currency converted—even on Saturday and Sunday from 10 a.m. to 6 p.m.

The **Villard Houses** between 50th and 51st Streets were built in 1882 for Henry Villard, founder of the Northern Pacific Railroad, and were later shared by Random House and the Archdiocese of New York (**St. Patrick's Cathedral** is right across the street). Then, in one of the strangest bedfellow deals in recent memory, they were sold and "incorporated" into the **Palace Hotel** *(455 Madison)* (see Hotels page 27) which rises like a Phoenix behind the graceful Florentine Renaissance palazzo styling of the original facades.

The measure of the Madison Avenue man, is still **Brooks Brothers** *(346 Madison; ☎ 682-8800)* which has been in style since 1818. Synonymous with the "Ivy" look and button-down shirts, it is probably least well known for the fact that Abraham Lincoln was wearing a Brooks Brothers suit the night he was shot.

Once down past 42nd Street, Madison dissolves into **Murray Hill**.

The good news is that when midtown Madison reaches 59th Street, it becomes Bond Street, the rue St. Honore and the Via Veneto all wrapped up in one package. In the '60s, '70s, and '80s, Madison was the New York address of the greatest designers in the world. They keep the créme de la créme in stitches and the rest of us in credit card hell. With the exception of the **Whitney Museum** (see page 214.) Madison has nothing of redeeming social value to distract you from counting your change and pocketing your receipts.

Agenda Shopping/Madison Avenue
59th to 86th Street
(A Selective, Follow-the Numbers Shop-Till-You-Drop Guide)

635 / Bottega Veneta
635 Madison Avenue; ☎ 319-0303.
Italian leathers so beautiful and so expensive they could be put on a shelf at home for exhibit.

645 / Lana Marks
645 Madison Avenue; ☎ 355-6135.
Lana focuses on Alligators and Crocodiles with the dedication of Captain Hook. Her handbags are famous for reptilian luxury.

650 / Crate & Barrel

650 Madison Avenue; ☎ *308-0011.*

Fresh from Chicago this mega-home-furnishings and tableware bonanza is bursting with color and design.

654 / Calvin Klein

654 Madison Avenue; ☎ *292-9000.*

You can now get your Calvins in a 22,000 sq. ft. emporium that holds a lot more than jeans and tee shirts. Old Cal has now come up with sexier clothes, accessories and even home furnishings.

660 / Barney's

660 Madison Avenue; ☎ *826-8900.*

Until a few years ago the only Barney's in town, located in Chelsea, set such a wide and expensive swath in the neighborhood that it gentrified the whole area. Young designers, young clientele, and a young spirit made it as much of a sight as a shopping experience. Then Barney's added an even swankier outpost on Madison Avenue where it again set a merry pace for all the avid Madison mavens to follow. Unfortunately, not as many of the crowd followed as they had supposed and today Barney's is long on style but short on cash. There are seven floors of pure "swank" where price tags are usually in three figures (for the moment, that is).

679 / Sherry-Lehmann

679 Madison Avenue; ☎ *838-7500.*

The Rolls Royce of wine shops. A must for anopheles, the selection is dazzling and beautifully displayed. At the very least, bring your wine-lover back home a Sherry's catalog.

680 / Crystal Lalique

680 Madison Avenue; ☎ *355-6550.*

Straight from the rue Royale and not about to throw stones are the artists who produce some of the most ravishing crystal in the city. Museum quality at prices to match.

683 / Georg Jensen

683 Madison Avenue; ☎ *759-6457.*

Superb Scandinavian silver, china, and pottery. Everything you buy here carries a warranty for elegance. Worth every Kroner.

687 / Julie Artisans Gallery

687 Madison Avenue; ☎ *688-2345.*

The motto here is wear it or hang it. Each piece of clothing is a work of art. For the woman who wants to paint a statement everything here will put her right in the picture.

703 / Floris

703 Madison Avenue; ☎ *935-9100.*

A royal warrant from QE II herself and all the English Lavender anyone could want dating back to 1730. Come here for the sweet smell of success.

717 / Erica Wilson

717 Madison Avenue; ☎ *832-7290.*

For those who believe in a stitch in time. Needlework buffs from all over the planet come to Erica Wilson's.

Museums

85	BMW Gallery, 320 Park Av	E18
90	City Gallery, 2 Columbus Circle	D17
99	IBM Gallery of Science & Art, Madison Av at E 56 St	E18
100	International Center of Photography Midtown, 1133 Av of Americas	D19
102	Intrepid Sea-Air-Space Museum, Hudson River, foot of W46 St	B18
103	Japan Society, 333 E 47 St	F18
105	Lladro Gallery & Museum, 43 W 57 St	E17
106	Lever House Gallery, 390 Park Av	E18
111	Museum of Modern Art, 11 W 53 St	D18
112	Museum of Television & Radio, 25 W 52 St	E18
118	Nikon House, in Rockefeller Center, 625 5 Av near 50 St	E18
119	Pierpont Morgan Library, 29 E 36 St	E20
123	Takashimaya New York, 680 Fifth Av	E18
127	Whitney Museum of American Art, at Equitable Center: 787 Seventh Av	D18
129	at 51 St at Philip Morris: Park Av & E 42 St	E19

Places of Interest

31	Carnegie Hall, 154 W 57 St	D18
34	Chrysler Bldg, Lexington Av & E 42 St	E19
38	Empire State Bldg, Fifth Av & 34 St	E20
49	NY Convention & Visitors Bureau, Executive Offices and Information Center, 2 Columbus Circle	D17
50	NY Public Library, 5 Av & 42 St	E19
53	Radio City Music Hall Entertainment Center, in Rockefeller Center, Av of the Americas & 50 St	D18
54	Rockefeller Center	E18
61	Times Square, Bway from W 42 to 47 Sts	D19
62	TKTS, W 47 & Bway	D19
65	United Nations, 1 Av & E 45 St	F19
66	UNICEF House, 3 United Nations Plaza	F18

Transportation Terminals

10	Airlines Ticket Office, 100 E 42 St	E19
13	East Side Airlines Terminal, E 37 St & First Av	F19
15	Grand Central Station, Park Av & E 42 St	E19
16	Island Helicopter, 34 St Heliport, 34 St & East River	F20
17	Passenger Ship Terminal, W 47–52 Sts & 12 Av	B18
21	Port Authority Bus Terminal, 8 Av & W 42 St	C19

Foreign Currency Exchange

705	American Express, Macy's Herald Sq at 34 St 695-8075	D20
720	American Express, 150 E 42 St 687-3700	E19
730	American Express, 374 Park Av 421-8240	E18
740	American Express, 59 St & Lexington Av 705-3171	E17
743	Chemical Bank, 970 Eighth Av 935-9935	D18
744	Chemical Bank, 969 Eighth Av 974-1594	D17
745	Chemical Bank, 1501 Bway 719-2180	D19
746	Chemical Bank, 270 Park Av 450-7814	E18
747	Chemical Bank, 1 UN Plaza 688-7095	F19
748	Chemical Bank, 11 W 51 St 307-8743	E18
750	Chequepoint USA, 22 Central Park So 750-2400	E17
755	Chequepoint USA, 551 Madison Av 980-6443	E18
760	Chequepoint USA, 1568 Bway 869-6281	D18
780	Harold Reuter & Co, Inc. 200 Park Av 800-258-0456	E19
795	Piano Remittance Corp, 645 Fifth Av 800-554-5613	E18
800	Reusch International, 608 Fifth Av 800-292-4685	E18

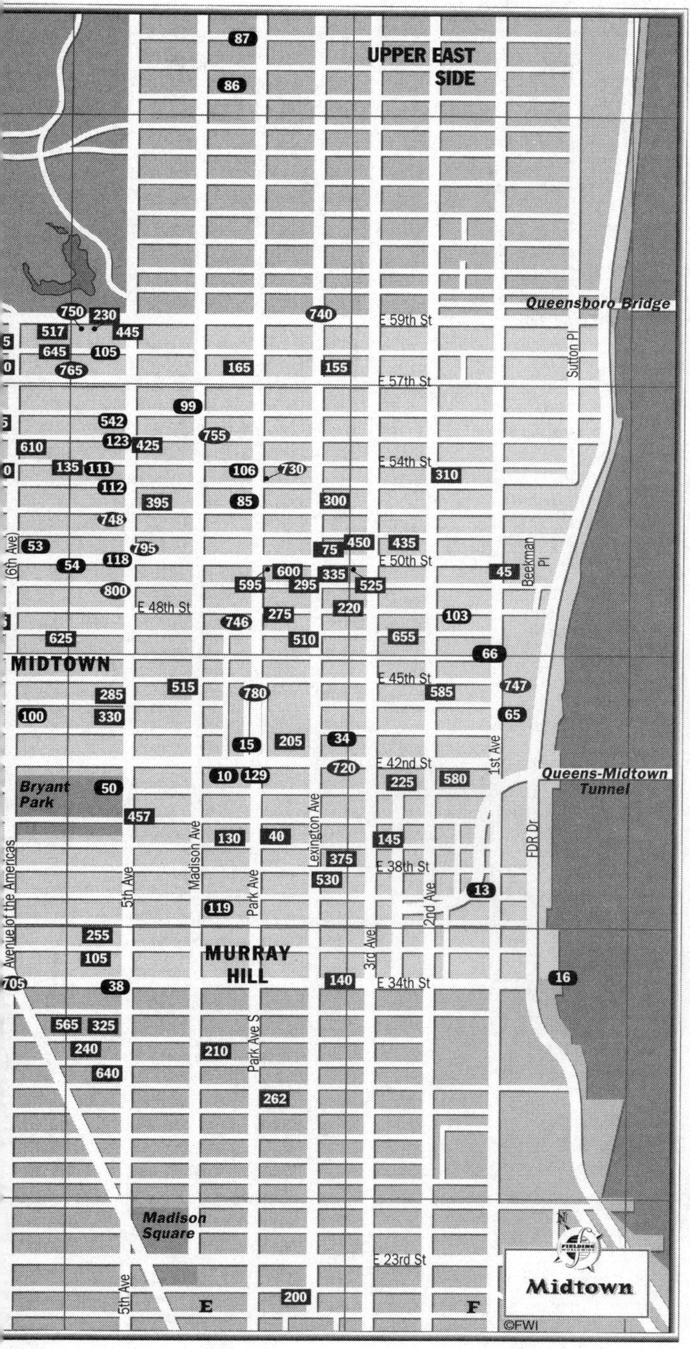

UPPER EAST SIDE
Queensboro Bridge
E 59th St
Sutton Pl
E 57th St
E 54th St
E 50th St
Beekman Pl
E 48th St
MIDTOWN
E 45th St
E 42nd St
1st Ave
Queens-Midtown Tunnel
Bryant Park
Avenue of the Americas
(6th Ave)
5th Ave
Madison Ave
Park Ave
Lexington Ave
E 38th St
2nd Ave
FDR Dr
3rd Ave
MURRAY HILL
E 34th St
Park Ave S
Madison Square
E 23rd St
E
F
Midtown
©FWI
87
86
750
230
517
445
645
105
765
740
165
155
99
542
755
123
425
610
135
111
106
730
310
112
395
85
300
748
53
795
75
450
435
54
118
600
335
45
595
295
525
800
275
220
103
746
625
510
655
66
515
747
285
780
585
100
330
65
15
205
34
720
10
129
225
580
50
457
130
40
145
375
530
13
119
255
105
140
16
705
38
565
325
240
210
640
262
200

Hotel Accommodations

25	Ameritania, 1701 Bway	D18
40	Bedford, 118 E 40 St	E19
45	Beekman Tower Suite, 3 Mitchell Pl	F18
50	Best Western President, 234 W 48 St	D18
65	Best Western Woodward, 210 W 55 St	D18
75	Beverly, 125 E 50 St	E18
105	Comfort Inn Murray Hill, 42 W 35 St	E19
110	Consulate, 224 W 49 St	D18
112	Crowne Plaza, 1605 Bway	D18
115	Days Hotel, 790 Eighth Av	D18
130	Doral Park Avenue, 70 Park Av	E19
135	Dorset, 30 W 54 St	E18
140	Dumont Plaza, 150 E 34 St	E20
145	Eastgate Tower Suite, 222 E 39 St	F19
155	Fitzpatrick Manhattan, 687 Lexington Av	E17
165	Four Seasons, 57 E 57 St	E17
185	Friendship Inn, 765 Eighth Av	D18
195	Gorham, 136 W 55 St	D18
205	Grand Hyatt, Park Av at Grand Central	E19
210	Grand Union, 34 E 32 St	E20
215	Guest Quarters Suites, 1568 Bway	D18
220	Helmsley Middletowne, 148 E 48 St	E18
225	Helmsley New York, 212 E 42 St	E19
230	Helmsley Park Lane, 36 Central Park S	E17
235	Helmsley Windsor, 100 W 58 St	D17
240	Herald Square, 19 W 31 St	E20
250	Hilton and Towers, 1335 Av of the Americas	D18
255	Hotel Metro, 45 W 35 St	D20
260	Hotel Pennsylvania, 401 Seventh Av	D20
262	Howard Johnson on Park, 429 Park Av S	E20
265	Howard Johnson Plaza, 851 Eighth Av	D18
275	Inter-Continental, 111 E 48 St	E18
285	Iroquois, 49 W 44 St	E19
295	Lexington, 511 Lexington Av	E18
300	Loews New York, 569 Lexington Av	E18
310	Lyden House Suite, 320 E 53 St	F18
315	Macklowe/Macklowe Conference Ctr, 145 W 44 St	D19
325	The Manhattan, 17 W 32 St	E20
330	Mansfield Hotel, 12 W 44 St	E19

335	Marriott East Side, 525 Lexington Av	E18
345	Marriott Marquis, 1535 Bway	D19
365	Milford Plaza, 270 W 45 St	D19
375	Murray Hill East, 149 E 39 St	E19
385	Novotel, 226 W 52 St	D18
395	Omni-Berkshire Place, 21 E 52 St	E18
405	Paramount, 235 W 46 St	D18
407	Park Inn International, 440 W 57 St	C18
415	Park Savoy, 158 W 58 St	D17
425	Peninsula, 700 Fifth Av	E18
430	Penn Plaza, 215 W 34 St	D20
435	Pickwick Arms, 230 E 51 St	F18
445	The Plaza, Fifth Av at Central Park S	E17
450	Plaza Fifty Suite, 155 E 50 St	E19
455	Portland Square, 132 W 47 St	D18
457	Quality Hotel, 3 E 40 St	E19
490	Remington, 129 W 46 St	D18
493	Renaissance Hotel, 2 Times Sq	D18
495	Righa Royal, 151 W 54 St	D18
500	Ritz-Carlton, 112 Central Park S	D17
510	Roger Smith, 501 Lexington Av	E18
515	Roosevelt, 45th St & Madison Av	E19
517	St. Moritz On the Park, 50 Central Park S	D17
520	Salisbury, 123 W 57 St	D19
525	San Carlos, 150 E 50 St	E18
530	Shelburne Suite, 303 Lexington Av	E19
535	Sheraton Hotel & Towers, 811 Seventh Av	D18
540	Sheraton Manhattan, 790 Seventh Av	D18
542	The Shoreham Hotel, 35 W 55 St	E18
545	Skyline Manhattan, 725 Tenth Av	C18
555	Southgate Tower Suite, 371 Seventh Av	D20
565	Stanford, 43 W 32 St	D20
575	Travel Inn, 515 W 42 St	B19
580	Tudor, 304 E 42 St	F19
585	UN Plaza-Park Hyatt, 1 United Nations Plaza	F19
595	Waldorf-Astoria, 301 Park Av	E18
600	Waldorf Towers, 100 E 50 St	E18
610	Warwick, 65 W 54 St	D18
620	Wellington, 7 Av & 55 St	D18
625	Wentworth, 59 W 46 St	D18
635	Westpark, 308 W 58 St	D17
640	Wolcott, 4 W 31 St	E20
645	Wyndham, 42 W 58 St	D17
655	YMCA Vanderbilt Branch, 224 E 47 St	F18

NEIGHBORHOODS

760 / Patricia Pastor

760 Madison Avenue; ☎ *734-4673.*

Old clothes never looked so new in her collection of vintage duds from the '20s to the '50s. Prices go from $75 to a possible four-digits.

773 / Fred Leighton

773 Madison Avenue; ☎ *288-1872.*

Extraordinary collection of antique jewelry. The Czarina and Lillian Russell would be equally at home. Prices for these once-in-a-lifetime pieces match the quality.

AGENDA TIP

For heaven's sake, keep your eyes open as you cross the street. There are all sorts of hidden treasures tucked into the blocks between Madison and Fifth, and Madison and Park. Be sure not to miss gems such as **Tender Buttons** ☎ *758-7004 (143 East 62nd Street) for what may well be the country's most complete collection of buttons for every occasion.*

---

789 / Montenapoleone

789 Madison Avenue; ☎ *532-2660.*

Luscious lingerie for sybaritic ladies if you can just manage to spell their name. For the fab femme fatale.

792 / Emmanuel Ungaro

792 Madison Avenue; ☎ *249-4090.*

Clothing of the same name.

793 / Godiva Chocolates

793 Madison Avenue; ☎ *249-9444.*

When is a Godiva not like all the other Godivas? When it serves coffee, tea, and exquisite pastries along with its usual take-home goodies.

799 / Frette

799 Madison Avenue; ☎ *988-5221.*

The one and only to get between the sheets with. Their linen is coveted by every grand hotel in the world.

809 / Puiforcat

809 Madison Avenue; ☎ *734-3838.*

Their crystal clear view of the world includes not only their own stemware and china but also the Saint Louis and Hermes collections.

812 / Billy Martin

812 Madison Avenue; ☎ *861-3100.*

What the well-dressed cowpoke will wear. Gorgeous handmade silver belt buckles, extravagant boots. Must be well-heeled to shop here.

813 / Maxmara

813 Madison Avenue; ☎ *879-6100.*

Sharp Italian designs by a sharp Italian designer. Bring many lira.

815 / Giorgio Armani

815 Madison Avenue; ☎ *988-9191.*

His usual impeccable tailoring and romantic designs are all present and accounted for.

816-817 / Gianni Versace

816–817 Madison Avenue; ☎ *650-0497.*

No unisex approach here for this very hot, very trendy designer. 816 has clothes for Signors, 817 for Signoras.

823 / Valentino

823 Madison Avenue; ☎ *772-6969.*

More Italian designs for your *dolce vita.*

824 / MacKenzie-Childs Ltd.

824 Madison Avenue; ☎ *570-6050.*

The most original looking shop on the avenue. A cross between Hans Christian Andersen and Tivoli, the inside could be a cottage in the middle of a fairy tale. Gilded ribbons festoon the ceiling and in the center of the store is a floor to ceiling bird cage filled with roosters and guinea hens. The collection of pottery, furniture, linens and glassware have all been hand fashioned or painted in romantic designs.

829 / Pratesi

829 Madison Avenue; ☎ *288-2315.*

Sheet-maker to the stars. Barbra won't sleep on anything else. Sinatra's linen closet is filled with them. Liz buys sheets and lingerie.

835 / The Metropolitan Opera Shop

835 Madison Avenue; ☎ *734-8406.*

If a tight schedule has made you a Phantom at the Opera this trip, you can still buy a musical memento "to go" at this uptown outpost.

836 / Missoni

836 Madison Avenue; ☎ *517-9339.*

The Missoni family have knitted and purled their way to sweater fame. Their wooly wonders are collected like treasures.

844 / Minna Rosenblatt

844 Madison Avenue; ☎ *288-0257.*

A woman who can spell Tiffany. The glass lamps are dazzling. She has fabled collector's items at fabled prices.

849 / Mabel's

849 Madison Avenue; ☎ *734-3263.*

A store devoted to feline fantasies. Categorically unique, it's filled with sweaters, toys, jewelry, furniture, and primitive art all celebrating Mabel's descendants. Mabel was an elegant black-and-white cat. The shop is *purrrr*fectly enchanting.

855 / St. Laurent Rive Gauche (Boutique Femme)

855 Madison Avenue; ☎ *988-8169.*

The Master speaks!

859 / St. Laurent Rive Gauche (Boutique Homme)

859 Madison Avenue; ☎ *988-8169.*

The Master speaks again!

867 / Ralph Lauren's Polo

867 Madison Avenue; ☎ *606-2100.*

Housed in one of New York's most beautiful mansions, this is the flagship store that carries everything Lauren designs from clothes to home furnishings. Magnificent interior.

870 / Pierre Deux

870 Madison Avenue; ☎ *570-9343.*

French fabrics, china, glassware, personal and home accessories. Fabrics are translated into bags, luggage, table-linen, wallets, and lots more.

870 / Oilily

870 Madison Avenue; ☎ *628-0100.*
A dutch treat for kids, from Holland. The whole store vibrates with the bright floral designs that makes Oilily the happiest place for the carriage trade in NY.

888 / Ralph Lauren's Double R.L.

888 Madison Avenue; ☎ *606-2100.*
The world of Polo has taken over what probably are the two most expensive pieces of real estate on Madison Avenue; both corner stores on 72nd Street. Opposite each other. The new double R.L. is sleek and nouveau southwest with an open fireplace and a sporty outlook on life.

895 / Portantina

895 Madison Avenue; ☎ *472-0636.*
Devoted to Italian brocades for upholstering you or your furniture. Some of the most luxurious fabric in the world.

939 / Books & Co.

939 Madison Avenue; ☎ *737-1450.*
More than just books, this is where you'll find people who eat, drink, and sleep books. Judy Krantz and Jackie Collins take back seats here to literary movers and shakers.

943 / Store Next Store

943 Madison Avenue; ☎ *570-3676.*
A new gift shop for the Whitney Museum that's filled with "made in America" goodies.

954 / Givenchy Boutique for Women

954 Madison Avenue; ☎ *772-1040.*
Le plus grand even if you're not Audrey Hepburn.

974 / Villeroy & Boch

974 Madison Avenue; ☎ *535-2500.*
Most of the world's elegant restaurants have you eating off this china. A full selection of all patterns.

987 / Judith Leiber

987 Madison Avenue; ☎ *327-4003.*
Evening bags and luscious leather that become instant collector's items. Her pavé crystal minaudieres can cost thousands. Leiber has created her own art-form.

991 / Vera Wang

991 Madison Avenue; ☎ *628-3400.*
Here come a lot of brides who know that Vera Wang can make a trip down the aisle a breathtaking experience (when she's not stitching up skating outfits for Nancy Kerrigan or frocks for Sharon Stone).

992 / Issey Miyake

992 Madison Avenue; ☎ *439-7822.*
The sun rises over this boutique for both men and women. Loose fitting elegant designs and tailoring for fashions playthings.

1015 / Linda Horn Antiques

1015 Madison Avenue; ☎ *772-1122.*

Chock full of terrific treasures that Linda Horn couldn't find room for at home. Has the look of an Italian palazzo: anything that doesn't have a burnished glow, twinkles.

1064 / EAT

1064 Madison Avenue; ☎ *772-0022.*

These people claim they are running a "sandwich shop." They sell soup at $8 a bowl and a side of mashed potatoes for $5. Stand outside and read the prices in the window: it's good for a laugh.

Agenda Best Bites/Madison Avenue

Sushisay $$$

38 E 51st Street; ☎ *755-1780.*
Cuisine: Japanese. Avg. $45–$60.
Lunch: Noon–2 p.m., Mon.–Fri.
Dinner: 5:30–10 p.m., Mon.–Sat.

Fresh from Tokyo, but fresher still is the exquisite raw fish that makes up the Sushi arrangements in this Japanese businessmens' "deli." Try to sit near the Sushi Master for one of the best shows in town. Credit Cards: All major.

Typhoon Brewery $$$

22 E 54th Street; ☎ *754-9006.*
Cuisine: Thai. Avg. $45–$60.
Lunch: Noon–2:30 p.m., Mon.–Sat.
Dinner: 5:30–10:30 p.m., Mon.–Sat.

There is no doubt that a big, fragrant wind has blown this chi chi micro-brewery to the thirsty Madison Avenue denizens who cram themselves into it. Aside from the boutique brewskis, the Thai food is delectable. The dumplings and ribs are served with a sauce that's hotter than the people who fight for a place at the bar. Everything on the menu is Thai-namic! Credit Cards: All major.

Viand Coffee Shop $

673 Madison; ☎ *751-6622.*
Hours: 8 a.m.–6 p.m., Mon.–Sat. Avg. $10–$15.

One of the last places left that you can get a turkey sandwich cut right from the bird. Add a little Russian Dressing and you're back in the '50s. Credit Cards: Cash only.

Le Bistro de Maxims $$$

680 Madison; ☎ *980-6988.*
Cuisine: French. Avg. $45–$60.
Lunch: 11:30 a.m.–4 p.m., 7 days.
Dinner: 5–10:30 p.m., 7 days.

Not as glorious as the one and only that used to be here, but the scaled down menu is a comfort when you need a quick aperitif. They also carry a line of take-away goodies with the big M label. Credit Cards: All major.

Arcadia $$$

21 E 62nd Street; ☎ *223-2900.*
Cuisine: American. Avg. $45–$60.
Lunch: Noon–2:30 p.m., Mon.–Sat.
Dinner: 6–10 p.m., Mon.–Sat.
Anne Rosenzweig has created the kind of atmosphere that makes lunch an escape to a cozy port in the midst of Madison mayhem. The fantasy mural that wraps around the room takes you "Into the Woods." Aside from the intelligence she brings to her kitchen she's put her Lobster Club sandwich and chocolate bread pudding on the New York culinary map. Credit Cards: All major.

Coco Puzzo $$$

23 E 74th Street; ☎ *794-0205.*
Cuisine: Italian. Avg. $45–$60.
Lunch: Noon–3 p.m., Mon.–Sat.
Dinner: 5:30–11:30 p.m., Mon.–Sat.
High profile Chef Pino Luongo who has a few fab pasta parlors around town, is stirring up his usual mix of hearty ragus and heady hype. Great for carbo loading in the midst of Madison. Credit Cards: All major.

Le Relais $$$

712 Madison Avenue; ☎ *751-5108.*
Cuisine: French. Avg. $45–$60.
Lunch: Noon–3:30 p.m., 7 days.
Dinner: 6–11 p.m., 7 days.
Aside from "haute" snacks and bistro bites the most popular feature is their sidewalk cafe. It's one of the trendiest in town. All the Beautiful people can watch all the other BP's as they stroll by. Credit Cards: All major.

Soup Burg

922 Madison Avenue; ☎ *734-6964.*
Hours: 5 a.m.–midnight. 7 days.
Cheap, quick, good and a decent bowl of soup. Hard to find all three on Madison. Credit Cards: Cash only.

Sant Ambroeus $$

1000 Madison Avenue; ☎ *570-2211.*
Cuisine: Continental. Avg. $20–$35.
Hours: 9:30 a.m.–10:30 p.m., Mon.–Sat.; Sun. 10 a.m.–6 p.m.
Though they serve full lunches and dinners here, the real story is the Creamy Italian gelati and pastries to soothe the sweetest of teeth. Credit Cards: All major.

Nector Coffee Shop

1090 Madison; ☎ *772-0916.*
Hours: 7 a.m.–10 p.m., 7 days. Avg. $10–$15.
The nectar will seem even sweeter after you've spent the morning wearing yourself out at the fabulous Metropolitan Museum of Art. This classic coffee shop is only a rosetta's stones throw away. Credit Cards: Cash only.

Sofia Fabulous Pizza $$

1022 Madison Avenue; ☎ *734-2676.*
Cuisine: Italian. Avg. $20–$35.
Hours: Noon–midnight, 7 days.

Good, crispy pizza in a very snazzy setting that covers two floors. The lights dim in the evening and Presto—pizza becomes romantic. Credit Cards: All major.

Lobster Club, The $$

24 E 80th Street; ☎ *249-6500.*

Cuisine: American. Avg. $20–$40.

Lunch: 11 a.m.–3 p.m., 7 days.

Dinner: 5:30–10:30 p.m., 7 days.

Named after Ann Rosenzweig's famous sandwich which she introduced at Arcadia—her first east-side triumph. Not only the lobster club but the rest of the menu here is informal, relaxed and delicious. The locals love it. Credit Cards: All major.

Park Avenue

It seems unbelievable that such a boring stretch of New York real estate could represent to the world the ultimate glamour of capitalism. With a few very important exceptions it's stone, steel and glass as far as the eye can see.

Once past 60th Street there are no shops to speak of so there is no shopping agenda for Park and unless you're checking out the neighborhood, there are no attractions to draw anyone except those who live there.

59th and Park is one of my favorite corners because of **Christie's** *(*☎ *546-1000)*, the fine arts auction house that has been making headlines for over 200 years. Be sure to check the papers for pre-sale exhibits; there's no more New Yorkish way to spend an afternoon than browsing and perhaps bidding on some of their goodies.

The **Mercedes-Benz showroom** at 430 Park is more notable in being the first NY work by Frank Lloyd Wright than for what it actually is. Park continues downtown attracting business headquarters because of the cache attached to its name.

St. Bartholomew's Church between 50th and 51st Streets, is located on a piece of land that formerly housed the Schaefer Brewing Company back in the late 1800's. St. Bart's is one of the avenue's oldest structures and certainly its most Byzantine. The salmon-colored exterior bricks were handmade and the ornate portico is by Standard White.

If you've heard of New York, you've heard of the **Waldorf**. From the day it opened, October 1, 1931, in the midst of the Great Depression, the **Waldorf** (see Hotels) has been making news. The former **New York Central Building** on 46th Street was built in 1929 as a coda to the avenue (it stands behind **Grand Central Station** and faces uptown). Later it became **The Helmsley Building** without any loss to its former self. It is a lovely structure, daunted only by the monolithic, ugly, and intrusive **Pan Am Building** *(200 Park Avenue)* that squeezed itself in behind the New York Central Building and has been a blot on the vista down Park since the day it opened.

The Park Avenue that continues on the other side of Grand Central Station is legally Park Avenue but is more identifiable with its Murray Hill location than its uptown provenance.

Agenda Best Bites/Park Avenue

Akbar $$

475 Park Avenue; ☎ *838-1717.*
Cuisine: Indian. Avg. $20–$35.
Lunch: 11 a.m.–3 p.m., Mon.–Sat.
Dinner: 5:30–11 p.m., Mon.–Sun.
First rate Indian cuisine in a Park Avenue setting as well as prices that would be low on the Lower East side. Credit Cards: All major.

Park Avenue Cafe $$$

100 E 63rd Street; ☎ *644-1900.*
Cuisine: American. Avg. $40–$60.
Lunch: 11:30 a.m.–2:30 p.m.; 11:15 p.m.–1:30 a.m., Sat.–Sun. only.
Dinner: 5:30–10:30 p.m., Mon.–Sat.
A cafe in the true sense of the word. Hustle, bustle, people dressed to the nines in a trendy atmosphere that definitely rates as "ten." David Burke brought his pots, pans and success from the River Cafe and is now serving up his own brand of American cuisine. Credit Cards: All major.

7th Regiment Armory $$

643 Park Avenue; ☎ *744-4107.*
Cuisine: American. Avg. $20–$35.
Hours: Tues.–Sat., 5–9:30 p.m.
You're in the Army now, but only in the magnificent mess hall, surrounded by the designs of Louis Comfort Tiffany. A truly amazing setting (including the moose head) that dates back to 1880. This has to be the most unique dinner spot in the city. The food may not rate a salute but the place does. Credit Cards: Cash only.

Lexington Avenue

If you need me to tell you that **Bloomingdale's** is on the corner of 59th Street and Lexington, where have you been? The most important retail establishment aside from the souvenir counter at Lourdes, Bloomies is the classic example of being in the right place at the right time.

When the Third Avenue El came down in 1954, the East Side suddenly became a "hot" location. **Bloomingdale's**, which had been a lower middle-class store, changed its image more rapidly than a chameleon on a rainbow. Quite literally, people thronged to Bloomingdale's on a daily basis. It was, in the late fifties and into the sixties, magic.

Alas, today, it is more fashionable to complain about **Bloomingdale's** than to adore it. The decision about whether to spend time heading up Lex from Bloomie's will depend upon how shopped-out you are.

The stretch down Lexington from 59th to the **Citicorp Center** between 53rd and 54th is six blocks in search of a character. There's nothing of major import here. Things literally look up at 54th with the white aluminum Citicorp Center that is topped off with a slanted 45-degree roof that can't be missed. It's part of the cityscape.

Since 1977, **The Market at Citicorp Center** (☎ *559-9992*) has offered New Yorkers a midtown shopping mall complete with some better than usual food possibilities and offbeat shopping. However, you don't have to do either and can still enjoy the multi-storied atrium space for its free concerts, movies, exhibits, and good public bathrooms.

If you're looking for an upbeat respite from the city, **Saint Peter's Church** (☎ *935-2200*), which is tucked in at the 54th Street corner and has a chapel created by sculptor Louise Nevelson, has been dubbed "the jazz ministry" and offers jazz vespers (Sun., 5 p.m.) and midday jazz (Wed, 12:30 p.m.).

Caswell-Massey, *518 Lexington at 48th Street* (☎ *755-2254*) is understandably proud of being the oldest pharmacy in the U.S. and is the only drugstore we've ever been to that has crystal chandeliers and carved wood paneling. They sell their own line of products, including the cologne favored by George Washington.

With the very notable exception of the fabulous **Chrysler Building** (see Priorities) which is not to be missed, Lexington loses its cache the closer it gets to **Grand Central Station** at 42nd Street. Grand Central is an outstanding feat of engineering, as well as a stunning example of Renaissance-style architecture. There are two levels of tracks to accommodate more than 500 trains daily. Its main concourse is one of the largest rooms in the world.

The Chanin Building (*122 East 42nd Street*) is a true Deco treasure with its interesting exterior bas reliefs and inner lobby of marble and bronze.

By the time Lexington reaches the lower 40s, it's passionately into its **Murray Hill** mode, almost as a last ditch effort to avoid the low 30s and upper 20s where it becomes (dare we say it?) ethnic: lots of quiet little Indian restaurants and shops for those who live in the neighborhood.

Third Avenue

Like Sixth Avenue on the West Side, Third is an urban Cinderella story. Most people who haven't been to New York recently still retain the "toidy-toid and toid" image of an avenue made infamous in the alcoholic nightmares of the movie, *The Lost Weekend*. By the mid 1950's, with all traces of the eyesore "El" gone, Third Avenue turned around faster than a pickpocket in a crowd. Once the domain of derelicts and pawnbrokers, the creepy crawly caterpillar sprouted commercial wings. The tenements are long gone and in their place, are the generic office buildings that finally made the area blandly respectable.

59th Street and Third is movie heaven. There are four theaters alone between 59th and 60th, with others tucked away in the downtown cross streets. You wouldn't be the first person to have a terrific NY day by wandering through **Bloomies**, stopping for a hot dog and then recuperating at an early movie. As you head down Third there are funky ground-level plazas and yet another atrium and even a Philip Johnson original that's been nicknamed the "lipstick" building. You won't have any trouble finding it.

Agenda Shopping/Lexington/Third

Saint-Remy

818 Lexington Avenue; ☎ *486-2018, 10:35 a.m.–5:30 p.m., Mon.–Sat.*
Another sweet shop, this one filled with dried flowers, sachets, nee-
dlepoint and lace from Provence. Tres French in feeling, a treat to
inhale, and sure to have that little something you need to bring someone back home.

April Cornell

860 Lexington Avenue; ☎ *570-1816, 10 a.m.–7 p.m., 7 days.*
A perfectly stenciled copy of the original on Columbus Avenue.
Indian prints for linens and clothes in delectable colors.

Ashanti

872 Lexington Avenue; ☎ *535-0740, 10 a.m.–6 p.m., Mon.–Sat.; 11
a.m.–5 p.m., Sun.*
Designer quality dresses in sizes 14-24. Elegant fabrics and styles.
Kate Moss need not apply.

Sylvia Pine

1102 Lexington Avenue; ☎ *744-5141, 10 a.m.–6 p.m., Mon.–Sat.*
Known for her extraordinary collection of antique beaded bags. Some
of the frames are silver, some are jeweled, all are one of a kind. She
also has antique jewelry with an emphasis on fine marcasite pieces dating from the twenties and thirties.

Big City Kite Co., Inc.

1210 Lexington Avenue; ☎ *472-2623, 11 a.m.–6:30 p.m., Mon.–Sat.*
Their extraordinary collection of kites makes you itch to experience
Central Park at the end of a string.

New York Women's Exchange

1095 Third Avenue; ☎ *753-2330, 10 a.m.–6 p.m., Mon.–Sat.*
Back in the dark ages before Hillary Clinton and Gloria Steinem and
Betty Friedan, women who wanted to work did so discretely behind
closed doors. Then they sent their beautiful handmades to the
Women's Exchange. They started that in 1878 and they're still doing
it.

Grace's Marketplace

1237 Third Avenue; ☎ *737-0600, 7 a.m.–8:30 p.m., Mon.–Sat.; 8 a.m.–
7 p.m., Sun.*
Grace's is to this neighborhood what Balducci's is to the Village.
Small wonder: Grace is a member of the Balducci dynasty who wandered north.

Agenda Best Bites/Lexington/Third

Gino   **$$**

780 Lexington Avenue; ☎ *758-4466.*
Cuisine: Italian. Avg. $20–$35.
Hours: Noon–10 p.m., 7 days.
A chance for you to see New Yorkers who have been in love with this hangout for years. Always crowded and noisy. If Damon Runyon had a yen for spaghetti and meatballs, this is where he'd have shown up.
Credit Cards: Cash only.

Sette Mezzo   **$$**

969 Lexington Avenue; ☎ *472-0400.*
Cuisine: Italian. Avg. $20–$40.
Lunch: Noon–2:30 p.m., 7 days.
Dinner: 5 p.m.–midnight, 7 days.
Wonderful homemade pasta pleasures in a "molto hectico" cafe—very *in* New York. Credit Cards: All major.

Mortimer's   **$$$**

1057 Lexington Avenue; ☎ *517-6400.*
Cuisine: American. Avg. $40–$60.
Lunch: Noon–3:30 p.m., Mon.–Fri.; 12:15-4:30 p.m., Sat.–Sun.
Dinner: 6 p.m.–midnight, Mon.–Fri.
In the guise of being a restaurant, Mortimer's feeds the New York passion to "do" lunch. This is one of those everyone-knows-everyone places that attracts all the big names in fashion and society (the two not being redundant terms in the least). People like to knock Mortimer's for the very reason it's successful. Not fair. Especially when there's so much else to knock. Credit Cards: All major.

Trois Jean   **$$**

154 E 79th Street; ☎ *988-4858.*
Cuisine: French. Avg. $20–$40.
Lunch: Noon–2:30 p.m., 7 days.
Dinner: 5:30–10:30 p.m., 7 days.
Three Jeans for the price of one. No matter which one is in the kitchen, the Bistro food is first rate. One of the few places around town you can drop into for a snack or dessert and coffee without making a major monetary commitment. Credit Cards: All major.

Vong   **$$$**

200 E 54th Street at Third Avenue; ☎ *486-9592.*
Cuisine: Thai. Avg. $40–$60.
Lunch: 12:30–2:30 p.m., 7 days.
Dinner: 5:30–10 p.m., 7 days.
Jean-Georges Vongerichten is the chef who not only brought flavored oils, but the kind of cuisine that makes strong critics weep, to the city. At Vong, he's translated Thai food into his extravagantly French menu. The best way to approach it is—a plate of this, a taste of that. You won't want to linger because the place is noisier than New Year's Eve. Credit Cards: All major.

Lipstick Cafe $$

885 Third Avenue; ☎ *486-8664.*
Cuisine: American. Avg. $20–$35.
Hours: 8 a.m.–3 p.m., Mon.–Fri.
Located in the lobby of a building whose nickname came from its shape, this trendy favorite with the office lunch crowd serves really good soups, salads and very original sandwiches. It's open for breakfast and lunch only. Credit Cards: All major.

Contrapunto $$

200 E 60th Street; ☎ *751-8616.*
Cuisine: Italian. Avg. $20–$40.
Hours: 11:30 a.m.–11:45 p.m., 7 days.
One flight up and right opposite "Bloomies," pastas are the story here. Home-made and in all shapes and sizes for dedicated carbo-cuties. Always crowded and always terrific. Credit Cards: All major.

Yellowfingers $

200 E 60th Street at Third Avenue; ☎ *751-8615.*
Cuisine: Italian. Avg. $10–$20.
Lunch: Noon–3 p.m., 7 days.
Dinner: 5:30–10 p.m., 7 days.
Even though this sounds like a place that serves too much mustard, in reality it's the place shopping and movie mavens on Third go for good pizza and maybe a skim milk cappuccino. Credit Cards: Cash only.

Arizona 206 $$

206 E 60th Street; ☎ *751-8615.*
Cuisine: Southwestern. Avg. $20–$40.
Lunch: Noon–3 p.m., 7 days.
Dinner: 5:30–10 p.m., 7 days.
Southwest dining in a totally citified restaurant. There are adobe walls, bleached floors and straight-back wooden chairs at wooden tables and a hint of jalapeño in the air. The bar is ten deep with cow-pokes from Bloomingdale's. Credit Cards: All major.

Matthew's $$$

1030 Third Avenue at 61st Street; ☎ *838-4343.*
Cuisine: American. Avg. $40–$60.
Lunch: Noon–5 p.m., 7 days.
Dinner: 6–10:30 p.m., 7 days.
Chef Matthew Kenny looks about fifteen-years-old and cooks with the finesse of a young Bocuse. His food is simple, classic and a breath of the freshest culinary air around. So is the restaurant which is open, bright and as comfortable as Matthew is with his very stylish menu. Credit Cards: All major.

E. J.'s Luncheonette $

1271 Third Avenue; ☎ *472-0600.*
Hours: 8 a.m.–11 p.m., 7 days. Avg. $10–$20.
B.L.T.'s, sodas, shakes in everyone's misty recollection of their old hangout. Fun to sit back, sip your time away and dream of Elvis. Credit Cards: All major.

S. G. Mellon $$

1291 Third Avenue; ☎ *650-1310.*
Cuisine: American. Avg. $15–$30.
Hours: 11:30 a.m.–2:30 a.m., 7 days.

One of New York's really meaty hamburger joints, not to mention the great french fries and beer that flows like wine. Credit Cards: Cash only.

Second Avenue

Second Avenue is the kitchen of the East Side. There are more restaurants here than in many emerging nations, not to mention more Italian eateries than Rome. Restaurants to the right, restaurants to the left, into the valley of pasta...

Part of what keeps Second smiling is the fact that it still retains an ethnic identity more meaningful than alligators on sport shirts. There are German, Hungarian, and Czech populations that give Second Avenue in the upper seventies and eighties (and part of First Avenue as well) a gentle reminder that there was life before the "Me" Decade.

The major sight at 59th and Second is traffic, traffic, traffic, as cars pile onto and off the **Queensboro Bridge**. However, if you take a ride on the overhead bright red **Roosevelt Island Tram** (think cable car), the traffic actually looks good.

Roosevelt (formerly Welfare) Island was reconceived as a "new town" way back in the 1970s, an urban utopia with no cars. A people-place to live in the middle of the East River with smashing views of the East Side skyline. I'll stick to a tram ride at night on the Rube Goldbergesque tinkertoy. Located between 59th and 60th streets on Second Avenue, it does not run all night (Monday through Thursday, 6 a.m. to 2 a.m.; Friday and Saturday until 3:30 a.m.; Sunday until 3 a.m.). Leaves every 15 minutes, $1.50.

Agenda Shopping/Second Avenue

Manhattan Arts & Antiques Center

1050 Second Avenue; ☎ *355-4400; Open Mon. thru Sat. from 10:30 a.m. to 6 p.m., Sun. from noon to 6 p.m.*
You could spend the entire week here. There are three levels of shops. The main floor is heavy on jewelry and silver with the two lower levels covering everything from china to furniture to glass and beyond. A favorite beyond is on the second concourse, the Hemingway African Gallery.

Joia

1151 Second Avenue at 60th Street; ☎ *754-9017, 10 a.m.–6 p.m. Mon.–Sat.*
If living in the past makes your heart beat faster then Joia can dress you for the part. Antique clothing for baby from the '30s and '40s.

AccScentiques

1418 Second Avenue; ☎ *288-3289, 11 a.m.–7 p.m., Tues.–Sun.*
Smelling like a rose, or in fact, most other blooms, the shop is one of the best places to inhale in the city. They also have tapestries and pillows in lush fabrics.

Agenda Best Bites/Second Avenue

Pamir $$
1437 Second Avenue; ☎ *734-3791.*
Cuisine: Afghan. Avg. $20–$40.
Dinner: 4:30 p.m.–1 a.m., Tues.–Sat.
Where to go when you're in the mood for chick peas, kabobs and yogurt. The Afghan cooking at this restaurant has won kudos from critics and locals alike. Credit Cards: All major.

Cafe Crocodile $$
354 E 74th Street; ☎ *249-6619.*
Cuisine: Mediterranean. Avg. $20–$40.
Dinner: 5:30–10:30 p.m., Tues.–Sun.
Very original menu featuring everything the chef loves which looks like just about everything. A nod to the Greeks, a stir of the Italian and a caravan of North African favorites. Credit Cards: All major.

Quatorize Biz $$
323 E 79th Street; ☎ *535-1414.*
Cuisine: French. Avg. $20–$40.
Lunch: Noon–2:30 p.m., 7 days.
Dinner: 5:30–11 p.m., 7 days.
Attention Bistro fans: Thick rich bouillabaisse, cassoulet, choucroute and all the other stars of a real bistro menu are appearing here daily. We have to stop ourselves from doing the same. Credit Cards: All major.

Lusardi's $$
1494 Second Avenue; ☎ *249-2020.*
Cuisine: Italian. Avg. $20–$40.
Lunch: Noon–3 p.m., Mon.–Fri.
Dinner: 5 p.m.–midnight, 7 days.
This old beauty has been here for years attracting the crema of Italian society. Even if you are not, the food can be impressive. Credit Cards: All major.

Pig Heaven $$
1540 Second Avenue; ☎ *744-4333.*
Cuisine: Chinese. Avg. $20–$40.
Hours: 11:30 a.m.–midnight, 7 days.
This may not be Miss Piggy's favorite hangout, but it's a really good-natured place where David Keh's porcine preferences translate into some of the best Chinese pork you're going to get in the city. Ribs, suckling pig, and the scallion-and-turnip pancakes are enough to make you smile when you say, "Th-th-th-that's all, folks!" Credit Cards: All major.

Sistina
1555 Second Avenue; ☎ *861-7660.*
Cuisine: Italian. Avg. $20–$40.
Lunch: Noon–2:30 p.m., 7 days.
Dinner: 5 p.m.–midnight, 7 days.

They cook in two directions here—Northern and Southern Italy. Both are top notch. You can mix and match your way around the whole country. Credit Cards: All major.

Mocca   **$**

1588 Second Avenue; ☎ *734-6470.*
Cuisine: Hungarian. Avg. $15–$25.
Hours: 11:30 a.m.–10 p.m., 7 days.
This is the closest you can get to Budapest on a budget. Paprika is the spice of choice here and it's dusted over breaded mushrooms, stuffed cabbage and almost everything else except the dessert chestnut puree and palacsinta. Not spa cuisine but a real bargain. Credit Cards: Cash only.

Elio's   **$$$**

1621 Second Avenue; ☎ *772-2242.*
Cuisine: Italian. Avg. $40–$60.
Dinner: 5:30–midnight, 7 days.
Don't expect great food but they give great atmosphere. When you're at Elio's you always feel like you're "In"—"In" with L.A. "In" with Wall Street and "In" with everybody else who wants to be "In." Elio's is always fun. Credit Cards: All major.

Elaine's   **$$$**

1703 Second Avenue; ☎ *534-8103.*
Cuisine: Italian. Avg. $40–$60.
Dinner: 6 p.m.–2 a.m., 7 days.
Everyone has heard about the legendary Elaine's where the literati meet the linguini. On any given evening (after 10 p.m.) you'll find the room filled with more scribes than ancient Egypt. Because Elaine's virtually (re) invented the power-restaurant concept, it's taken the rap for bad manners and bad food from precisely those people who should never be here. Elaine's masquerades as a restaurant but it's really a club. Approach at your own peril. Credit Cards: All major.

First and York Avenues

First Avenue

Former capital of the Swinging Singles Scene, the one-time boulevard of bars is beginning to show its age. The yuppies have begun finding grey hairs in the bristles of their military brushes and are suddenly starting to realize there's a price tag on everything.

Tack First Avenue onto your trek down Second. Turn the corner on Second Avenue and 42nd Street and head east. **United Nations Headquarters** is located on an 18-acre parcel of land donated by John D. Rockefeller, Jr. that is now international territory, the UN's signature structure is the **Secretariat Building**. The **General Assembly Building**, with its curved roof and central dome, is an integral part of the UN profile.

An international team of architects worked on the design, but the most dramatic aspects are credited generally to Le Corbusier. Works of art from all major nations are on display, most notably British sculptor Barbara Hepworth's abstraction dedicated to UN secretary-general Dag Hammarskjkold who was killed in a 1961 air crash while on a peace mission in Africa.

The United Nations displays the flags of its member countries along the plaza at First Avenue and 45th St.

Visitors enter on the north side of the **General Assembly Building** (45th Street) through one of seven nickel-bronze doors donated by Canada. Inside the lobby you'll see the Tamayo mural titled, "Brotherhood" which was a gift from Mexico, and above you is a Soviet gift, a replica of their 1957 Sputnik. Take note of the Chagall windows in the lobby. Stop at the information desk: there are a limited number of free tickets to open sessions of the General Assembly which are usually held at 10:30 a.m. and 3:30 p.m.; call ☎ *963-1234* in advance. Tours are given every half hour from 9:15 to 4:45. Admission. and they cover not only the history of the UN but also the art collections. Check at the Tour Desk in the lobby or call ☎ *963-7713*.

The **UN Gift Center** is a place that savvy New Yorkers have been patronizing ever since it opened and not merely because there's no city sales tax. You'll find jewelry, art objects, and handicrafts from member nations sold at very favorable prices. The selection is terrific and if you can't at least find enough to fill a Christmas stocking, surrender your credit cards at the door. Open 7 days from 9:15 a.m. to 5:15 p.m.; ☎ *963-7700*.

HIDDEN AGENDA

*The best kept secret in New York is the **Delegates' Dining Room**. With its terrific view of the East River and the UN gardens, it is open to the public for lunch between 11:30 a.m. and 2:30 p.m., Mon.-Fri. Aside from not knowing who's likely to be pow-wowing at the next table, the menu keeps changing with a list of international specials from member nations. Reservations are a must (☎ 963-7625).*

York Avenue

No doubt about it, unless you're heading for New York Hospital (and I hope you aren't), the star of York Avenue is **Sotheby's** at 72nd Street *(1334 York)*. As a Fine Arts auction house, Sotheby's has been operating since 1744 in England and in New York, after merging with Parke Bernet since 1964. By all means, do not leave the city without attending an auction: it's high drama, gambling, and art all rolled into one. Sotheby's arcade Auctions held approximately every other week have items within the potential of mere mortals. Even if there isn't a sale, it's worth going to one of the exhibitions. Unlike a museum, you can touch things at an auction house—and learn a great deal as you watch the dealers appraise the goods before they buy.

Another sight I personally might not take time for in a tight schedule is **Gracie Mansion**, since 1942 the home of the Mayor. On the other hand, if you find yourself in **Carl Schurz Park** on 90th Street and East End Avenue, you might take a peek. Diehards can call ☎ *570-4747* for tour information.

Agenda Shopping/
First and York Avenues

Applefield Gallery

1372 York Avenue; ☎ 988-7835, Mon.–Fri., 10 a.m.–5:30 p.m.
Browsers heaven, with shelves lined with rare editions and out of print treasures. A bit of London in New York.

Agenda Best Bites/
First and York Avenues

Red Tulip, The   **$$**

439 E 75 Street (York & 1st Avenue); ☎ 734-4893.
Cuisine: Hungarian. Avg. $20–$40.
Dinner: 6–11 p.m., Wed.–Sun.

Tulips are part of the folk art of this Hungarian boite. The food is ladled out with no restraint which is all to the good because the goulash soup is addictive. If you're counting fat grams leave your calculator at home. Credit Cards: All major.

Peppermint Park $

1225 First Avenue; ☎ 288-5054.
Cuisine: Ice Cream Parlor. Avg. $10–$15.
Hours: 10 a.m.–midnight, 7 days.
Sundaes on Monday not to mention a zillion homemade ice creams, splits, shakes and other confections of the devil. Hog heaven for kids. Credit Cards: All major.

Petaluma $$$

1356 First Avenue; ☎ 772-8800.
Cuisine: Italian. Avg. $40–$60.
Lunch: 11:30 a.m.–3 p.m., 7 days.
Dinner: 5:30 p.m.–midnight, 7 days.
A good place for pizza on First. The place vibrates with sound and color. The setting is just right for casual clothes and a casual Italian mind-set. Credit Cards: All major.

Voulez Vous $$

1462 First Avenue; ☎ 249-1776.
Cuisine: French. Avg. $40–$60.
Lunch: 11:30 a.m.–3 p.m., 7 days.
Dinner: 5:15 p.m.–midnight, 7 days.
A very relaxed French bistro with a relaxed menu as well. Tuck into the duck comfit, or the very respectable coq au vin. How scrumptiously retro can you get. Credit Cards: All major.

Upper West Side

N/S - 86th Street to 59th Street
E/W - Central Park West to Riverside Drive

Upscale professionals occupy the sought-after West 70s townhouses.

If Pinkerton had married Madame Butterfly, or if things had worked out differently for Anna Karenina and Count Vronsky, chances are they would have wound up on the Upper West Side. This is not the side of town for marriages of convenience. Everything on the West Side is inconvenient, or at least West Siders make it seem that way. Nothing is cool or pragmatic. Everything is passionate, a fight to the finish: be it for the love of your life or being next on the lox line at **Zabar's**. The West Side is the East Side with a short fuse—always wearing its heart on its sleeve.

The West Side jealously guards its position as the Left Bank of New York. It imposes no dress or behavior codes. It accepts the homeless and the beggars as it does the "first amendment" peddlers who narrow the sidewalks by lining them with elaborate displays of unwanted magazines and dog-eared books. There are falling-down drunks on the street in front of trendy new boutiques. Now, you must understand that this suits most West Siders just fine: they are, typically, liberals who feel guilty for having it better than others.

The official point of entry to the Upper West Side is **Columbus Circle** where Central Park South (59th Street), Broadway, and Eighth Avenue meet in a head-on traffic collision beneath the statue of Columbus erected in 1894. Since then, the area has had more ups and downs than the Santa Maria. The ill-fated Gallery of Modern Art appeared in 1965 amid heckles that its Middle Eastern white marble facade was in conflict with everything else in sight. The Gallery soon closed and the building limped along for a while until it became the **New York Convention and Visitors Bureau** where the Visitors Information Center *(2 Columbus Circle, ☎ 397-8222)* dispenses brochures, TV tickets, half-price theater tickets, and information. Today there are still rumblings about razing it and moving the Convention and Visitors Bureau to 42nd Street.

Then, there was the **New York Coliseum** which also went up in 1965 to a chorus of jeers about its nondescript design. With all the trade shows having changed their venues to the more modern Javits Convention Center, the Coliseum's future is in doubt. The **Gulf & Western building** once a sore thumb opposite **Columbus Circle** was recently bought by Donald Trump and is now in the process of being transformed into "the most expensive hotel and apartment residence in the world." This is a direct quote from that Trumpet of understatement, the Big D himself. Stay tuned! Thank God for the glorious baroque excess of the **Maine Memorial** (park entrance on Columbus Circle) that observes the sinking of the battleship *Maine* and the start of the Spanish-American War.

Central Park West

At 59th Street, Eighth Avenue's name was changed to **Central Park West** in order to stimulate real estate development on the western border of newly-completed Central Park. What we have today is the city's most elegant boulevard of apartment houses. The attention to detail, the sheer opulence of design, and the incredible variety of styles are not duplicated on any single stretch in New York.

Begin your walk on the park side of Central Park West, taking note of the following buildings:

Century Apartments
25 Central Park West.
Art deco.

N.Y. Society for Ethical Culture
2 W 64th.
Art nouveau.

HARLEM

Marcus Garvey Park

Upper West Side

©FWi

N

FIELDING

Henry Hudson Pkwy

Morningside Dr

Morningside Ave

Manhattan Ave

St. Nicholas Ave

W. 116th St

Cathedral Pkwy

Central Park N

Riverside Park

Columbus Ave

Central Park West

West End Ave

Amsterdam Ave

Broadway

5th Ave

Madison Ave

20

93

113

W. 96th St

101

104 **605**

114 **92**

97

68 **UPPER WEST SIDE**

The Reservoir

W. 86th St

88

Central Park

109

736 W. 79th St **81**

330

570

126

W. 72nd St

96

5th Ave

Madison Ave

Central Park West

Amsterdam Ave

Broadway

Columbus Ave

11

a

f,g b

d **46**

c e

9th Ave

660

32

West End Ave

215

11

8th Ave

Central Park S

W. 57th St

B **C** **D** **E**

11 12 13 14 15 16 17

Fielding

NEW YORK CITY

CENTRAL PARK TOUR

New Yorkers are rightfully proud of their 843 acre park. Scenic hills, lakes and meadows are framed by picturesque bridges, legendary highrise apartment buildings and must-see museums.

Bow Bridge

This decorative cast iron bridge leads from the Bramble over the lake to Cherry Hill.

Strawberry Fields

This tranquil area of the park contains 161 plants sent from all over the world as a tribute to the late John Lennon. Naples, Italy donated the mosaic in the pathway inscribed "Imagine."

The Lake

CENTRAL PARK WEST

Sheep Meadow

The Mall

FIFTH AVENUE

CENTRAL PARK SOUTH

The Pond

58TH STREET

MADISON AVENUE

The Dairy

The area that now houses the park information center was once an oper- ational dairy. The beautifully restored carousel is fun for all ages.

Wollman Rink

Ice skaters flock to this rink in winter and concert-goers enjoy it in the summer.

The Ramble

This 37 acre wooded area is a favorite with bird-watchers. The park reportedly has more than 250 species.

Belvedere Castle

The Central Park Learning Center is housed here and the terraces offer spectacular city views.

CENTRAL PARK NORTH

The Great Hill

The Cliff

Harlem Mere

Reservoir

Great Lawn

Metropolitan Museum of Art

Conservatory Water

A bronze statue of Alice in Wonderland characters is one of this area's most famous sights. Model boats float on the lake from March to November.

Bethesda Fountain and Terrace

This area near the lake and the Ramble is one of the park's best people-watching spots.

Central Park Wildlife Conservation Center

More than 100 species of animals are featured in climate zones including Polar, Tropics, Rainforest and California Coast.

The Plaza Hotel

Romantic carriage rides through Central Park often begin and end at the legendary hotel.

Carriage rides through Central Park are still one of New York City's most romantic experiences.

Prasada Apartments

50 Central Park West.
French Empire.

55 Central Park West.
More deco.

Hotel des Artistes

1 W 67th.
One of the city's most lavish apartment houses where the roster of tenants included Isadora Duncan, Noel Coward, Fannie Hurst, and Norman Rockwell. At the very least, peek in through the neo-Gothic facade at the devastatingly romantic Cafe des Artistes (see Restaurants) on the ground floor.

Majestic Apartments

115 Central Park West.
Note the window treatment that wraps around corners of this deco building designed by Irwin Chanin.

Dakota Apartments

1 W 72nd.
Perhaps the most famous residence in New York. Designed by Henry J. Hardenbergh who was also responsible for the Plaza Hotel (see

Hotels), on a site so far from the city's center that wags in 1884 said "it might as well be in the Dakota territory." The ultimate in luxury living and the setting for the film *Rosemary's Baby*, it has long attracted celebrities from the arts as tenants: Lauren Bacall, Leonard Bernstein, Boris Karloff, etc. Resident John Lennon was shot as he was about to enter.

San Remo Apartments
145-146 Central Park West.
One of the twin-towered buildings that's a familiar part of the skyline: these are topped with Roman temples yet. Hot and cold running celebrities.

Beresford, The
211 Central Park West.
Baroque towers top this blocklong building.

While strolling along the avenue, be sure to look down the blocks, especially 67th, 68th, 71st, 74th, 75th and 76th Streets for some prime examples of the "New York Brownstone."

The Museums that are located along Central Park West are covered in depth in the Museum Agenda (page 207).

Columbus Avenue

It's at 59th Street that Ninth Avenue loses control and becomes **Columbus**. Although renamed in 1890 to enhance the value of its real estate, it wasn't until the 1970s (a decade after the arrival of neighboring Lincoln Center) that Columbus began to get its sea legs. It seemed as though every shopkeeper in Paris, Milan, and Tokyo rushed to open a boutique on Columbus. Bars were transformed into pubs, and restaurants popped up like hives after a strawberry festival.

Today the whole nature of the street has changed. Columbus was a street for the 80s—Yuppie heaven, bankers and investment brokers. Gold card to Gold card with Euro trash and California cuties. But it's the 90s and Columbus is having an attack of glitz withdrawal.

It still hums on a sunny Sunday but not quite as feverishly as before. Caffeine has become the drug of choice on Columbus, coffee bars are seen from one end of the Avenue to the other and stores are now mostly Mall to Mall boring.

If that weren't bad enough, it's trying valiantly to recover from over two years of traffic-stopping street repairs. Visitors should still be prepared for traffic tie-ups and plenty of N.Y. chaos.

Agenda Shopping/Columbus Avenue
Betsy Johnson
248 Columbus Avenue; ☎ *362-3364, 11 a.m.–8 p.m., 7 days.*

A designer for the young at heart. Always witty, trendy, really creative clothes in crayon colors. Fun for the extrovert, with a very conservative price tag.

To Boot

256 Columbus Avenue; ☎ *724-8249, 11 a.m.–8 p.m., 7 days.*
Custom-made boots to please any Texas ranger. Exotic leathers make this a shoe-in for original craftsmanship.

Exotica

284 Columbus Avenue; ☎ *721-4394, 11 a.m.–10 p.m., 7 days.*
Lush jumble of masks, carved animals, jewelry and gifts from Mexico, Africa, India. One of the more intriguing stores on the avenue.

Only Hearts

386 Columbus Avenue; ☎ *724-5608, 11 a.m.–8 p.m., 7 days.*
Jewelry, sachets, delicate undies and even molds for fried eggs. Have a heart, these are great gifts.

Penny Whistle Toys

448 Columbus Avenue; ☎ *873-9090, 9 a.m.–6 p.m., Mon.–Sat.; 11 a.m.–5 p.m., Sun.*
An instant neighborhood hit opened by Meredeth Brokaw, Tom's wife. A must stop if you have kids, know kids or were one yourself.

Maxilla & Mandible

453 Columbus Avenue; ☎ *724-6173, 11 a.m.–8 p.m., Mon.–Sat.; 11 a.m.–5 p.m., Sun.*
If you want to pick a bone with someone, this is the place to come. Bleached cattle skulls, human tibias, vertebrae from reptiles, and other anatomical kitsch.

Agenda Best Bites/Columbus Avenue

Rikyu $$

210 Columbus Avenue; ☎ *799-7847.*
Cuisine: Japanese. Avg. $20–$40.
Hours: 11:30 a.m.–11:30 p.m., 7 days.
This place has been here forever, pre-yuppiedom. It's cheap, good and you don't have to sit up straight. Credit Cards: All major.

Godiva $$

245 Columbus Avenue; ☎ *787-5804.*
Cuisine: Coffee House. Avg. $15–$20.
Hours: 10 a.m.–9 p.m., Mon.–Sat; Noon–8 p.m., Sun.
The most European of the coffee shops in town. You can almost see the Danube from the window. Chock-full of confections and schlegg as far as the eye can see. Credit Cards: All major.

Dallas BBQ $

27 West 72nd Street; ☎ *873-2004.*
Cuisine: Western. Avg. $10–$25.
Hours: Noon–midnight, 7 days.
This is strictly for someone suffering from rib withdrawal. Grease isn't just the name of a hit on Broadway, here. Credit Cards: All major.

China Fun $

246 Columbus Avenue (72nd Street); ☎ *580-1516.*
Cuisine: Chinese. Avg. $10–$20.
Hours: 11 a.m.–midnight, 7 days.
Noodles, dumplings, lots of noise and indeed, lots of fun. They say
the menu has over 200 dishes—I guess it depends on how hungry you
are. Credit Cards: All major.

Scaletta $$

50 W 77th Street; ☎ *769-9191.*
Cuisine: Italian. Avg. $20–$40.
Dinner: 5–11 p.m., Mon.–Sat; 4–10 p.m., Sun.
One of the West Side's best Italian eateries. The risottos in particular
are creamy, melting, delights. The antipasto is another yummy
choice. Perfect if you're off to the theatre. Credit Cards: All major.

Mughlai $$

320 Columbus Avenue; ☎ *724-6363.*
Cuisine: Indian. Avg. $20–$40.
Hours: Noon–11 p.m., 7 days.
A bit of the Raj on the avenue. The food is hot but the homemade
chutneys keep the curries under control. Credit Cards: All major.

Isabella $$

359 Columbus Avenue; ☎ *724-2100.*
Cuisine: Italian. Avg. $20–$40.
Lunch: 11:30 a.m.–4 p.m., 7 days.
Dinner: 5:30 p.m.–midnight, 7 days.
This is an equal opportunity restaurant. They serve good Italian, good
grills and good salads. Nothing is memorable but on the other hand
the setting is very pretty and the spirit is more than willing. Credit
Cards: All major.

Museum Cafe

366 Columbus Avenue; ☎ *799-0150.*
Cuisine: Hamburgers. Avg. $15–$35.
Hours: 11:30 a.m.–midnight, 7 days.
A good burger is the good news here. The best news is that it's right
across the street from the American Museum of Natural History.
After all that T-Rex viewing you'll be feeling carnivorous to the max.
Credit Cards: All major.

Main Street $$

446 Columbus Avenue; ☎ *873-5025.*
Cuisine: American. Avg. $20–$40.
Hours: Mon.–Thurs., 5:30–11 p.m.; Fri.–Sun., 5:30 p.m.–midnight.
Big, airy, roomy tables, wall to wall comfort. Food served family style.
Mom-style home cooking. Favorites: Chicken Pot Pie, Meat Loaf,
mashed potatoes to die for. There are tables for two but at Main
Street the more people the more fun. Credit Cards: All major.

Rain $$$

100 W 82nd Street; ☎ *501-0776.*
Cuisine: International. Avg. $40–$60.
Lunch: Noon–3 p.m., 7 days.
Dinner: 6–11 p.m., 7 days.
The confusion about "Fusion cuisine" continues as French restau-
rants add bok choy to their paté and Italian's put foie gras on top of
pizza. At Rain all is finally revealed. They serve three separate though

equal cuisines. [Thai, Vietnamese and Malaysian] and they're all wonderful. Credit Cards: All major.

Amsterdam Avenue

Before the Upper West Side put on its top hat, white tie and tails. Amsterdam was the ugly duckling of the three "service" avenues—Columbus, Broadway and Amsterdam. It still is. But the West Side's frame of reference has changed so drastically that it's like a reviewer calling Pavarotti someone who can carry a tune.

Once the domain of Hispanic groceries and fixit shops, Amsterdam has gone from bilingual to bicoastal. But not entirely. It still suffers from urban schizophrenia: there are probably few avenues in the entire country that have boutiques, a gas station, a funeral home, trendy new restaurants, a public school, and bodegas where English is barely spoken, all within a few blocks. Amsterdam has also picked up the restaurant ball after Columbus dropped it, and there are some terrific new shops since Columbus lost its explorer's edge. It's at 72nd Street that Amsterdam crisscrosses Broadway and begins to hit its stride.

Agenda Shopping/Amsterdam Avenue

Star Magic
275 Amsterdam Avenue; ☎ *769-2020, 10 a.m.–10 p.m., 7 days.*
Right on the corner of 73rd Street is a heavenly store that covers all the stars except those in Hollywood. This is where astrology meets astronomy.

Granny Made
381 Amsterdam Avenue; ☎ *496-1222, 11 a.m.–6 p.m., 7 days.*
Even the Big Bad Wolf would snuggle up to the handmade sweaters and other knitted goodies for assorted generations.

Avventura
461 Amsterdam Avenue; ☎ *769-2510, 10:30 a.m.–7 p.m., Mon.–Fri. Closed Sat. 11 a.m.–5 p.m., Sun.*
Not as much fun as picking up your Venetian glass around the corner from the Grand Canal but the crystal and china designs are some of the best in the city. Very Nouvelle Italian. Don't bring your pit bull.

Agenda Best Bites/Amsterdam Avenue

Vinnie's Pizza   **$**
285 Amsterdam Avenue; ☎ *874-4382.*
Hours: 11 a.m.–midnight, 7 days. Avg. $10–$15.

The crust here is crispier than new money. Just the place for a quick slice to refuel for the journey ahead. Credit Cards: Cash only.

Shark Bar $$
307 Amsterdam Avenue; ☎ *874-8500.*
Cuisine: Cajun. Avg. $20–$40.
Lunch: 11 a.m.–3 p.m., Wed.–Fri.
Dinner: 5–11:30 p.m., Mon.–Fri.; 5–11:30 p.m., Sat.–Sun.
Cajun and soul food in a trendy setting. The room hums with model-speak and the young and the restless. Atmosphere and fried chicken to sink your teeth into. Credit Cards: All major.

Mingala West $$
325 Amsterdam Avenue; ☎ *873-0787.*
Cuisine: Burmese. Avg. $20–$40.
Hours: Daily, Noon–11 p.m.
A taste of Burma in a very unlikely place. Lavender walls and gilded tapestries create an exotic backdrop for genuine Burmese cuisine which is a combination of the best of Chinese and Indian. Some of it may be too hot to handle. Credit Cards: All major.

Emack and Bolio's $
389 Amsterdam Avenue; ☎ *362-2747.*
Cuisine: Ice Cream. Avg. $2.50.
Hours: Daily, 4 p.m.–midnight.
In Boston they all scream for E & B's ice cream fantasies. Now they've turned up on the upper West Side in a tiny parlor devoted to candy bar choices such as Peppermint Patty and Almond Joy. The sophisticates in your group can veer toward chocolate mousse. My cone runneth over. Credit Cards: Cash only.

Baci $$
412 Amsterdam Avenue; ☎ *496-1550.*
Cuisine: Italian. Avg. $20–$40.
Lunch: Noon–4 p.m., 7 days.
Dinner: 5:30–11 p.m., 7 days.
Yuppie Italian. Minimal setting but homemade sauces to the max. Designer carbo-cals that would have inspired Michelangelo to paint faster. Always crowded. Credit Cards: All major.

Sarabeth's Kitchen $$
423 Amsterdam Avenue; ☎ *496-6280.*
Cuisine: American. $20–$40.
Breakfast: 8–11 a.m., 7 days.
Lunch: 11 a.m.–3:30 p.m., 7 days.
Dinner: 6–10:30 p.m., 7 days. Avg.
THE place for brunch. Terrifically wholesome and always filled with the "literati" of the West Side. Good place to lose the bends from being trendy. Credit Cards: All major.

Cafe Con Leche $
424 Amsterdam Avenue; ☎ *595-7000.*
Cuisine: Cuban. Avg. $10–$20.
Hours: 8 a.m.–midnight, 7 days.
Tiny cantina with Cuban food that is respected by NY's Cuban community. Serves the only Cuban breakfast in this part of town, and throughout the day it specializes in Cuban sandwiches and powerhouse Cuban coffee. Credit Cards: Cash only.

Monsoon   **$**

435 Amsterdam Avenue (81st Street); ☎ *580-8686.*
Cuisine: Vietnamese. Avg. $10–$20.
Hours: 11:30 a.m.–midnight, 7 days.
There's always a line at dinnertime to experience their delicate Viet-
namese specialties. It is definitely worth the wait. Credit Cards: All major.

Good Enough To Eat   **$$**

483 Amsterdam Avenue; ☎ *496-0163.*
Cuisine: American. Avg. $20–$30.
Breakfast: 8–11 a.m., 7 days.
Lunch: Noon–4 p.m., 7 days.
Dinner: 4–10 p.m., 7 days.
Small cheery place for down-home cooking that runs the gamut from
comfort to Cajun. The lines form at breakfast for homemade scones,
continue through lunch for bowls of thick, rich soup, and through
dinner that finishes with a flourish of dynamic desserts. Credit Cards: All
major.

Tibet Shambala   **$**

488 Amsterdam Avenue; ☎ *721-1270.*
Cuisine: Tibetan. Avg. $10–$20.
Hours: 11 a.m.–midnight, 7 days.
Shangri-La with dumplings. A lot easier to stop off here than climb
the Himalayas. Real Tibetan home cooking like llama used to make.
Insiders tip (Tibetans put butter in their tea). Credit Cards: Cash only.

Barney Greengrass   **$**

541 Amsterdam Avenue (86th-87th); ☎ *724-4707.*
Cuisine: Jewish. Avg. $10–$20.
Hours: 8:45 a.m.–4 p.m., Tues.–Fri.; 8:45 a.m.–5 p.m., Sat.–Sun.
Preceding Zabars by a decade or two (1929) and slightly up stream,
Barney was the only lox game on the West Side for a while. After
opening he was crowned the sturgeon king but I'm not sure if the
title isn't just a fish story today. There's a small crowded cafe next
door that serves a pretty decent lox and bagel combo and a lot of local
color. Credit Cards: Cash only.

Broadway

Although Broadway is the only West Side avenue that doesn't change its
name after crossing 59th Street, it undergoes no less a transformation. The
downtown razzmatazz comes to an abrupt halt. Honky-tonk is put on hold
as it metamorphoses into as gracious a boulevard as one might find in Eu-
rope. Indeed, city planners in 1866 designed Broadway to follow the path
of the old Bloomingdale Road, anticipating it would be lined with posh pri-
vate homes. Like Park Avenue, there are "islands" of greenery to separate
the north- and southbound traffic. Both sides of the street are filled instead
with large apartment houses and with shops, shoppers, window shoppers,
and street vendors selling things you don't even want to know about.

Everyone who lives on the Upper West Side has a special part of Broad-
way that belongs to them. Every three or four blocks is its own small town.
Self-contained. Unique. Even the beggars (yes, Virginia, there are beggars
on Broadway) and crazies define their turf according to this most organic
of thoroughfares. Sidewalk space is at a premium on weekends because ev-

eryone has an urgent, chic or indulgent reason for being there, and Broadway becomes Calcutta, Paris, or Baghdad.

Lincoln Center

Lincoln Center is the home of the Metropolitan Opera, New York Philharmonic and American Ballet Theater.

The one part of Broadway that belongs to everyone including West Siders is a few blocks north of Columbus Circle at the **Lincoln Center for the Performing Arts**. The 14-acre complex of six building is devoted to theater, music, and dance. It's where you'll find the **Metropolitan Opera**, the **New York Philharmonic**, the **New York City Ballet**, the **New York City Opera**, **Lincoln Center Theater**, and the **Chamber Music Society of Lincoln Center**. Lincoln Center became a hit despite urban planners objecting to the traffic congestion, and architecture critics who panned the project for its lack of proper aesthetics (they may have had a point).

To be fair, **Lincoln Center** has taken it on the chin for years, and rather unfairly. I've often been there when all four theaters break, and it's quite manageable—if somewhat difficult to get a taxi. (So what else is new?) The most outstanding debit seems to be the lack of imagination in building the three major properties that form a U around the black marble fountain in the plaza: **Avery Fisher Hall** (formerly Philharmonic Hall), the **Metropolitan Opera**, and the **New York State Theater**.

Sadly, the decor of the Met and the NY State Theater is perilously close to the **Old Chinese Restaurant School of Design**. All that gorgeous travertine marble supporting a complex that attracts an audience of more than 5 million people annually should have been as demanding in concept as in performance.

AGENDA OBSERVATION: LINCOLN CENTER TOURS

A Totally Objective View

According to the "Lyons Guide to Empty Theaters," (a very short book, indeed), one-hour tours of the Met, Avery Fisher Hall, and the NY State Theater are given with alarming frequency and are incomprehensibly popular. Call 875-5351, if you can't figure out what else to do with $8.25.

AGENDA OBSERVATION: LINCOLN CENTER TOURS

*The best vantage point from which to experience **Lincoln Center** au naturel is standing in the center of the plaza near the fountain. As you face the ten-story high facade of the **Metropolitan Opera House**, at the curve of the U, the focal point shifts to the two Chagall murals. The one to your left, as you face the Met, is Le Triomphe de la Musique; to your right is Les Sources de la Musique. The latter has a King David-like figure, a Tree of Life in the Hudson River, while the former updates the sources into a montage of performers against the New York skyline.*

***Avery Fisher Hall** is the home of the New York Philharmonic. The most arresting piece of art here is in the main foyer (partially visible from the plaza): a two-part hanging metal sculpture by Richard Lippold—Orpheus and Apollo. The lobby here has a bar and two restaurants.*

*The **New York State Theater** has some brilliant pieces of art on display, most notably two enormous marble statues by Elie Nadelman: **Two Nudes**, and **Two Circus Women**. Be sure to see them.*

*Between Avery Fisher and the Met is the entrance to the Library and the Eero Saarinen-designed **Vivian Beaumont Theater**, surely the best looking structure of the lot. But the real star is the reflecting pool with its two-piece bronze by Henry Moore, aptly titled, Lincoln Center Reclining Figure. Also, don't miss the Calder black steel mobile near the entrance to the Library.*

Agenda Best Bites/Lincoln Center

Gabriel's $$$

11 W 60th Street; ☎ *956-4600.*
Cuisine: Italian. Avg. $40–$60.
Lunch: Noon–4 p.m., Mon.–Sat.
Dinner: 5:30–11 p.m., Mon.–Sat.

New, hot, '90s spin on Tuscan food. Buckwheat Polenta, Goat cheese cannoli, shank of lamb; really earthy Italian food. Better to go after the concert or theater—otherwise bring a pillow. Credit Cards: All major.

Fiorello's Roman Cafe $$

1500 Broadway; ☎ *595-5330.*
Cuisine: Italian. Avg. $20–$40.
Lunch: 11:30 a.m.–3 p.m., 7 days.
Dinner: 5:30–11:30 p.m., 7 days.

A riot of color from the dazzling array on the antipasto table that greets you. Make a do-it-yourself dinner that's too tempting to miss. Also crispy little pizzas make a perfect second act. Credit Cards: All major.

The Saloon $$

1920 Broadway; ☎ *874-1500.*
Cuisine: American. Avg. $15–$30.
Hours: 11:30–midnight, 7 days.

It goes every which way: Tex to Mex to Cajun to Slavic and back to Asian. If you can't find at least six major choices, you're hopeless. Great for people watching: The Saloon is one of the few places in the city where a sidewalk cafe really works. Credit Cards: All major.

Picholine $$$

35 W 64th Street; ☎ *724-8585.*
Cuisine: French. Avg. $40–$60.
Lunch: Noon–2:30 p.m., 7 days.
Dinner: 5:30–11:30 p.m., 7 days.
Mediterranean neighborhood bistro. Very pretty little place right off L.C. with a menu that has enough fish choices to make a comfortable pre-theater dinner. Credit Cards: All major.

O'Neals $$

49 W 64th Street; ☎ *787-4663.*
Cuisine: American. Avg. $20–$40.
Hours: 8 a.m.–midnight, 7 days.
A new home for the first restaurant to open in the Lincoln Center area. The famous Ginger Man has metamorphosed into O'Neals, same owners, much more space, but a menu that keeps all the "regulars" happy and some new wrinkles, (a toy chest for kids of all ages as you come in) Now you can have a hamburger and fries, with a teddy bear on the side. Credit Cards: All major.

Sfuzzi $$

58 West 65th Street; ☎ *873-3700.*
Cuisine: Italian. Avg. $20–$40.
Lunch: 11:30 a.m.–3 p.m., 7 days.
Dinner: 5–11 p.m., 7 days.
High-tech Italian design is coupled with first-rate pasta. Sfuzzi means "fun food" in Italy as well as on 65th Street. The menu works and so does the glitzy setting that attracts a savvy crowd. Be prepared for a crush. Credit Cards: All major.

Opera Espresso $

1928 Broadway; ☎ *799-3050.*
Hours: 7:30 a.m.–midnight. Avg. $10–$20.
Perfect for a dish of gelato, an ice-cream soda, or a sandwich. Maybe even a little tea and symphony. Credit Cards: All major.

Lincoln Square Coffee Shop $

2 Lincoln Square (64-65th Sts); ☎ *799-4000.*
Hours: 8 a.m.–midnight, 7 days. Avg. $10–$20.
A sprawling coffee shop with an extensive salad bar. Sheer heaven for bargain hunters. Credit Cards: Cash only.

West 63rd Street Steakhouse $$$

44 W 63rd Street; ☎ *246-6363.*
Cuisine: American. Avg. $40–$60.
Dinner: 5–11 p.m., Mon.–Sat.
On the second floor of the Empire Hotel they take their steaks very seriously. Amid a wood-paneled room filled with flowers and a view of Lincoln Center that is panoramic, the steaks are as impressive as the setting. Prime cuts are the order of the day. They easily match the bravura of the performances across the street. At last, a genteel steakhouse, lacking the usual saw-dust mentality. That's really music to my ears. Credit Cards: All major.

Ollie's Noodle Shop and Grill   **$**

> *1991 Broadway (67th Street);* ☎ *599-8181.*
>
> *Cuisine: Chinese. Avg. $10–$20.*
>
> *Hours: 11 a.m.–midnight, 7 days.*
>
> If you really want to use your noodle, you'll stop in before or after seeing a movie across the street at the Sony Complex, and flex your chopsticks at Ollie's. Upstairs a full menu of doughy delights. Downstairs a quick cup of tasty soup or a plate of the cutest dumplings this side of Shanghai. Credit Cards: All major.

The **Sony Theaters Lincoln Center Complex** at *Broadway and 68th Street* (☎ *336-5000)* has brought a whole new exciting way to view movies, with their introduction of IMAX 3-D. The 600 seat IMAX theater is equipped to show 3-D films with special headsets that provide the 3-D image as well as translations in the language of your choice. Will New York wonders never cease!

AGENDA'S "WURST" MOMENT

At the corner of Broadway and 72nd street is the best frankfurter stand in the city, Gray's Papaya. The price is a mere 50¢ for a juicy, hot dog, fresh from the grill. My drink of choice as accompaniment is a vintage Coconut Champagne. Now that's really putting on the dog!

At 73rd and Broadway is the **Ansonia**, a Beaux Arts fantasy with a high mansard roof, rounded corners, iron balconies and terra cotta ornamentation. It was built in 1904 as one of the largest apartment hotels in the world, fronting all of Broadway from 73rd to 74th Streets. Toscanini, Caruso, and Stravinsky all lived here. Upper Broadway comes into its own as a major artery right in front of the Ansonia. Although Columbus and Amsterdam have developed into fatal attractions for people from all over the city, Broadway is still the underbelly of the West Side. The **Apthorp Apartments** take the entire block between 78th and 79th Streets and Broadway and West End Avenue. Small wonder. If you've ever been inside an Apthorp apartment, you know why it takes up an entire block. They are grand in the great tradition of luxury living. Peek in through the gates to the large interior court. Some movie studio or other is forever filming at the Apthorp.

On the corner of 81st Street, a wonderful bookstore, **Shakespeare & Company** where regulars stop in on their way home after a night on the town. Best browsing on the West Side. Mmmmm. Did I mention **Zabar's**?

There are lots of restaurants along this stretch of Broadway, but my personal favorite is **Restaurant Two Two Two**, *222 West 74th Street,* ☎ *799-0400. (Expensive. Credit cards)* If you know who is buried in Grant's Tomb you can figure out where the restaurant's name came from. Set in a little townhouse off Broadway it is an uncharacteristically elegant spot in the midst of the West Side. The skyline makes the crystal chandelier dance and the wood-paneled, painting lined walls set the tone for some of the best food in the city. The menu is American cuisine and the sauces are awash with truffles and heavy cream. Desserts are equally formidable. It's all "two two" divine.

Hidden Agenda

HOW TO ZABAR

Zabar's *began as a small kosher deli in the 1930's and has developed into the MGM of gourmet markets. This place has taken on the cache of a national monument as though it were The Tomb of the Unknown Herring. Better than the Polo Lounge for bumping into celebs. Retired partner Murray Klein used to say that if you can still see floor between the feet of the mobs that line up here, they're not doing enough business. Just hang around out front (if you can find a place among the beggars, activists, and people selling things we all know accidentally "fell off a truck") and you'll see overachieving West Siders hot on the trail of a perfect piece of brie, or blue-haired Riverside Drive matrons picking up their weekly five pounds of smoked salmon for the family's Sunday brunch, and (hold on to your hats!) a busload of Japanese businessmen taking pictures in front of the salamis.*

Even if you're not planning a snack in your penthouse suite at the Pierre, it's worth taking a turn around Zabar's to see what all the excitement is about. The sheer variety of products on display is staggering. Especially when you realize that nothing, absolutely nothing, they sell is required for the continuation of life as we know it on this planet.

The things to remember are:

You'll need to take a number for purchases at the cheese, deli, and smoked fish counters and the wait on weekends can be as long as an hour, generally speaking, you are entitled to a taste of anything that is being cut for you.

They will ship for you—what better way to take home a bite of the Big Apple?

There's a super-sized **Barnes & Noble bookstore** on the corner of 82nd Street with a cafe and the aroma of fresh-brewed coffee wafting through the stacks.

The **Children's Museum of Manhattan** is dedicated to self-discovery and participation for toddlers to teenagers. (See Museums page 209)

West End Avenue

Once north of 72nd Street, West End is not zoned for commerce. It is strictly a residential avenue in the European tradition, this is where you find family living at its peak. For visitors, it has little excitement to offer—especially with the competition on Broadway that's only one block west.

Riverside Drive

Riverside, like Central Park West and Fifth Avenue, fronts a park and has the added benefit of the Hudson River. For sheer drama, nothing in the city beats **Riverside Drive**. It is open, airy, offers river views, and a landscape that includes the skyline or the **George Washington Bridge**. The blocks along the Drive are dotted with some superb architecture, notably along 75th, 77th, 80th and 81st Streets.

Riverside Park itself is a sliver of green, window dressing at times to obscure the West Side Highway, but still a cherished part of the neighborhood. Designed by Olmsted and Vaux of Central Park fame, it (unlike Central Park) doesn't have to be shared with the East Side and is guarded jealously by all those who live west of Broadway. A special feature is the

79th Street Boat Basin where some hardy New Yorkers live year round on their boats while others use the dock seasonally.

Gramercy Park and the Flatiron District

E/W - Fifth Avenue to the East River
N/S - 14th Street to 27th Street

If you ask a New Yorker where the **Flatiron district** is they'll tell you it's the block that the **Flatiron building** occupies in all its triangular splendor. If you ask an out-of-towner, he'll tell you with great excitement that it runs from river to river, from the 20s to the village, and that it's new, hot, in and where everything "cool" is happening. Luckily for the city both assessments are right. **The Flatiron Building** sits like the huge prow of a ship having made enormous waves in the downtown area.

The first new group to colonize the area was the publishing industry. Low rents, big spaces and enough spectacular restaurants for a century of Editor, Author, Agent lunches. Then came a bouquet of boutiques so that if you had any time after your very productive lunch, you could then spend a fortune. Last but not least came aliens from the outer boroughs who discovered that there was life after SoHo.

Gramercy Park, which is east of the Flatiron district, is a triumph for realtors, who speak about it in the same reverent tones usually reserved for The Queen Mother. To be sure, there are gorgeous blocks here, especially 19th Street between Third Avenue and Irving Place, and those houses on the perimeter of the park, some of which have been designated national landmarks. (**The Players Club** at 16 Gramercy Park South is a Gothic Revival townhouse remodeled by Stanford White after actor Edwin Booth donated it as a private club for his cohorts in the theater.)

The park itself is most exclusive. A pocket of green for those with green in their pockets. It is locked. The keys are bestowed upon residents of the area deemed worthy (whatever that may mean.) There is even a dress code for those in the park. Give me a break!

Fourteenth Street, which forms the border with **Greenwich Village** was once a very classy boulevard: it was "uptown" New York, the center of the theatrical district, site of the legendary Luchow's restaurant. The park was a hotbed of radical outrage in the early 1900's. This is the place that angry New Yorkers stepped onto their soapboxes, where leftists pulled no verbal punches, and the place you could always find anarchist Emma Goldman clenching her fists.

The most radical thing to be found in **Union Square** these days is the sprawling **Greenmarket** which is an astonishing sight to behold in the middle of the urban confusion of 14th street. Farmers bring the cream of the crop as well as muffins, cheese, plants, and honey to the market on Wednesdays and Saturdays. It's wonderful to stroll through and have a pick-up lunch of cheese and fruit practically fresh from the tree.

19

7th Ave
6th Ave
5th Ave
Madison Ave
Park Ave
Lexington Ave

730
MURRAY HILL

E. 34th St

East River

52 60 432
19
20 555
331
565 640
245 190
210

87
263

85

20

650

Madison Square

Park Ave South

3rd Ave
2nd Ave
1st Ave

E. 23rd St

21

200
Gramercy Park

117

8th Ave
7th Ave
5th Ave

CHELSEA

Union Square

124

Ave C
Ave D

W. 14th St

94

4

GREENWICH VILLAGE

EAST VILLAGE

22

Fourth Ave

735

E. 8th St

St. Marks

East River Park

Greenwich Ave

615

70

Washington Square Park

Christopher St

Bleecker St

Lafayette St

Broadway

Houston St

23

Columbia St

Williamsburg Bridge

Houston St
Washington St
Greenwich St
Houston St

SOHO

115
98
57

Allen St

390

Pitt St

116

Hubert St
Ericsson Pl

West Broadway

Spring St
Broome St

Kenmare St

LITTLE ITALY

Bowery

Christie St

Holland Tunnel

Canal St

260

47

24

TRIBECA

Broadway

Church St

CHINA-TOWN

740

Manhattan Bridge

63

Chambers St

Centre St

33

25

35
City Hall Park

340

18

Fulton St

60

71
710
590

72
750

370
128
39

725
41
58

325

64
745
40

Broad St
Pearl St

Wall St

26

30
51

715
110
108

93

69

95

Battery Park

23

24

22

N

Downtown

FIELDING
©FWI

27

NEIGHBORHOODS

37

59 121

Brooklyn-Battery Tunnel

D   **E**   **F**   **G**

Museums

91	Dia Center for the Arts, 548 W 22 St.	C21
94	Forbes Magazine Galleries, 60 Fifth Av at 12 St.	E22
95	Fraunces Tavern Museum, Broad & Pearl Sts	E26
98	Guggenheim SoHo, Prince St. & Bway	E23
107	Lower East Side Tenement Museum, 97 Orchard St.	F24
108	Museum of American Financial History, 24 Bway	E26
110	National Museum of the American Indian, 1 Bowling Green	E27
115	New Museum of Contemporary Art, 583 Bway, So of Houston	E23
116	NYC Fire Museum, 278 Spring St.	D24
117	NYC Police Museum, 235 E 20 St	F21
121	Statue of Liberty Museum, Liberty Island, New York Bay	E27
124	Ukrainian Museum, 203 2 Av	F22
128	Whitney Museum of American Art, at Federal Reserve Plaza: 33 Maiden Lane at Nassau St	E26

Places of Interest

30	American Stock Exchange, 78 Trinity Pl	E26
33	Chinatown, Chatham Sq, Mott, Pell, & Doyer Sts	F25
35	City Hall, Bway & Murray Sts	E25
36	East Village	F22
37	Ellis Island, NY Harbor	E27
39	Federal Hall National Memorial, Wall & Nassau Sts	E26
40	Federal Reserve Bank of NY, 33 Liberty St	E26
41	Fulton Fish Market, in South Street Seaport, South & Fulton Sts	F26
44	Greenwich Village	D22
47	Little Italy	F24
48	Historic Orchard St District	G24
51	Post Office (Main), 8th Av, W 31 to W 33 Sts	C20
52	NY Stock Exchange, Wall & Broad Sts	E26
57	SoHo, Bway, Canal, Av of the Americas & Houston Sts	E23
58	South Street Seaport, Fulton St & Pier 16	F26
59	Statue of Liberty, NY Bay	E27
60	The Paramount, Madison Square Garden	D20
63	TriBeCa	D25
64	Trinity Church (PE), Bway & Wall St	E26
69	Vietnam Veterans Memorial, Lower Manhattan	F26
70	Washington Arch, Washington Sq & Fifth Av	E22
71	World Financial Center, 200 Liberty St	D26
72	World Trade Center, btwn West, Church, Liberty, Vesey Sts	E26

Transportation Terminals

12	Air Pegasus Heliport, Liberty Helicopter, W 30 St & 12 Av	B20
	PATH (Hudson Tubes),	
18	at World Trade Center,	E26
19	at Av of the Americas & 33 St	D20
20	Pennsylvania RR Station, Seventh Av & W 33 St	D20
22	Staten Island Ferry Terminal, Battery Park, South Ferry	F27
23	Wall St Heliport, Pier 6	F27
24	World Trade Center-Battery Park City Heliport, Hudson River	E27

Foreign Currency Exchanges

710	American Express, World Financial Center 640-4885	D26
715	American Express, 65 Bway 493-6500	E26
725	American Express, 199 Water St 943-6947	F26
730	Chemical Bank, 349 Fifth Av 696-3252	E20
735	Chemical Bank, 756 Bway 777-5866	E22
740	Chemical Bank, 180 Canal St 334-9686	F24
745	Chemical Bank, 16 Wall St 577-1460	E26
750	Chemical Bank, 2 World Trade Ctr 321-1686	E26

Hotel Accommodations

60	Best Western Seaport Inn, 33 Peck Slip (Front St)	F26
85	Carlton on Madison Av, 22 E 29 St	E21
87	Deauville Hotel, 103 E 29 St	E20
93	Downtown Athletic Club, 19 West St	E26
190	Gershwin, 3 E 27 St	E20
200	Gramercy Park, 2 Lexington Av	E21
210	Grand Union, 34 E 32 St	E20
245	Herald Square, 19 W 31 St	E20
260	Holiday Inn Downtown, 138 Lafayette St	E24
263	Howard Johnson on Park, 429 Park Av S	E20
325	Manhattan Seaport Suites, 129 Front St	F26
331	The Manhattan, 17 W 32 St	E20
340	Marriott Financial Ctr, 85 West St	D26
370	Millennium Hilton, 55 Church St	E26
390	Off-Soho Suites, 11 Rivington St	F23
432	Hotel Pennsylvania, 401 Seventh Av	D20
555	Southgate Tower Suite, 371 Seventh Av	D20
565	Stanford, 43 W 32 St	E20
590	Vista International, 3 World Trade Center	D26
615	Washington Square, 103 Waverly Pl	E22
640	Wolcott, 4 W 31 St	E20
650	YMCA McBurney, 206 W 24 St	D21

NEIGHBORHOODS

Agenda Shopping/Gramercy Park/ Flatiron District

Strand Books

828 Broadway (12th Street); ☎ *473-1452, 9 a.m.–9:30 p.m., Mon.–Sat.; 9 a.m.–5 p.m., Sun.*

Bargain books by the billions. This is one of the most fabled bookstores in the world. Crammed with second-hand, rare, and review copy books that are unloaded by critics (who will remain anonymous.) at an up to 85% discount. There is a private rare book room upstairs where the price tags have many zeros.

Paragon Sporting Goods

871 Broadway (18th Street); ☎ *255-8036, 10 a.m.–8 p.m., Mon.–Sat.; 11 a.m.–6:30 p.m., Sun.*

If you're really a good sport you won't leave the city without a puptent or a pair of skis. It's as big as all outdoors.

A.B.C. Carpet

888 Broadway (19th Street); ☎ *473-3000, 10 a.m.–8 p.m., Mon.–Sat.; 11 a.m.–6:30 p.m., Sun.*

I'm not suggesting you buy 10 or 12 yards of broadloom to take home with you. It's just that ABC Carpet is so much more fun then rugs and furniture. The main floor is laid out as what they call the Parlor. Really it's a wonderland of gifts and accessories that will make your charge card salivate at the sight of it all. There are also miles of exotic ephemera from India and Asia as well as luxurious fabrics and tabletop wares. A.B.C. has taken over the mantle of "A New York Legend" from Bloomingdales and wears it with great panache! Don't miss at least having a peek if you're in the nabe.

Fan Club, The

22 W 19th Street; ☎ *929-3349, Noon–7 p.m., Tues.–Sat.*

Tired of collecting autographs? You can go to the next glam level and collect the clothes of your favorite star. There are little numbers worn by Dolly Parton, Marlo Thomas and for the big spenders, the castoffs of Dorothy Lamour.

Saint Laurie Limited

897 Broadway (20th Street); ☎ *473-0100, 10 a.m.–6:30 p.m., Mon.–Fri.; 11 a.m.–5 p.m., Sat.*

Suits everybody to a tee. The wholesale prices for the huge suit collection are only available at this outlet. Otherwise, Saint Laurie manufactures exclusively for out-of-town distributors. They even have a museum to show how they make the clothes you'll be tucking into your suitcase.

Darts

30 E 20th Street; ☎ *533-8684, Noon–6 p.m., Mon.–Fri., 11 a.m.–5 p.m., Sat.*

This place hits the bulls-eye for one of the most unusual shops in New York. An entire store just for darts! Square-tipped, round-tipped, pointed, blunt—not to mention dartboards up to the ceiling. These guys come right to the point.

AGENDA TIP

Perfume Row is the name given to 17th Street between Broadway and Fifth Avenue. It's lined with shops selling brand name perfumes and toiletries at a discount of 10-20% off department store prices. Although these are rough-and-tumble establishments, the goods are real. Except for some knock-off fragrances clearly marked as Fake Opium, Fake Giorgio, etc. Sniff a whiff at **Jay's Perfume Bar** *(28 E 17th),* **Perfume Encounter** *(25 E. 17th) or* **M&P Perfumes** *(24 E 17th).*

New York Cake

34 W 22nd Street; ☎ *675-2253, 9:30 a.m.–6 p.m., Mon.–Sat.; 11 a.m.–6 p.m., Sun.*

Nothing half-baked about this place. They have just the right equipment to turn out enough cakes and candies for Willie Wonka's most extravagant dreams. Gadgets galore for the serious baker.

Agenda Best Bites/Gramercy Park/ Flatiron District

Coffee Shop $

29 Union Square West (E 16th Street); ☎ *243-7969.*
Hours: Open 23 hours a day, 7 days. Avg. $10–$20.

A definite "scene." Tables filled with the on-the-brink, almost recognizable, look-at-me set, in a ditsy Brazilian setting. Credit Cards: Cash only.

Republic $

37 Union Square (16th & 17th Streets); ☎ *627-7172.*
Cuisine: Asian. Avg. $10–$30.
Hours: Noon–11 p.m., 7 days.

A wonderful place to noodle around. Pan Asian specialties in a big informal fun setting. Udon, Soba and Raman to wrap around your chopsticks. Won't cost a lot of dough either. Credit Cards: All major.

Pete's Tavern $$

129 E 18th Street; ☎ *473-7676.*
Cuisine: American. Avg. $20–$40.
Hours: 10–1 a.m., 7 days.

Legend has it that this is where O Henry wrote "The Gift of the Magi." Booth No. 1, please. Pete's is a comfortable place for burgers, omelettes, and other forms of yuppie cuisine downed by the stockbrokers who come to trade tips. Still a favorite with gloomy freelance writers, and editors with souls. Credit Cards: All major.

A.B.C. Cafe; A.B.C. Carpet $

888 Broadway (19th Street); ☎ *473-3000.*
Cuisine: American. Avg. $10–$20.
Hours: 10 a.m.–6 p.m., 7 days.

Tucked away in the back of ABC in a cozy corner they will serve you up a slice of quiche a cappuccino or a scrumptious dessert. The Cafe is as magical as the rest of A.B.C., so it's the perfect place to ponder your purchases. Credit Cards: All major.

Friend of a Farmer $$

77 Irving Place (18–19th Streets); ☎ *477-2188.*
Cuisine: American. Avg. $15–$40.
Hours: 8 a.m.–10 p.m., Mon.–Fri.; 8 a.m.–11 p.m., Sat.–Sun.
This is a charming little country restaurant filled to the brim with comfort pot pies, spinach meatloaf, and some of the best breads around. Credit Cards: All major.

America $

9 E 18th Street; ☎ *505-2110.*
Cuisine: American. Avg. $10–$20.
Hours: 11 a.m.–midnight, 7 days.
There are a dozen good reasons for going to a restaurant besides great food. What about deafening noise, cavernous spaces seating at last count, 350 diners, that still manage to be packed, great people watching. After all—this is America isn't it? Credit Cards: All major.

Gramercy Tavern $$$

42 E 20 Street; ☎ *477-0777.*
Cuisine: American. Avg. $40–$60.
Lunch: Noon–2 p.m., 7 days.
Dinner: 5:30–10 p.m., 7 days.
Danny Meyer has struck again, this time with a more elegant version of his mega-successful Union Square Cafe. (see Restaurants). The menu is focused on Americana that includes fragrant chowders and perfectly done grills. The black truffle ragout is a sybaritic show-stopper. Credit Cards: All major.

Aja $$$

937 Broadway; ☎ *473-8388.*
Cuisine: Asian. Avg. $30–$50.
Lunch: Noon–3 p.m., 7 days.
Dinner: 6–11 p.m., 7 days.
All the spices of the Orient are mingled here to produce an enchanting menu—China, India, Japan and Thailand are all deliciously represented. Credit Cards: All major.

Campagna $$$

24 E 21st Street; ☎ *460-0900.*
Cuisine: Italian. Avg. $40–$60.
Lunch: Noon–2:45 p.m., 7 days.
Dinner: 6–11:30 p.m., 7 days.
Mark Strausman, the Chef here has created an Italian restaurant that can sometimes resemble a Bar-Mitzvah reception. People blow kisses to friends across the room and amble back and forth to schmooz. But familiarity sure doesn't breed contempt here because the food is great. Robust flavors, very personal and original offerings that would make Mama Leone spin in her grave. Credit Cards: All major.

Cals $$

55 W 21st Street; ☎ *929-0740.*
Cuisine: American. Avg. $40–$60.
Lunch: 11:30 a.m.–5 p.m., Mon.–Fri.
Dinner: 5 p.m.–midnight, 7 days.

Everybody likes Cal, but it's hard to pin them down about why. It's just a big, handsome place, with a gorgeous bar and a very relaxed pace. All this and good food seem the way to go for us. Credit Cards: All major.

Bolo $$$

23 E 22nd Street; ☎ *228-2200.*
Cuisine: Spanish. Avg. $40–$60.
Lunch: Noon–2:30 p.m., Mon.–Fri.
Dinner: 5:30–11:30 p.m., 7 days.

Bolo is more than a restaurant. It's really a state of mind and your mind is on Spain as soon as you walk through the door. The look is Madrid on a busy night (of course, every night is a busy night in Madrid). Bobby Flay the energetic maestro of the very spicy Mesa Grill (see 5th Avenue page 58) has gone across the Atlantic to capture the flavor of Spain on a very sunny day. Paella of Lobster, Crisp Grilled Squid, and a Catalan specialty called Frideus made of fine noodles poached in a rich fish stock. As Hemingway might have said, the Bolo tolls for thee. Credit Cards: All major.

Follonico $$

6 W 24th Street; ☎ *691-6359.*
Cuisine: Italian. Avg. $20–$40.
Lunch: Noon–3 p.m., Mon.–Fri.
Dinner: 6–11 p.m., 7 days.

Toothsome Tuscan treats in a cozy room, complete with brick oven aromas to inhale. Pastas are homemade and the sauces robust enough for any big apple peasant. Credit Cards: All major.

Les Halles $$$

411 Park Avenue South (28–29th Streets); ☎ *679-4111.*
Cuisine: French. Avg. $40–$60.
Hours: Noon–midnight, 7 days.

A French Butcher Shop that metamorphosed into a "hot" bistro. Onion soup and frites in a boisterous setting. You can hear a steak drop. Credit Cards: All major.

Park Bistro $$$$

414 Park Avenue South (28–29th Streets); ☎ *689-1360.*
Cuisine: American. Avg. $40–$80.
Lunch: Noon–3 p.m., Mon.–Fri.
Dinner: 6–11 p.m., 7 days.

Owned by the same monsieurs who have Les Halles, the menu here is much more sophisticated and eclectic. They're both bistros but this one is tres chic. Credit Cards: All major.

Chelsea

E/W - Fifth Avenue to the Hudson River
N/S - 14th Street to 30th Street

The problem with gentrification is that it takes no prisoners. Today, a fix-it shop; tomorrow, the Gap. Nothing works but it looks good. If you're planning to visit **Chelsea**, do it fast while there are still dry cleaners, hardware stores, a bodega here, a carniceria there. Uh oh. Another boutique. Junk shop to junque shoppe.

The Jacob Javits Centre hosts hundreds of major conventions each year in its halls the size of 15 football fields.

The land acquired by Thomas Clarke in 1750 was a tract that went from what is now Eighth Avenue to the Hudson and from 14th to 24th Streets. Reportedly, he named the estate Chelsea after London's Chelsea Hospital. A century later, grandson Clement Clarke Moore thought it 'twas a good area to develop into a residential district. (Yes, the very same C. C. Moore who wrote "Twas the Night Before Christmas".) Hence, the catalog of Gothic and Greek Revival, and Italianate townhouses that make it such a joy to walk up and down 20th and 21st Streets between Ninth and Tenth Avenues.

Chelsea's other landmark is the description-defying **Hotel Chelsea** *(222 W 23rd Street, between Seventh and Eighth Avenues,* ☎ *243-3700)* where Thomas Wolfe, Brendan Behan, Arthur C. Clarke, Arthur Miller and William Burroughs wrote, Virgil Thompson and Bob Dylan composed, Sid Vicious and Dylan Thomas died. Far too eccentric to be included under "Hotels," the Chelsea is, for some people, a real treasure. Walking into the lobby is comparable to stepping on stage in the midst of "You Can't Take it with You," the play about a nuttier-than-a-fruitcake family with a heart of gold. The pink brick and iron grillwork Victorian Gothic exterior of this first building in the city to be designated a New York Landmark in no way prepares you for the near chaos of a gallery-lobby filled with enormous and sometimes quite wonderful canvases, sculptures, and more characters than a Fellini movie. The people who stay here love it, the ones who don't are mystified by it all.

Today, **Chelsea** is undergoing even more changes. The stretch that runs from 14th Street to 23rd Street, on 6th Avenue, was known as **Ladies Mile**. Huge, very fashionable department stores opened there after the Civil War, to cater to the carriage trade. Today it has been recolonized by mega-merchandisers such as Barnes & Noble, Bed, Bath and Beyond, Today's Man, Old Navy, Burlington Coat Factory, Filene's Basement and on and on. The whole area has become a shopping magnet, so the calm, unhurried pace of Chelsea may really be a thing of the past. Last but definitely not least, someone has finally decided to use some of New York's extraordinary river frontage for fun and games. The brand new **Chelsea Piers**, which run from 17th to 23rd Street on the river is a colossal sports, entertainment, dining complex that even has a film and T.V. production company on premises. Miles and miles of sports activities make this 100 million dollar play-pen peerless for the sporting life. Admission depends on the activity chosen. *West 23rd Street and the Hudson River.* ☎ *336-6666.*

Agenda Shopping/Chelsea

Barney's New York

106 Seventh Avenue (17th Street); ☎ *929-9000, 10 a.m.–9 p.m., Mon.–Thurs.; 10 a.m.–8 p.m., Fri.–Sat.; Noon–6 p.m., Sun.*

This is the original, the store that put Chelsea on the map (for better or worse) before deciding to invade Madison Avenue with an even glitzier version. We respond emotionally to this one because this former frog of a discount men's store has been transformed into the city's most expensive and avant garde designer shop for men and women of all sexes. Valentino, Armani, Cerutti, Versace & Co.— you'll find them hanging out here. The Co-Op, is a slightly less expensive women's shop within the store, which is good news if you're an 18-year old willowy model saving every penny for a new Porsche. For the rest of us, it's a treat just to rub elbows while browsing.

Tobacco Products Company

137 Eighth Avenue (17th Street); ☎ *989-3900, 9:30 a.m.–5:30 p.m., Mon.–Fri.; 10 a.m.–4 p.m., Sat.*

An old-fashioned place where they huff and puff from making cigars and reading the Surgeon General's report. It's the kind of shop you hardly ever find anymore and might be the end of your search for a gift for Uncle Sylvester.

Chrisholm-Prats Gallery

145 Eighth Avenue (17th Street); ☎ *741-1703, 11 a.m.–6 p.m., Tues.–Sat.*

A tres bon collection of antique French posters and some cinema posters as well.

Movie Star News

134 W 18th Street; ☎ *620-8160, 10 a.m.–6 p.m., Mon.–Sat.*

8 by 10 glossies of all your favorites plus memorabilia, magazines, and enough other kitsch to keep stars in your eyes for years to come.

Old Navy

610 6th Avenue (18th Street); ☎ *645-0663, 9:30 a.m.–9 p.m., Mon.–Sat.; 11 a.m.–7 p.m., Sun.*

The Gap done up in a sailor suit. The clothes are a bit more nautical but it all boils down to the same cookie-cutter look. The whole family can shop here and have a sandwich and a soda in the Old Navy Coffee Shop.

Jam Envelope and Paper Discount Outlet

621 Avenue of the Americas (19th Street); ☎ *255-4593, 8:30 a.m.–7 p.m., Mon.–Fri.; 10 a.m.–6 p.m., Sat.–Sun.*

For dedicated paper hounds only. If you're tickled pink at the thought of shocking pink computer paper and chrome-yellow interoffice envelopes, the prices are right.

Bed Bath and Beyond

620 6th Avenue (19th Street); ☎ *255-3550, 9:30 a.m.–9 p.m., Mon.–Sat.; 10 a.m.–8 p.m., Sun.*

The beauty of the building that houses this mega-mart of toilet seats and towels is enough to make you stop by. Hard to believe the outside is landmarked and the inside is discount-marked.

Filene's Basement

620 6th Avenue (19th Street); ☎ *620-3100, 9:30 a.m.–9 p.m., Mon.–Sat.; 11 a.m.–7 p.m., Sat.*

Very stylish clothes for both sexes that have been discounted. The occasional designer label pops up from time to time just to keep you guessing.

Somethin' Else!

182 9th Avenue (21st Street); ☎ *924-0006, 11 a.m.–7:30 p.m., Mon.–Sat.; 1–6 p.m., Sun.*

Places like this make an antique buff's heart beat faster. Lots to browse through, pick up, finger and unprofessionally appraise.

Agenda Best Bites/Chelsea

da Umberto $$$

101 West 17th Street; ☎ *989-0303.*
Cuisine: Italian. Avg. $40–$60.
Lunch: 12–3 p.m., Mon.–Sat.
Dinner: 5:30–11 p.m., Mon.–Sat.

Try to get past the antipasto that seems to overflow it's display table, we dare you. They specialize in Tuscan game dishes, but the best game here is trying to decide what to order. Everything is molto scrumptious. Credit Cards: All major.

La Luncheonette $$$

130 10th Avenue (18th Street); ☎ *675-0342.*
Cuisine: French. Avg. $30–$50.
Lunch: Noon–3 p.m., Mon.–Fri.
Dinner: 6–11:30 p.m., 7 days.

Don't be misled by the name—it's meant to be playful, not accurate. This is a little bistro, tucked out of the way, but worth the trudge. Country-cooking to make Mama proud. Credit Cards: All major.

Le Madri $$$

168 W 18th Street (7th Avenue); ☎ *727-8022.*
Cuisine: Italian. Avg. $40–$60.
Lunch: Noon–2:30 p.m., 7 days.
Dinner: 5:30–11 p.m., 7 days.

Offers Italian home-cooking with the ambience of a Tuscan villa. It doesn't hurt either that a couple of motherly Italian women stir up the linguini. Credit Cards: All major.

Gascogne $$$

158 8th Avenue (18th Street); ☎ *675-6564.*
Cuisine: French. Avg. $40–$60.
Lunch: Noon–3 p.m., 7 days.
Dinner: 6–10:30 p.m., 7 days.
Yet another chapter in the on-going French Revolution in Chelsea. Lots of foie gras, lots of fish chowders, and all your other favorite Gascogne goodies. I'm nuts about the prune ice cream at the end. There's a pretty little garden in the back. Credit Cards: All major.

Claire $$$

156 Seventh Avenue (bet 19 and 20th Streets); ☎ *255-1955.*
Cuisine: American. Avg. $30–$50.
Hours: Noon–12:30 a.m., 7 days.
Fine seafood in a very'90s setting by Robin Wagner, set designer for *A Chorus Line.* Credit Cards: All major.

Bright Food Shop $

216 8th Avenue (21st St.); ☎ *243-4433.*
Cuisine: Asian. Avg. $10–$20.
Hours: 11 a.m.–10:30 p.m., 7 days.
It doesn't look like anything more than your average greasy spoon but wait—inhale the aroma of the Orient. Great, creative Asian cuisine in a spartan atmosphere. Credit Cards: All major.

Luma $$

200 9th Avenue (22nd Street); ☎ *633-8033.*
Cuisine: Vegetarian. Avg. $20–$40.
Dinner: 6–10 p.m., 7 days.
Say M.S.G. in this tummy temple of health food and they'll say scram. This is not your usual sprouts and tofu joint. Their menu is imaginative and elegant. A plate of grilled veggies will make you forget that yen for pastrami Credit Cards: All major.

Empire Diner $$

210 Tenth Avenue (22nd Street); ☎ *243-2736.*
Cuisine: Burgers. Avg. $20–$40.
Hours: 24 hours, 7 days.
This is where people who wouldn't be caught dead in a diner, go. It's open 24 hours a day for insomniac models and guilt-ridden stockbrokers who kid themselves into thinking that life is a cabaret. Credit Cards: All major.

Chelsea Central $$

227 10th Avenue (23rd Street); ☎ *620-0230.*
Cuisine: American. Avg. $20–$40.
Lunch: Noon–3 p.m., 7 days.
Dinner: 6–11 p.m., 7 days.
If you love old saloons and good burgers, this is the place for you. Its been around forever and is still cozy and comfortable. And if you want to go beyond burgers, the menu has terrific grills, steaks and desserts. Credit Cards: All major.

Greenwich Village

N/S - 14th Street to Houston Street
E/W - Broadway to the Hudson River

Greenwich Village still attracts the artistic and political.

When I was growing up in Manhattan, it seemed to me that anything that was exciting in New York—with the exception of Ethel Merman—was happening in the Village. There was, in those days, only one Village. Of course, everyone said (even way back then) that the Village wasn't what it used to be.

In that respect, nothing has changed: **Greenwich Village** still isn't what it used to be. The former Camelot of creativity is trapped in the nostalgia of everyone's memories and hasn't redefined itself. There are still coffee houses and jewelers and off-Broadway theaters and Italian restaurants. But the only parts of the Village in which one is likely to succumb to deja vu is along **Bleecker Street**, or south of Washington Square Park along MacDougal, Sullivan and Thompson Streets. Dear old Eighth Street has been vandalized by fast foodies and discounters. Today, it has all the charm of a subway station. While I was watching the East Village, SoHo and Chelsea and the Upper West Side, someone came and stole Greenwich Village.

However cranky one is with the Village for not realizing its potential as the "Left Bank" of New York, it did, at the very least, attract a more diverse list of creative talent than anywhere else in the city. It was here that Eugene O'Neill got his first break at the **Provincetown Playhouse** *(133 MacDougal Street)*. Artists from Winslow Homer to Diego Rivera, most of the jazz greats, and even latter day folk heroes such as Bob Dylan strutted their stuff in the Village.

Today's major strutters are members of the gay community who fought long and hard for their rights in private and then in public. The Village, with a history of nurturing artistic and social passions, supported vigorously the "gay pride" movement that gained momentum in its backyard.

The Village, at first glance, seems somewhat daunting. Its geography is as nonconformist as its residents. The best way to psych things out is a walk along **Bleecker Street**, named for 19th-century scholar Anthony Bleecker who gave the land for the street to the city. Start at the Abingdon Square end and go east.

Bank Street is the first intersection and here you'll find some of the Village's nicest homes, 19th century row houses: Nos. 16–34, 37 (noted as one of the best examples of Greek Revival in the area), 55, 57, 68, 74, 76, 128, and 130.

Christopher Street (sometimes called the Gay White Way) crosses **Bleecker** and as it heads toward the river becomes the official parade ground (usually on the weekend) for the most baroque members of the homosexual community. While gawking is definitely out of place, the order of the day is to be flamboyant and so no matter your level of sophistication, you may well find your eyes widening a bit. Although some of the "heavy metal" gay bars have shut down, the area near the river should be approached, if at all, with discretion.

The part of **Bleecker** that runs between Seventh Avenue South and Sixth Avenue is the last remaining block of ethnic Bleecker Street. You'll find Italian bakeries and butchers and grocers that will make you wish they delivered back home. To complete the day's excursion, head north on La Guardia to **Washington Square Park** which is recognized generally as the heart (if not the soul) of the Village. This is the park in which Robert Redford was "Barefoot in the..", and the center of street life on weekends. You'll find mimes and thieves, artists and drug dealers, an almost medieval mix of professions seeking voluntary and involuntary compensation.

Agenda Shopping/Greenwich Village

Li-Lac Chocolates
120 Christopher Street; ☎ *242-7374, Noon–8 p.m., Mon.–Sat.; Noon–5 p.m., Sun.*
Hand-dipped goodies some say are the best around. This nirvana for fudge fanatics has been here for over 60 years and will ship almost anywhere.

Balducci's
424 Avenue of the Americas (bet. 9-10th Streets); ☎ *673-2600, 7 a.m.–8:30 p.m., 7 days.*
Almost everything in this foodie fantasma is available for tasting, the selection is miraculous, and the quality simply can't be beat. Have a picnic.

Pierre Deux
367 Bleecker Street; ☎ *243-7740, 10 a.m.–6 p.m., Mon.–Sat.*
French country furniture and fabrics. They make it easy for anyone to live in a farmhouse minus the farm.

Biography Bookshop
400 Bleecker Street; ☎ *807-8655, Noon–8 p.m., Mon.–Sat.; 11 a.m.–7 p.m., Sun.*
Everything you've ever wanted to know about everyone, all on the shelves of one store.

Greenwich
Village

©FWi

EAST
VILLAGE

GREENWICH
VILLAGE

Washington
Square Park

Tompkins
Square

124

735

94

615

70

44

E. 14th St
E. 12th St
E. 10th St
E. 6th St
E. 4th St
E. 2nd St
Avenue A
First Ave
Second Ave
Third Ave
Fourth Ave
Bowery
Houston St
Allen St
St. Marks Pl
Lafayette St
Broadway
Mercer St
W. 4th St
W. 3rd St
Bleecker St
La Guardia Pl
Fifth Ave
Sullivan St
MacDougal St
E. 4th St
University Pl
Fifth Ave
E. 8th St
E. 10th St
E. 12th St
E. 14th St
W. 8th St
W. 10th St
W. 12th St
W. 14th St
Broadway
Waverly Pl
Avenue of the Americas
Washington Pl
W. 4th St
7th Ave South
Greenwich Ave
Eighth Ave
Bleecker St
Bank St
Bethune St
Perry St
Charles St
W. 4th St
W. 11th St
W. 10th St
Weehawken St
Greenwich St
Hudson St
Christopher St
Barrow St
Grove St
Morton St
Leroy St
Bleecker St
Clarkson St
Washington

NEIGHBORHOODS

Pink Pussycat Boutique

167 W 4th Street; ☎ *243-0077, 10 a.m.–2 a.m., 7 days.*

A real Village landmark. By today's standards this Pussycat has no claws but it was one of the first shops to sell (right out in the open) things that belong behind closed doors. It used to be the village at its naughtiest.

Agenda Best Bites/Greenwich Village

John's Pizzeria $

278 Bleecker Street; ☎ *243-1680.*
Cuisine: Italian. Avg. $10–$20.
Hours: 11:30 a.m.–midnight, 7 days.

A counter-chic menu for close encounters of the crispy kind. Always crowded, this is the place for pre-designer pizza. Credit Cards: All major.

Chumley's $$

86 Bedford Street; ☎ *675-4449.*
Cuisine: American. Avg. $20–$40.
Dinner: 5 p.m.–1 a.m., Mon.–Fri.; 5–11 p.m., Sat.–Sun.

One of the hardest bars in the city to find. Look for an unmarked door with a grill on it, between Barrow and Grove Streets. If it opens into a former speakeasy that's filled with uptown yuppies, you're in the right place. In its earlier days Chumley's was the favored haunt of Ernest Hemingway, J.D. Salinger and William Faulkner among others. Credit Cards: All major.

Moondog $

378 Bleecker Street; ☎ *675-4540.*
Cuisine: Ice Cream. Avg. $5.
Hours: 2–10:30 p.m., Mon.–Fri.; Noon–11 p.m., Sat.–Sun.

A great ice-cream parlor that has over 100 flavors in its repertoire. They don't appear all at once but if you're lucky you'll hit Chocolate Guiness Stout. Credit Cards: Cash only.

Pink Teacup, The $$

42 Grove Street; ☎ *807-6755.*
Cuisine: Southern. Avg. $15–$30.
Hours: 8 a.m.–midnight, Mon.–Fri.; 8 a.m.–1 a.m., Sat.–Sun.

This cubbyhole has nothing to do with New York except that it attracts hungry New Yorkers who scarf down huge platters of grits and eggs, fried pork chops, or barbecue chicken. Southern comfort that's inexpensive, homey, and hearty. Credit Cards: Cash only.

Chez Brigitte $

77 Greenwich Avenue; ☎ *929-6736.*
Cuisine: French. Avg. $10–$20.
Hours: 11 a.m.–10 p.m., Mon.–Sat.

French home cooking at downtown prices. No tables, only a counter, but it's laden with retro things like blanquette de veau and coq au vin. So it's not Lutece! Credit Cards: Cash only.

13 Barrow Street   **$$**

13 Barrow Street (7th Avenue & 4th Street); ☎ *727-1300.*
Cuisine: American. Avg. $20–$40.
Dinner: 6 p.m.–12:30 a.m., 7 days.
An instant hit as soon as it opened. A lovely setting (vaulted ceilings) and good seafood has brought out the troops in great numbers. Oysters are a specialty. Credit Cards: All major.

One If By Land, Two If By Sea   **$$$**

17 Barrow Street (W 4th Street); ☎ *228-0822.*
Cuisine: Continental. Avg. $40–$60.
Dinner: 5:30–11:30 p.m., 7 days.
Once Aaron Burr's coach house, today it's just a lovely spot to have an intimate dinner. The food itself wouldn't bring Aaron back for a bite, but the atmosphere is really heavenly. Credit Cards: All major.

Custard Beach

33 East 8th Street; ☎ *420-6039.*
Hours: Noon–9 p.m., Mon.–Fri.; Noon–10 p.m., Fri.–Sat. Avg. $5.
The créme de la créme of the world of custard. Thick enough to supply instant ecstasy for the serious custard connoisseur. This could very well be custards' last stand. Credit Cards: Cash only.

La Metairie   **$$$**

189 W 10th Street; ☎ *989-0343.*
Cuisine: French. Avg. $40–$60.
Dinner: 5–11 p.m., Mon.–Sat.; 5–10 p.m., Sun. Closed Mon.
Yet another itsy-bitsy country-French restaurant in the village, but this one has more than just a pretty face. The foie gras flows and the duck is crispier than a new franc note. Not for the claustrophobic or Roseanne and Dan. Credit Cards: All major.

Home   **$$**

20 Cornelia Street (Bleecker & West 4th); ☎ *243-9579.*
Cuisine: American. Avg. $20–$40.
Hours: 9 a.m.–8 p.m., Mon.–Sat.; 6–11 p.m., Mon.–Sat.
The chef here is definitely home on the range in this very charming, welcoming spot. He turns out his creations with great flair and sometimes a hint of curry or fennel for good measure. Credit Cards: All major.

Po's   **$$**

31 Cornelia Street (Bleecker); ☎ *645-2189.*
Cuisine: Italian. Avg. $20–$40.
Lunch: 11:30 a.m.–2:30 p.m.; Wed.–Sun.;
Dinner: 5:30–11 p.m., Tues.–Sun. Closed Mon.
No relation to Edgar Allen but people are raving about the homemade pastas here. The menu lists a whole bunch of "pastas di journo" and none is better than the other. Credit Cards: All major.

Caffe Dante   **$**

79-81 MacDougal Street; ☎ *982-5275.*
Cuisine: Coffee. Avg. $10–$15.
Hours: 10 a.m.–2 a.m., 7 days.
One of the most famous of the famous village coffee houses, you can sit forever, watch the world go by or just savor some of the best espresso around. Credit Cards: Cash only.

Caffe Reggio   **$**

119 MacDougal Street; ☎ *674-9589.*
Cuisine: Coffee. Avg. $10–$15.

Hours: 10 a.m.–2 a.m., 7 days.

Dates back to the 18th century but it's still brewing its cappuccino without a let-up. This is the coffee house Hollywood always uses when it needs one *(Godfather II)*. Credit Cards: Cash only.

Anglers & Writers $$

420 Hudson Street; ☎ *675-0810.*
Cuisine: Country. Avg. $20–$40.
Hours: 9 a.m.–11 p.m., Mon.–Sat.; 10 a.m.–10 p.m., Sun.

A truly distinctive restaurant that is part library and part restaurant. They serve wholesome food and a great collection of books to go with it. You're actually encouraged to sit back, relax and read a page or two. All of this and a wonderful "full tea" every afternoon. Credit Cards: All major.

White Horse Tavern $

567 Hudson Street; ☎ *243-9260.*
Cuisine: Burgers. Avg. $10–$20.
Hours: 11 a.m.–2 a.m., Mon.–Fri.; 11 a.m.–4 a.m., Sat.

One block west of Bleecker on 11th Street, the Whitehorse is famous as a writer's hangout which translates as inexpensive for a burger and brew. The bar dates back to 1880, but is really a landmark because Dylan Thomas was a regular in the early '50s. Credit Cards: All major.

Restaurant Florent $$

69 Gansevoort Street (Greenwich-Washington Streets); ☎ *989-5779.*
Cuisine: French. Avg. $20–$40.
Hours: 9 a.m.–5 a.m., Mon.–Fri.; 24 hours, Sat.–Sun.

So far west, it's almost in the river, this place rocks around the clock. Because Florent is in the middle of the wholesale meat district you could be rubbing shoulders with a butcher or a bachelor looking for a great bowl of onion soup. All your bistro favorites perform here on a 24 hour basis. Credit Cards: Cash only.

East Village

**E/W - Broadway to Avenue A or B or C depending upon whom you ask.
N/S - 14th Street to Houston Street**

If ever a neighborhood wore its heart on its sleeve, that's the **East Village**. Situated geographically, and emotionally, between the Lower East Side and Greenwich Village, the area is as ethnic as Zorba the Greek and every bit as passionate. Life-support systems are fueled by a finely adjusted blend of oxygen, rebellion, and sturm und drang.

The creative spirits who live east of Broadway are not yet successful enough to move away. The citizens of Alphabet City (the avenues east of First Avenue are Avenue A, B, and C) cannot afford the West (Greenwich) Village or SoHo—and it is unthinkable to them that anything worthwhile in life could ever happen north of 14th Street. The good news is there's enough excitement down here to keep them, and you, hopping.

The official point of entry into the East Village is **St. Mark's Place** which is, in reality, East 8th Street. A fashionable place to promenade in the 19th century (townhouses are set back from the street giving the block a boulevardish appearance) when the area was part of the Lower East Side ethnic stew, and the accents were heavily German, then Polish, Ukrainian, and Russian. Next came the hippies, flower children, runaways, rockers, druggies, and even members of Andy Warhol's Velvet Underground. While most everyone else has moved on, one loyal group remains: Hell's Angels. You'll find their headquarters on East 3rd Street, between First and Second Avenues. It's hard to miss. Lots of bikes out front. Lots of guys you just know never eat quiche.

Second Avenue, the main artery of the East Village, was once the great white way for New York's Yiddish Theater. Then it became home to the equally legendary Fillmore East where every group worth its groupies rocked the rafters. What remains today is a creative anarchy that produces paintings, clothes, jewelry, and theater you won't find elsewhere.

HIDDEN AGENDA

Gem Spa *(13 Second Avenue, at St. Mark's Place) is where you'll find one of the great staples of Manhattan life: the egg cream. This beverage is to NYC what mint juleps were to Scarlett O'Hara. Made with neither egg nor cream, The Official NYC Egg Cream is a chocolate soda with milk that has more controversy surrounding ingredients and techniques than any dry martini we ever met. Gem is one of two recognized dispensers of the authentic brew.*

THE OFFICIAL NYC EGG CREAM RECIPE

One 8 ounce glass
One spoon
Fox's U-Bet Chocolate Syrup (No substitutes, please.)
Whole milk
Seltzer in a pressurized cylinder (no bottles, please)
Put one inch of syrup into the glass. Add one inch of milk. Tilt the glass as you aim seltzer onto the spoon. You should get a big chocolaty foam. Stir, shake your head approvingly, and drink. Smile knowingly. Eat your heart out, Moet et Chandon!

Agenda Shopping/The East Village

Screaming Mimi's

22 E 4th Street; ☎ *677-6464, 11 a.m.–8 p.m., 7 days.*
This looks like the kind of shop where Madonna buys her "truth or date" outfits. Choice used duds for the unisex crowd.

Trash and Vauderville

4 Street Marks Place; ☎ *982-3590, Noon–8 p.m., Mon.–Sat.; 1–7:30 p.m., Sun.*
If you need a new look, this is the place to come. Vintage '50s right through 2001. Anything goes, but don't expect to do your Christmas shopping here.

Bowl & Board

8th Street at St. Mark's Place; ☎ *673-1724, 11 a.m.–7 p.m., 7 days.*
The interior would drive a self-respecting woodpecker crazy. Wooden spoons, bowls, toys, trays, but they won't take any wooden nickels.

Back From Guatemala

306 E 6th Street; ☎ *260-7010, Noon–10:30 p.m., 7 days.*
Just in time, too, if you're interested in exotic designs and marvelous wood carvings. Indian masks mingle with fashions and jewelry from guess where.

Dinosaur Hill

306 E 9th Street (2nd&3rd Aves); ☎ *473-5850, 11 a.m.–7 p.m., 7 days.*
All the prehistoric monsters here are stuffed and so cute you just have to hug the nearest T-Rex. There are also clothes for your favorite little cave person as well as nifty togs and games.

Enchantments

341 E 9th Street; ☎ *228-4394, Noon–9 p.m., Mon.–Sat.; Noon–8 p.m., Sun.*
Halloween all year round. This is a veritable witches boutique with everything for the "complete coven." You hardly know which way to look.

Little Rickie's

49-1/2 1st Avenue (3rd Street); ☎ *505-6467, 11 a.m.–8 p.m., Mon.–Fri.; Noon–7 p.m., Sat.–Sun.*
Rubber chickens, musical toilet paper and fetishes created in Haiti. But seriously folks, some really interesting crafts from around the world.

Cobblestones

314 E 9th Street; ☎ *673-5372, 1–7 p.m., Tues.–Sat.; 1–6 p.m., Sun.*
Eclectic kitsch from all over. Ceramics, glassware, '50s jewelry. A real treasure chest.

Arka

26 1st Avenue; ☎ *473-3550, 11 a.m.–5 p.m., Mon.–Sat.*
Beautiful hand-painted Ukrainian Easter eggs all year round, as well as embroidery crafts and recorded folk music from the Ukraine.

Geomancy

337 E 9th Street; ☎ *777-2733, 12:30–7 p.m., Tues.–Sun.*
Like visiting someone's fascinating apartment and then being able to buy everything. They have furniture and crafts from all over the world. Truly unique.

Kiehl's Pharmacy

109 Third Avenue (13th Street); ☎ *475-3400, 9 a.m.–8 p.m., Mon.–Sat.*
Headquarters for herbal and homeopathic remedies. Kiehl's has been selling natural substances since 1851 as well as fragrances, tonics, and creams to soothe the savage beast in all of us.

Agenda Best Bites/East Village

Baby Jake's $$

14 1st Avenue (1–2nd Street); ☎ *254-2229.*
Cuisine: Southern. Avg. $20–$40.
Hours: 10 a.m.–midnight, Mon.–Fri.; 10 a.m.–4 a.m., Sat.–Sun.

The Bayou may be miles away but the mind-set at Baby Jake's is Po Boy Sandwiches and Muffelattas. Their crab cakes add a lot of spice to 1st. Credit Cards: All major.

Old Devil Moon $$
511 E 12th Street; ☎ *475-4357.*
Cuisine: Southern. Avg. $20–$40.
Hours: 5–11 p.m., Mon.–Fri.; 10 a.m.–11 p.m., Sat.–Sun.
Since they serve homemade, old-fashioned baked ham, brunch is a real event here. At other times they just serve huge portions of country cooking. Credit Cards: All major.

Ukrainian East Village Restaurant, The $
140 Second Avenue; ☎ *529-5024.*
Cuisine: Ukrainian. Avg. $10–$20.
Hours: Noon–11 p.m., 7 days.
1950 prices and 19th century portions make this the bargain of the 20th century. You can hear Ukrainian folk songs while sipping a $1.75 bowl of (what else?) Ukrainian borscht or inhaling a platter of Pierogi, cabbage, and kielbasa—which sounds like a Ukrainian law firm. Credit Cards: Cash only.

McSorley's Old Ale House $
15 E 7th Street; ☎ *473-9148.*
Cuisine: Beer-Burgers. Avg. $10–$20.
Hours: 11 a.m.–1 a.m., Mon.–Sat; 1 p.m.–1 a.m. Sun.
They've been here since 1854 and they have finally allowed women to belly up to their bar after a 1970 court battle. Lincoln, Roosevelt, and Kennedy are said to have quaffed a few here. Draft ale, good sandwiches and a large helping of atmosphere. Credit Cards: All major.

Miracle Grill, The $$
112 First Avenue (7th Street); ☎ *254-2353.*
Cuisine: Southwestern. Avg. $20–$40.
Hours: 5:30–11:30 p.m., 7 days.
No loaves or fishes or walking or water, but the appearance of the tomatillo on 7th Street is probably as close as you can get. Great Chili and steaks with chipotle and a velvety flan to end with. There's a really pretty garden to ponder your jalapeño's in. Credit Cards: All major.

Veselka $
144 Second Avenue; ☎ *228-9682.*
Cuisine: Russian. Avg. $10–$20.
Hours: 24 hours, 7 days.
Twenty four kinds of homemade soups to be followed by huge plates of steaming kielbasa. So ethnic you'll be able to play the Warsaw concerto by the time you leave. Credit Cards: All major.

Kiev Coffee Shop, The $
117 Second Avenue (7th Street); ☎ *674-4040.*
Cuisine: Russian. Avg. $10–$20.
Hours: 24 hours, 7 days.
Vaguely Russian dishes here that can be had for less than a Czar's ransom—i.e., there is a $1.50 minimum at the tables. Credit Cards: Cash only.

Mitali $
334 E 6th Street; ☎ *533-2508; Inexpensive.*
Cuisine: Indian. Avg. $10–$20.

Hours: Noon–midnight, 7 days.

One of many Indian restaurants on East 6th (known as little India) but my very favorite. They offer Northern cuisine at deliciously low prices. Credit Cards: All major.

Three of Cups   **$$**

83 First Avenue (5th Street); ☎ *388-0059.*
Cuisine: Italian. Avg. $15–$30.
Hours: 6 p.m.–1 a.m., Mon.–Fri.; 6 p.m.–2 a.m., Sat.–Sun.

Right out of a deck of tarot cards. You're back in the Dark Ages except for the very "today" pizzas that pop out of their oven. Paper thin and covered with all kinds of terrific things, it's easy to predict that you'll love them, no matter what the cards say. Credit Cards: All major.

B&H Dairy Restaurant   **$**

127 Second Avenue (8th Street); ☎ *505-8065.*
Cuisine: Jewish. Avg. $10–$15.
Hous: 7 a.m.–10 p.m., 7 days.

Very narrow, crowded formica palace famous for borscht, blintzes and an entire catalogue of doughy/eggy things. Credit Cards: All major.

Cafe Tabac   **$$$**

232 E 9th Street (2–3rd Avenues); ☎ *674-7072.*
Cuisine: American. Avg. $40–$60.
Hours: 6 a.m.–2:30 a.m., 7 days.

So trendy that people go just for a glimpse of J.F.K. Jr. (and formerly Darryl). Nobody cares about the food, although it's pretty good. Celeb sighting is the dessert of choice. Credit Cards: All major.

Second Avenue Deli   **$$**

156 Second Avenue (10th Street); ☎ *677-0606.*
Cuisine: Jewish. Avg. $20–$30.
Hours: 7 a.m.–midnight, Mon.–Fri.; 7 a.m.–2 a.m., Sat.–Sun.

The Elaine's of New York's kosher mafia. Pastrami to the sky and wall-to-wall matzo balls. Credit Cards: All major.

SoHo/TriBeCa

E/W-Broadway to Avenue of the Americas (Sixth Avenue)
N/S-Houston Street to Canal, Lafayette and Chambers Streets

SoHo is a theme park for rich kids in their thirties and forties. The theme in this magic kingdom is that you don't have to be poor to be creative, and that there is life after divorce. (She keeps the co-op, he sacks out at the Harvard Club and has a brief but meaningless fling with the real estate agent from whom he winds up buying a loft in SoHo.) Voila! A neighborhood is born.

During the mid 1700's, **SoHo** was Indian territory: home of the self-same Indians against whom settlers built "the wall" for which Wall Street was named. By the 1850's, SoHo was the hub of the city but as the city center continued its move north, SoHo was no longer fashionable. The drop in real estate prices attracted manufacturers who filled their sweatshops with immigrant workers. In the 1950's, starving artists fleeing the rising rents in **Greenwich Village** began moving in illegally, renting substandard housing in return for unusually large studio space. In the '60s, SoHo went legit and was rezoned. Artists, realizing how much their space was now worth, didn't

Soho/Tribeca

Museums		
98	Guggenheim SoHo, Prince St & Bway	E23
115	New Museum of Contemporary Art, 583 Bway, So of Houston	E23
116	NYC Fire Museum, 278 Spring St	D24

Places of Interest		
57	SoHo, Bway, Canal, Av of the Americas & Houston Sts	E23
63	TriBeCa	D25

have to starve anymore. They sold and moved to Brooklyn or Hoboken. Suddenly, the community became a haven for the terminally trendy.

AGENDA INSIDE INFORMATION
WHAT THE NAMES MEAN

SoHo–South of Houston Street
(pronounced Howston not Hewston)
TriBeCa–Triangle below Canal Street
(pronouced Tri-Beck-a)
SoSo–South of Soho - Tribeca
NoHo–North of Houston Street
Dumbo–Down Under the Manhattan
Bridge Overpass - in Brooklyn

SoHo is one of the city's best attractions. It rivals 57th Street as the art capital of New York. It is an area filled with shops that sell the kind of classy goodies once associated with upper Madison Avenue before it smothered itself in chic Eurotrash. SoHo has restaurants for every taste and a weekend street life that is the talk of the town.

SoHo, once an industrial and artists' enclave, is now filled with trendy restaurants and boutiques.

As a visitor, your best day for **SoHo** is Saturday (Most galleries are closed on Sunday, everything is closed on Monday. The next best times—Tuesday through Friday—tend to be quiet). Nothing much is open before noon.

The most important architectural feature of the area is its concentration of cast-iron facades, the largest in the world. If you really want to test your mettle, head for **Greene Street**, the bull's eye in **SoHo's Cast-Iron Historic District**. There's more than a quarter mile of the late 19th century Italianate-ish structures that presaged modern steel-frame buildings.

The main "drag" is West Broadway, with Sullivan, Thompson, Wooster, Greene, and Mercer running parallel.

TriBeCa

E/W - Broadway to West Street
N/S - Canal Street to Chambers Street

The *Tri*angle *Be*low *Ca*nal Street is a triangle no more. This "son of SoHo" has outgrown its original boundaries to become, along with Battery Park, one of the city's most rapidly-changing areas.

There is still a sense of frontier in **TriBeCa**. All the streets and shops have not been conquered by the Army of the Chic. Hallelujah! There is ugliness to be seen! There are still grungy little coffee shops that would sooner die than serve red lettuce. On the other hand, you don't need a crystal ball to know what's going to happen down here.

If truth be told, this always was an interesting area for its oddball discount shopping. The reason to see **TriBeCa** today is that those stores will doubtless be replaced by the three B's: boutiques, Benettons, and brunch.

You could write an entire book just on the restaurants in **SoHo** and **TriBeCa**—low rents in this part of town have attracted the best of the new young chefs.

AGENDA TIP

The good news for all you fans of Architectural Digest is the Woolworth Building (233 Broadway) which in 1913 was the world's tallest, but not today. "The Cathedral of Commerce" built by the 5&10-cent king is anything but penny-pinching. The lobby in this American Gothic version of London's Houses of Parliament is one of NY's most elaborate. Woolworth personally picked out the mailboxes and bathroom fixtures. Discuss that one with your shrink.

Agenda Shopping/SoHo/TriBeCa

Rizzoli Bookstore
> *454 W Broadway;* ☎ *674-1677, 10:30 a.m.–9 p.m., Mon.–Sat.; Noon–7 p.m., Sun.*
> The latest in art books and art magazines.

Harriet Love
> *412 W Broadway;* ☎ *966-2280, 11:30 a.m.–7 p.m., 7 days.*
> Old clothes never had it so good. She made it fashionable to be retro.

Tootsie Plohound
> *413 W Broadway;* ☎ *925-8931, 11:30 a.m.–7:30 p.m., 7 days.*
> What else with a name like that? Shoes!

Zona
> *97 Greene Street;* ☎ *925-6750, 11 a.m.–7 p.m., Mon.–Sat.; Noon–6 p.m., Sun.*
> This is a biggie in SoHo. Dynamite collection of everything southwestern in a sprawling space that is handled in the most creative way.

Wolfman-Gold & Good Company

117 Mercer Street; ☎ *431-1888, 11 a.m.–6 p.m., Mon.–Sat.; Noon–5 p.m., Sun.*

The gold part stands for most of the prices here, but the store has some really beautiful gifts for the home. Most things are in shades of white, ivory, bone and beige. It's almost like being dropped in a bowl of cream.

Anna Sui Downtown

113 Greene Street; ☎ *941-8406, Noon–7 p.m., Mon.–Sat.; Noon–6 p.m., Sun.*

Oriental cum L.A. clothes for the very young, very rich and the very unselfconscious.

Morgan Le Fay

151 Spring Street; ☎ *925-0144, 11 a.m.–7 p.m., 7 days.*

Very cutting edge '90s duds for women who don't mind making a statement. Designs are done in luscious fabrics.

Second Coming, The

72 Greene Street; ☎ *431-4424, Noon–8 p.m., 7 days.*

Art Deco everything, from furniture to frocks. Definitely a fun scene.

Comme des Garcons

116 Wooster Street; ☎ *219-0661, 11 a.m.–7 p.m., Mon.–Sat.; Noon–6:30 p.m., Sun.*

Stark, elegant Japanese designs. Remember Julia Roberts wedding dress) Clunky accessories are a crime here.

FACE

110 Prince Street; ☎ *334-3900, 11 a.m.–7 p.m., Mon.–Sat.; Noon–6 p.m., Sun.*

This is a Face in the Swedish crowd. By yiminy, the make-up that you're faced with here is the counterpart that's found in its store of the same name in Stockholm. They have more nail polish shades than Barbra Streisand.

Metropolitan Museum of Art Gift Shop/Soho

113 Prince Street; ☎ *614-3000, 11 a.m.–7 p.m., Mon.–Fri.; 10 a.m.–7 p.m., Sun.*

The long arm of the Museum has reached down into SoHo to add a wonderful collection of gifts and reproductions of their treasures. It's a nice respite from swinging SoHo.

Il Bisonte

72 Thompson Street; ☎ *966-8773, Noon–6:30 p.m., Tues.–Sat.; Noon–6 p.m., Sun-Mon.*

Luscious leathers from Florence, all stamped with a buffalo. How many buffalo have you seen on the streets of Florence?

Enchanted Forest, The

85 Mercer Street; ☎ *925-6677, 11 a.m.–7 p.m., Mon.–Sat.; Noon–6 p.m., Sun.*

Leave enough time for this enchanting children's toy store, you'll never want to leave. You become part of the surroundings as you browse through books, play with the stuffed animals and happily regress.

Anbar Shoe Steal

60 Reade Street; ☎ *964-4017, 9 a.m.–6 p.m., Mon.–Sat.*

They're not kidding. They have a hot shoe line with designer names at down-at-the heel prices.

Coming to America

276 Lafayette Street; ☎ *343-2968, 11 a.m.–6 p.m., 7 days.*
Americana with unique finds in folk art and painted furniture.

"New York is a place of free spirits."

Drawing by Booth; ©1995, The New Yorker Magazine, Inc.

Agenda Best Bites/SoHo/TriBeCa

Odeon, The $$$

145 W Broadway; ☎ *233-0507.*
Cuisine: American. Avg. $40–$60.
Hours: Noon–2 a.m., Mon.–Sat.; 11 a.m.–2 a.m., Sun.
This place has historical (and from the noise level hysterical) signifi-cance in TriBeCa. It was the first hangout that started the restaurant scene there. Like Sardi's, it has a cache that transcends cuisine. A former cafeteria, the Odeon is best after midnight. Credit Cards: All major.

Barolo $$$

398 W Broadway; ☎ *226-1102.*
Cuisine: Italian. Avg. $40–$60.
Hours: Noon–midnight, Mon.–Sun.; Noon–1 a.m., Sat.

Italian food with a leaning toward fish and fresh pastas. The real story here is their outdoor garden that has eight big cherry trees—a wonderful escape if the season cooperates. Credit Cards: All major.

Cupping Room Cafe, The $$
359 W Broadway; ☎ *925-2898.*
Cuisine: American. Avg. $20–$40.
Hours: 7:30 a.m.–midnight, Mon.–Fri.; 7:30 a.m.–2 a.m., Weekend.
Perfect for a salad or sandwich in the middle of your gallery hopping. They also (don't ask us why) have a very good collection of wines from Australia. Credit Cards: All major.

El Teddy's $$
219 W Broadway; ☎ *941-7070.*
Cuisine: Mexican. Avg. $20–$40.
Lunch: Noon–3 p.m., 7 days.
Dinner: 6 p.m.–1 a.m., 7 days.
More tex than Mex, they serve a mean margarita to accompany the chili pepper of choice. The crowd is young, full of fun and usually full of margaritas. Credit Cards: All major.

Montrachet $$$
239 W Broadway; ☎ *219-2777.*
Cuisine: French. Avg. $40–$60.
Dinner: 5:30–10:45 p.m., Mon.–Sat.
Inventive chef, Debra Ponzek, keeps the level here right up to the sky. The food was the "nouvellest" of cuisine from the moment Montrachet opened years back, and the level is maintained with the same excellence today. One of our very best! Credit Cards: All major.

Kelly and Ping $
127 Greene Street; ☎ *228-1212.*
Cuisine: Chinese. Avg. $10–$20.
Lunch: 11:30 a.m.–5 p.m., 7 days.
Dinner: 6–11 p.m., 7 days.
The only Chinese grocery I know where you can get a Peking Duck sandwich. In the front are canned goods and cooking equipment, in the back you get some of the tastiest chinese snacks and stir fries around. They also serve mega-bowls of Cantonese Wonton soup. Credit Cards: All major.

SoHo Kitchen and Bar $$
103 Greene Street; ☎ *925-1866.*
Cuisine: American. Avg. $20–$40.
Hours: 11:30 a.m.–11:30 p.m., Mon.–Fri.; 11:30 a.m.–1 a.m., Weekends.
Great wine list, great burgers, great pizzas, what more is there to say! Credit Cards: All major.

Jerry's $
101 Prince Street; ☎ *966-9464.*
Cuisine: American. Avg. $10–$20.
Hours: 9 a.m.–11 p.m., Mon.–Fri.; 11 a.m.–11 p.m., Sat; 11 a.m.–5 p.m., Sun, 7 days.
Everybody here wears black, tries with excruciating dedication to appear Artsy-Fartsy and everybody seems to love Jerry's homey luncheonette menu. Credit Cards: All major.

Layla $$
211 West Broadway; ☎ *431-0700.*
Cuisine: Moroccan. Avg. $20–$40.

Lunch: Noon–2:30 p.m., 7 days.
Dinner: 5:30–10 p.m., 7 days.
From "souk" to nuts this madcap Moroccan fantasy is delicious fun. It's run by the De Niro group who also made the TriBeCa Grill hot. If you like belly dancers with your eggplant and falafel this may be your new favorite place. You can join in and hip your way through the menu. Credit Cards: All major.

Provence $$$

38 MacDougal Street; ☎ 475-7500.
Cuisine: French. Avg. $40–$60.
Lunch: Noon–2:30 p.m., 7 days.
Dinner: 6–11 p.m., 7 days.
Can you guess what kind of French food is dished out here? The flavors of Provence are brought to life in this very charming restaurant. There's a romantic garden out back, but even in the dead of winter, the food is wonderful. Credit Cards: All major.

Blue Ribbon $$$

97 Sullivan Street (Prince & Spring Streets); ☎ 274-0404.
Cuisine: American. Avg. $40–$60.
Hours: 4 p.m.–4 a.m., 7 days.
No reservations are taken here so people line up for the pleasure of Blue Ribbon's outstanding menu. It's a favorite stop for some of the best chefs in town, after work. They know they'll always find something intriguing on the menu. Credit Cards: All major.

Screening Room, The

54 Varick Street; ☎ 334-2100.
Cuisine: American. Avg. $20–$40.
Hours: 5 p.m.–2 a.m., 7 days.
Finally, an alternative to popcorn with your favorite flic. This 21st century place has food, drinks, movies, CD-Roms and God knows what other manner of interactive kitsch under one roof. Eat, drink and be bleary. Credit Cards: All major.

TriBeCa Grill $$$

375 Greenwich Street; ☎ 941-3900.
Cuisine: American. Avg. $40–$60.
Lunch: 11:30 a.m.–3 p.m., 7 days.
Dinner: 5:30–11 p.m., 7 days.
Twinkle, twinkle—big stars are everywhere from Julia Roberts to the super-model du jour, to co-owner Robert De Niro. But amazingly enough the staff is pretty decent to you even if you're from Des Moines. Simple, non-gussied-up American menu and a chance to try it in top, trendy, territory. Credit Cards: All major.

Arqua $$$

281 Church Street; ☎ 334-1888.
Cuisine: Italian. Avg. $40–$60.
Lunch: Noon–2:30 p.m., 7 days.
Dinner: 5:30–10 p.m., 7 days.
It may be minimalist in design but it's always decorated with people enjoying some extraordinary Northern Italian cuisine. Their homemade Pappardelle will linger all the way uptown. Credit Cards: All major.

Zeppole $$

186 Franklin Street; ☎ 431-1114.
Cuisine: Italian. Avg. $20–$40.

Lunch: Noon–3 p.m., Mon.–Sat.
Dinner: 6–10:30 p.m., Mon.–Sat.

Named after an Italian donutlike confection only served on special occasions. This casual, comfortable neighborhood hangout is just as delicious. The specialty of the casa is assorted plates of irresistible antipasto combinations. There are also five pastas and, of course, zeppole for dessert. Credit Cards: All major.

Chanterelle   **$$$**

2 Harrison Street; ☎ *966-6960.*
Cuisine: French. Avg. $40–$60.
Lunch: Noon–2:30 p.m., Mon.–Sat.
Dinner: 5:30–11 p.m., Mon.–Sat.

One of the city's preeminent tummy temples. Very serious in intent (perhaps a little too serious). You are expected to sit up straight and show some respect. Most of the time that's a fairly delightful task, but now and again you can't help wishing they would just "chill out" a little. Credit Cards: All major.

Agenda Lower Broadway, Astor Place

Lafayette Street & Lower Broadway

The gestalt of **Lower Broadway** really begins at Astor Place and Lafayette Street, once the most elegant and wealthiest residential areas in the city. This is where the Astors, the Delanos, and the Vanderbilts lived. **The Astor Library** is now the home of the **Public Theater**, founded by that theater's visionary Joseph Papp, and the birthplace of the musicals *Hair* and *A Chorus Line*. Another landmark on Lafayette street is the show-stopping **Puck Building**. The former home of the satiric magazine Puck, it is today, one of the grandest spaces for galleries, weddings and fabulous fetes.

Broadway from 12th Street down is more like SoHo which spills out into this energetic artery. And since it's on the fringe of **New York University**, the general feeling of the area is young, young, young! Both sides of the street are filled with new wave boutiques and a few old wave ethnic doodad emporiums. The whole place takes on a carnival atmosphere after dark and the restaurants and coffee houses are jammed. Not to be missed since it's the city's newest place for *la vie de boheme*.

Agenda Shopping/Lower Broadway

Canal Jean Co.

504 Broadway; ☎ *226-1130, 10:30 a.m.–8 p.m., Mon.–Thurs.; 10:30 a.m.–10 p.m., Fri.–Sun., 7 days.*

Not just jeans, which if you're lucky can cost just a couple of dollars here, but a huge assortment of surplus clothing. You can find everything from '40s satin pajama tops to antique furs (O.K. so that's not a politically correct purchase).

Tower Records

692 Broadway; ☎ *505-1500, 9 a.m.–midnight, 7 days.*

The selection here is so astonishing, you almost don't care about the show going on in the aisles.

Dean & DeLuca

560 Broadway; ☎ 431-8350, 10 a.m.–8 p.m., Mon.–Sat.; 10 a.m.–7 p.m., Sun.

Unquestionably the most heroic and extravagantly stocked gourmet food shop in the city. It seems to go on forever, with one delectable offering after another. In the back is an area for kitchen equipment and in the front an espresso bar where you can sample their "very parisienne" pastries. A definite foodie wonderland.

Broadway Panhandler

477 Brown Street; ☎ 966-3434, 10:30 a.m.–7 p.m., Mon.–Sat.

Too many cooks is just what this place is dedicated to. If over 8000 kitchen accessories make your whisk beat faster, prepare to bring oxygen with you.

Let There Be Neon

38 White Street (off Broadway); ☎ 226-4883, 10 a.m.–7 p.m., Mon.–Sat.

If you want your name in lights these guys will be more than happy to help. Other neon designs in accessories and furniture.

Rooms and Gardens

290 Lafayette Street (Houston); ☎ 431-1297, 10 a.m.–6 p.m., Mon.–Fri.; 11 a.m.–6 p.m., Sat.; Noon–6 p.m., Sun.

Imported French garden furniture that looks as nifty indoors. You can find anything from a zinc-topped table to an antique rooftop finial.

Agenda Best Bites/Lower Broadway

Indochine

430 Lafayette Street; ☎ 505-5111.
Cuisine: Vietnamese. Avg. $30–$50.
Hours: 5:30 p.m.–midnight, 7 days.

The blue plate specials here are Vietnamese but the reason people come is to watch the "cool" crowd. Credit Cards: All major.

Pravda $$$$

281 Lafayette Street; ☎ 226-4696.
Cuisine: Russian. Avg. $40–$60.
Hours: 5 p.m.–2 a.m., 7 days.

The headline here is all about caviar, blinis, and 75 ways to have vodka. My favorite is in the driest martini this side of the Kremlin. Be prepared to spend many rubles. Credit Cards: All major.

L'Ecole $$

462 Broadway; ☎ 219-3300.
Cuisine: French. Avg. $30–$50.
Lunch: Noon–1:45 p.m., Mon.–Thurs.
Dinner: 6–9:30 p.m., Fri.–Sat.

You may have seen chef Jacques Pepin potting around on T.V. but he's also the dean of the French Culinary Institute. The restaurant L'Ecole is run by his students. You can bet they watch their Ps and

Quinelles. As far as we're concerned most of them earn straight A's. Credit Cards: All major.

Lucky Strike $$$

59 Grand Street; ☎ *941-0479.*
Cuisine: American. Avg. $40–$60.
Hours: Noon–4 a.m., 7 days.

They carry on the bistro craze, and the fact that steak frites are under a thousand dollars here makes the "cutting edge" clientele even sharper. Credit Cards: All major.

Nobu $$$$

105 Hudson Street; ☎ *219-0500.*
Cuisine: Japanese. Avg. $60–$100.
Lunch: 11:45 a.m.–2:15 p.m., Mon.–Fri.
Dinner: 5:45–10:15 p.m., 7 days.

Despite what Horace Greeley advised, Nohu Matsuhisa went east. After becoming the darling of the L.A. sushi set, he looked for new tofu to climb and found them in a fantastic setting right here. The room has real peach trees with stylized wooden branches, cherry blossom stenciled on the floor, all very Zen. As we go to press, it's only been open for a few weeks so we still don't know what kind of clothes the emperor will be wearing. Credit Cards: All major.

Capsuto Freres $$$

451 Washington Street (at Watts); ☎ *966-4900.*
Cuisine: French. Avg. $40–$60.
Dinner: 5:30–11 p.m., 7 days.

Wonderful French food in a decidedly un-French area of town. Surrounded by the meat-packing industry, this is a gracious corner to have a substantial cassoulet or a gossamer souffle. Credit Cards: All major.

Lower East Side

E/W - Bowery to the East River
N/S - Houston Street to the East River

Tall ships from around the world are a stirring spectacle as they sail past New York for the July 4th festivities.

Think pickles—sweet, sour, kosher, pickle barrels, pushcarts, and immigrant dreams. Comedians, gangsters, intellectuals, activists, businessmen, songwriters—they all came out of the ghetto. The Jewish heritage of the Lower East Side has become part of New York's cultural heritage and belongs to every New Yorker.

At eye level, the area seems as hurly-burly and rundown as ever, except now Hispanics and Asians have begun moving into the old tenements above the discount handbag shops and the "appetizing" stores that put lox (smoked salmon) on the map. Still, visitors flock here from all over the country. The Lower East Side is a state of mind, it represents a universal struggle. Do not leave the area without a visit to the **Tenement Museum** (See Museums page 212) It's the best way to understand that heartbreaking struggle.

Although the streets are easier to navigate during the week, almost everyone comes on Sunday (shops are closed for the Jewish Sabbath from Friday afternoon through Saturday night). Simply, you can't have a ghetto without a crowd and the ghetto albeit one of affluent ex-patriots, is what many people come for, along with the shopping and eating, of course.

Agenda Shopping/Lower East Side

HIDDEN AGENDA

However facile you may be in the aisles at Saks, unless you've majored in Marrakesh Markets, a few words are in order. Everyone knows that the only reason to shop down here is to get a bargain. Shopping etiquette is strictly Early Souk. Reconfirm that you're prepared to buy but need a better price. Keep in mind that since most of us now live in a world filled with malls and discount outlets, the lower east side has lost a lot of its bargaining clout—real bargains down here have become an endangered species.

Most stores on the Lower East Side are closed on Saturday.

Fine & Kline
> *119 Orchard Street;* ☎ *674-6720, 8:30 a.m.–4;45 p.m., Sun.–Thurs.*
> For a handbag groupie—some small discounts, but this is not a place for dazzling savings. It's for a dazzling selection and leathers "like buttah."

Beckenstein
> *130 Orchard Street;* ☎ *475-4887, 9 a.m.–5:30 p.m., Sun.–Fri.*
> Fine cottons as well as other quality fabrics. They specialize in men's shirting, with the largest selection in the city.

Forman's
> *59,78,82 & 94 Orchard Street;* ☎ *228-2500, 9 a.m.–6 p.m., Mon.–Fri.;*
> *9 a.m.–2:30 p.m., Sun.*
> Each store caters to a different size customer, Petite, Plus, Regular and Designer Duds thrown in for extra good measure.

Klein's of Monticello
> *105 Orchard Street;* ☎ *966-1453, 10 a.m.–5 p.m., Sun.–Fri.*

Once known for their snazzy children's clothes, they're all grown up now. Elegant casual wear and designer originals but not a bargain in sight.

Economy Candy

108 Rivington Street; ☎ *254-1832, 8:30 a.m.–6 p.m., Sun.–Fri.*

After all the shopping and haggling, your blood sugar is sure to be low—head for Economy. They've been selling penny candy since 1937, when it really cost a penny.

Russ & Daughters

179 E Houston Street; ☎ *475-4880, 9 a.m.–6 p.m., Sun.–Fri.*

This delicious place goes way back to B.Z. (before Zabars). The granddaddy of New York "appetizing" stores, they overflow with Nova Scotia salmon (lox), smoked sturgeon and all the other good things that put a capital B in Brunch.

Agenda Best Bites/Lower East Side

Yonah Schimmel $

137 E Houston Street; ☎ *477-2858.*
Cuisine: Jewish. Avg. $5–$10.
Hours: 8 a.m.–6 p.m., Mon.–Sun. Closed Sat.

I suspect Olympic weightlifters could work out selling the potato, spinach, and kasha knishes. For those just arriving from Mars, knishes are large, stuffed, single-portion pastries, any one of which is filling enough to support life as we know it for some time to come. Credit Cards: Cash only.

Katz's $

205 E Houston Street; ☎ *254-2246.*
Cuisine: Jewish. Avg. $10–$15.
Hours: 8 a.m.–10 p.m., 7 days.

One of those places everyone has been saying "used to be better" since the day it opened. Katz's is a barn of a place, with about as much heart as a meter maid. Not anywhere as good as the Carnegie Deli. Credit Cards: Cash only.

Ratner's

138 Delancey Street; ☎ *677-5588.*
Cuisine: Jewish. Avg. $15–$30.
Hours: 8 a.m.–11:30 p.m., 7 days.

Oi vey, what would the Surgeon General say? Blintzes, sour cream, deep fried pierogi, and other dairy disasters, shoveled up in front of you with just a dash of cranky Jewish waiter thrown in. Ratner's has outlived most of its customers, even the ones who ate there last week.

Sammy's Famous Romanian
Jewish Steakhouse $$

157 Chrystie Street; ☎ *673-0330.*
Cuisine: Jewish. Avg. $20–$40.
Hours: 5–11 p.m., 7 days.

Places of Interest

33	Chinatown, Chatham Sq, Mott, Pell, & Doyer Sts	F25
47	Little Italy	F24

Foreign Currency Exchanges

740	Chemical Bank, 180 Canal St 334-9686	F24

The tables are set with syrup pitchers filled with chicken fat (schmaltz), bottles of seltzer, containers of milk, and jars of Fox's U-Bet chocolate syrup (for do-it-yourself egg creams). Meanwhile, tables are filled with people wolfing down Romanian tenderloins and side dishes of mashed potatoes with schmaltz and "greevens" (crispy bits of chicken skin) as though cholesterol were on sale. Credit Cards: All major.

Chinatown/Little Italy

(Bowery, Canal, Chatham Square, Mulberry Street)

To put it bluntly, I cannot imagine why any visitor without a degree in sociology would come to the **Bowery**. On the other hand, if you're in the mood to be grateful for small favors, the area is far more depressing than it is dangerous.

Hardy New Yorkers trudge down to the **Bowery**, albeit walking gingerly past the poor lost souls who sleep in flophouses and eat at the missions, for professional kitchen equipment (**Empire Food Service Equipment**, *114 Bowery*, ☎ *226-4447*, and **AAA Restaurant Equipment**, *280 Bowery*, 966-

1891) as well as to squint their way through some of the most eye-popping lighting fixture stores in town.

Canal Street runs further east than the Bowery (it goes under the **Manhattan Bridge**, with its wonderfully out of place Beaux Arts colonnade entrance, and into the Lower East Side). It's the official border between **Chinatown** and **Little Italy**.

Canal Street was so named because it had been proposed as a canal in the early 1800's to siphon off waters from the freshwater pond that covered Foley Square in what is now the civic center. Decades followed during which runaway slaves and immigrants were housed in substandard units as the city's focus and wealth moved north.

Today, **Canal** is a cornucopia of electronic parts, audio supplies, stationery, automotive goods, and wearables that have reached the end of the line.

Chinatown

Ten days of fireworks and celebrations between mid-January and early February herald Chinese New Year in Chinatown.

One of the reasons there are so many restaurants in Chinatown has to do with an old immigration law that allowed only Chinese *men* to enter the country. Restaurants and laundries (offering services usually provided by their wives) were the two businesses that Chinese immigrants were allowed to run since they were considered noncompetitive with jobs wanted by Caucasians. Chinatown is a true adventure and should be on everyone's agenda. You can eat better and less expensive Chinese food here than almost anywhere else in the country.

Important things to bear in mind are:

1) Chinese chefs come and go faster than a speeding egg roll. The restaurant that was great last week may have lost its edge while trying to find a replacement chef.

2) There truly is a ratio between the number of Chinese families in a restaurant and the quality of the food.

3) Chinatown Chinese is not "Uptown" Chinese. We're not talking L.A.-style "Chinois" or designer chic. Think formica, paper napkins

and cans of soda. If you're lucky, a paper tablecloth. Once in a while, a liquor license.

4) Many Chinese waiters belong to a school of service that begins and ends with carrying food from the kitchen. On the other hand there are no smiling faces to greet you with, "Hi, my name is Chang."

Little Italy

Once upon a time, when people were still discovering something magical called "tomato pie," and pasta was known as spaghetti, Little Italy was a wondrous place to which New Yorkers flocked for Italian home cooking. But the Italians aren't home anymore. The younger generation has integrated itself into more upmarket sections of the city, leaving behind an aging community rapidly being replaced by the expansion northward of **Chinatown**.

Still, in late September during the **Feast of San Gennaro**, when canopies of lights sparkle on **Mulberry Street**, outdoor stalls seduce your senses with the aroma of sausage and onions.

On a short walk along **Mott**, **Mulberry**, or **Grand Streets**, you'll find shops that are as wonderful as ever. Bursting with exotic salamis and cheeses and freshly-made pastas, cans of imported oils and tomatoes, breads studded with chunks of prosciutto, and pastries stuffed with ricotta—as the song says, "That's Amore."

Agenda Shopping/Canal/Chinatown/ Little Italy

Pearl Paint
308 Canal Street; ☎ *431-7932, 9 a.m.–6 p.m., 7 days.*
A bona-fide extravaganza for people who paint or draw or have carried on love affairs with papers and pens and lovely envelopes. Everything is priced low enough to satisfy dedicated skinflints.

Mazer Equipment
207 Bowery; ☎ *674-3450, 8 a.m.–7 p.m., 7 days.*
If you have room for a six-burner professional range in your suitcase, this is the place that sells them to most of the big cheeses in NY's food community. The last word in what's cooking.

Pearl River Market
277 Canal Street; ☎ *966-1010, 6 a.m.–10 p.m., 7 days.*
You'll find everything from woks to kids P.Js to restaurant crockery, to silk coolie jackets. One of the best places for fun gifts in the city.

Kam Man Food Products
200 Canal Street; ☎ *962-8414, 7 a.m.–10 p.m., 7 days.*
Don't hesitate going into this fragrant, Chinese grocery. Forget what looks like body parts floating in bottles and try some of the teas and spices. The basement has kitchenware.

Italian Food Center
186 Grand Street; ☎ *925-2954, 7 a.m.–11 p.m., 7 days.*

Provolones as big as the Ritz, mortadella to bring tears to the eyes. Prosciutto that melts on the tongue. Enter, inhale, we dare you to leave.

Agenda Best Bites/Chinatown/ Little Italy

Great Shanghai $

27 Division Street; ☎ *966-7663.*
Cuisine: Chinese. Avg. $10–$20.
Hours: 11 a.m.–2 a.m., 7 days.
A Chinatown experience to the max—great food (especially the fish), cheap, noisy, only minimal English spoken, but almost everything on the menu is great. Credit Cards: All major.

The Nice Restaurant $$

35 East Broadway; ☎ *406-9776.*
Cuisine: Chinese. Avg. $10–$20.
Hours: 6 a.m.–2 a.m., 7 days.
True to its name, it serves nice, tasty, Cantonese favorites including dim sum and melt-in-the-mouth duck. Chicken is baked in a salt crust that makes it fall off the bone. Credit Cards: All major.

Noodle Town $

28-1/2 Bowery; ☎ *349-0923.*
Cuisine: Chinese. Avg. $10–$20.
Hours: 8 a.m.–1 a.m., 7 days.
Among other carbo-classics, they specialize in Singapore-style noodles which are spiced with hot curries. Confucius meets Ghandi with great results. When they're not noodling around, they serve up *congee* (Chinese comfort food, like porridge with bits of meat) that is perfect for a chilly day or in our case, any day. Credit Cards: All major.

Mandarin Court $

61 Mott Street; ☎ *608-3838.*
Cuisine: Chinese. Avg. $10–$20.
Hours: 11 a.m.–2 a.m., 7 days.
Chinese tea lunch reaches supernal heights here in a less than supernal setting. Extraordinary selection of dim sum for next to nothing. Take your earmuffs and Mandarin dictionary. Credit Cards: All major.

Big Wong $

67 Mott Street; ☎ *964-0540.*
Cuisine: Chinese. Avg. $10–$20.
Hours: 6 a.m.–1 a.m., 7 days.
We know, we know, it sounds like a Chinese gangster runs this place, but it's really a very low-key (probably a real Chinese gangster) setting with high standard for ribs and noodles. Lots of Chinese families exercising their chopsticks. Credit Cards: Cash only.

Sween 'N' Tart Cafe $

76 Mott Street; ☎ *334-8088.*
Cuisine: Chinese. Avg. $10–$20.

Hours: 8 a.m.–midnight, 7 days.
Chinese "health-food" has come to Chinatown. This delightfully medicinal restaurant has sweet tonics that they use to rejuvenate the body and balance your yin and yang. The by-product is a chance to try something deliciously unfamiliar such as *congee*, a rice porridge studded with meat or fish. They also serve a mean Chinese cruller. Credit Cards: Cash only.

Silver Palace $

52 Bowery; ☎ 964-1204.
Cuisine: Chinese. Avg. $10–$20.
Hours: 6 a.m.–4 a.m., 7 days.
First of all, it's enormous, but perfect for beginners in the Dim Sum game. The menu is as enormous as the space and you may feel like you've entered the "Chinese twilight zone." As long as you can point, you'll never starve. Credit Cards: Cash only.

Peking Duck House $$

22 Mott Street; ☎ 227-1810.
Cuisine: Chinese. Avg. $20–$40.
Hours: 11 a.m.–2 a.m., 7 days.
If you've never had Peking duck, or if you don't want to go through the fuss some restaurants make about ordering it in advance, this is a real find. Good-naturedly rough and tumble. Don't let them talk you into appetizers or side dishes unless you're descended from Henry VIII. Credit Cards: All major.

Golden Unicorn $$$

18 East Broadway; ☎ 941-0911.
Cuisine: Chinese.
Hours: 11 a.m.–3 a.m., 7 days. Avg. $30–$60.
Unlike the usual Chinatown storefront eatery, this is a "real" restaurant with "real" decor—mirrors, cloth napkins, a wine list and some of the best food in the neighborhood. If you attempt to go for a tea lunch, they line up here at the crack of dawn. The regular menu is classical Cantonese at its very best. Credit Cards: All major.

Triple 8 Palace $$$

59 Division Street; ☎ 941-8886.
Cuisine: Chinese. Avg. $40–$60.
Hours: 7 a.m.–2 a.m., 7 days.
Another football-field sized space that is jammed almost all the time. It's perched on the top floor of a very forgettable mall overlooking the Manhattan Bridge. If you eat there once you're their prisoner for life. The food is exceptional and the variety staggering. Go with as many people as possible even if you have to "Shanghai" them. Credit Cards: All major.

Joe's Shanghai $

9 Pell Street; ☎ 233-8888.
Cuisine: Chinese. Avg. $10–$20.
Hours: 8 a.m.–midnight, 7 days.
Joe is usually nowhere in sight but his dumplings make their presence known in the most toothsome of ways, and they have a secret. They are soup dumplings. Liquid is magically hidden inside the dumpling dough and fills your mouth with a rich broth. That sly fox, Joe. Credit Cards: Cash only.

NHA Trang $

87 Baxter Street; ☎ 233-5948.
Cuisine: Vietnamese. Avg. $10–$20.
Hours: 6 a.m.–2 a.m., 7 days.

Vietnam is definitely making its presence felt in Chinatown and NHA Trang is a good spot for beginners to explore a very sophisticated cuisine. Crisp, dry spring rolls, spicy chicken with lemongrass, and grilled beef with peanuts are all intriguing new tastes. Credit Cards: Cash only.

Canton $$

45 Division Street; ☎ 226-4441.
Cuisine: Chinese. Avg. $20–$40.
Hours: 11 a.m.–2 a.m., 7 days.

Fish is the order of the day. Carp, sea bass, flounder are prepared with a light touch. One of the few restaurants in which you can ask questions and it's safe to stick with specials. For starters, try lettuce leaves that you stuff with beef, chicken or vegetables and fold into small packets. Credit Cards: Cash only.

Grotto Azzura $$

387 Broome Street; ☎ 226-9283.
Cuisine: Italian. Avg. $20–$40.
Hours: 11 a.m.–1 a.m., 7 days.

This is retro-dining at its most nostalgic. The walls of the "cave" are painted a bright blue with murals here and there as a background to an open kitchen, garrulous waiters, and barely enough breathing space between tables. Pitchers of wine with fruit, garlic bread that will keep you vampire-proof for years and a sea of tomato sauce atop everything in sight. Credit Cards: Cash only.

Luna $$

112 Mulberry Street; ☎ 226-8657.
Cuisine: Italian. Avg. $20–$40.
Hours: Noon–midnight, 7 days.

A sliver of a room that's always filled. Lots of southern Italian comfort food, ranging from garlicky artichokes to a terrific cannelloni. Credit Cards: Cash only.

Il Cortile $$$

125 Mulberry Street; ☎ 226-6060.
Cuisine: Italian. Avg. $40–$60.
Hours: Noon–1 a.m., 7 days.

It's northern Italian, chic and the garden room allows for relaxed conversation. Best of all you can get a martini with your osso-bocco. Credit Cards: All major.

Benito I $$

174 Mulberry Street; ☎ 226-9171.
Cuisine: Italian. Avg. $20–$40.
Hours: 11 a.m.–2 a.m., 7 days.

Benito I and Benito II are just across the street from each other and as if life weren't complicated enough you're faced with another decision. I'd stay with Benito I for the Sicilian menu, the perfect scaloppine and the adorable waiters. Credit Cards: Cash only.

Cafe Gitane $

242 Mott Street; ☎ 334-9552.
Cuisine: French. Avg. $10–$20.
Hours: 11 a.m.–midnight, 7 days.

A whiff of Paris in Little Italy. Great ham sandwiches "en baguette" or other light bites will put you right in the mood for a P.M. pasta pig-out! Credit Cards: All major.

Ferrara's $$

195 Grand Street; ☎ 226-6150.
Cuisine: Italian. Avg. $20–$40.
Hours: 8 a.m.–1 a.m., 7 days.
Very big, bright Italian bakery that's been a fixture down here for years. There's a sidewalk cafe so that you can ogle the locals while you sip your cappuccino. Credit Cards: All major.

Caffe Roma $$

385 Broome Street; ☎ 226-8413.
Cuisine: Italian. Avg. $10–$20.
Hours: 8 a.m.–midnight, 7 days.
Not as glitzy as Ferrara's with a well worn, less touristy feel. This one gets our vote and our cannoli business. Credit Cards: Cash only.

Along with its concrete and glass symbols of capitalism, Lower Manhattan offers stunning vistas of New York's waterways.

Lower Manhattan

N/S - Canal Street to Battery Park
E/W - East River to Hudson River

From **Bowling Green** where the Dutch bought the island from the Indians, to the **Statue of Liberty** welcoming "your tired, your poor," to the first boom on Wall Street that promised to make everyone rich—the fabulous skyline of Lower Manhattan silhouettes The Great American Dream.

If you have time to cover only one area in addition to Midtown, it should be Lower Manhattan. Not for its history, but for its perspective. The dissonance of architectural styles, the zig-zag of time frames, and the panoply of hopes they represent are staggering: **Trinity Church**, the **World Trade Center**, **Federal Hall** (where Washington took his oath as first President of the U.S.), the **New York Stock Exchange**, the **Fulton Fish Market**, **City Hall**, **Battery Park City**, and **Ellis Island** with its **National monument** and **Museum of Immigration**.

Unlike other New York neighborhoods, this part of town was open only during business hours. By 6 p.m., the streets were deserted. On weekends, the place was a ghost town. Not anymore.

The change began with the building of the **World Trade Center** by the **Port Authority of New York and New Jersey** to establish a downtown locus for international business. By the time the twin towers opened in 1973, interest peaked in restoring the **South Street Seaport** area.

Although it doesn't much matter where you start out, plan on winding up at the **South Street Seaport** for a little R&R before heading back uptown. Most people tend to head for the **World Trade Center**. Today, it seems unbelievable that in February 1993, terrorists were able to set-off a bomb that caused death and millions of dollars of destruction to this seemingly indestructible landmark. Today, no trace of that terrible day remains except in the minds of most New Yorkers. As you ride up to the 107th floor, you might think about this: you're travelling at a speed of up to 1600 feet per minute.

The **World Financial Center** on West Street, right across from the **World Trade Center** is much more elegant in design than the **Twin Towers** (money not only talks, it creates). Its public spaces are arrestingly dramatic. The courtyard done in the style of an outdoor square sports more marble than Carrara as well as sophisticated shops and restaurants. But the dramatic jewel in the Financial Center's crown is the **Winter Garden** with its 16 Palm trees that soar to meet its domed glass ceiling. A marble staircase sweeps down from the floor above, just made for Fred and Ginger to dance on. The total effect of this miragelike structure is one of open-mouthed disbelief.

The Twin Towers of the World Trade Center (1350 ft.) are eight stories taller than the Empire State Building.

The **Winter Garden** leads out onto a promenade that has gorgeous views of the Hudson. Benches make it possible to take full advantage of them.

Keep walking downtown to **Battery Park**. You'll see **Castle Clinton**, a 19th century fort that, prior to landfills, was 200 feet offshore. Now restored and manicured, it's about as fierce as a paper tiger

Museums

95	Fraunces Tavern Museum, Broad & Pearl Sts	E26
108	Museum of American Financial History, 24 Bway	E26
110	National Museum of the American Indian, 1 Bowling Green	E27
121	Statue of Liberty Museum, Liberty Island, New York Bay	E27
128	Whitney Museum of American Art, at Federal Reserve Plaza: 33 Maiden Lane at Nassau St	E26

Places of Interest

30	American Stock Exchange, 78 Trinity Pl	E26
37	Ellis Island, NY Harbor	E27
39	Federal Hall National Memorial, Wall & Nassau Sts	E26
40	Federal Reserve Bank of NY, 33 Liberty St	E26
41	Fulton Fish Market, in South Street Seaport, South & Fulton Sts	F26
51	Post Office (Main), 8th Av, W 31 to W 33 Sts	C20
58	South Street Seaport, Fulton St & Pier 16	F26
59	Statue of Liberty, NY Bay	E27
64	Trinity Church (PE), Bway & Wall St	E26
69	Vietnam Veterans Memorial, Lower Manhattan	F26
71	World Financial Center, 200 Liberty St	D26
72	World Trade Center, btwn West, Church, Liberty, Vesey Sts	E26

Follow the promenade along the river's edge and you'll reach one of my favorite structures, **Pier A** *(West Street and Battery Place)*—the 1885 fireboat station, jubilantly painted as though it were a set for a Disney film.

The **Battery** was named for the cannons that lined the shore to protect the Dutch settlers—the self-same group of Type-A over-achievers who, in 1653, built a wooden wall "uptown" (**Wall Street**) to protect their tushes from the Indians. Unlike the promissory notes on Wall Street, Battery Park offers a gracious expanse of green from which to view the harbor. The **Circle Line Ferry** *(☎ 269-5755)* to the **Statue of Liberty** leaves from here every day except Christmas, 9:30 a.m.–4:30 p.m. on the hour, with sailings every half hour (starting at 10:30 a.m.) on weekends during July and August. Round trip fare is $7; children under 11, $3 and seniors $5.

The **Staten Island Ferry** (at the foot of Whitehall Street) is one of those things you simply have to do. For the paltry sum of fifty cents, you will be treated to a mini-cruise that is second only in sensory thrill to being launched in outer space. The ferry leaves every half hour from 6:30 a.m. to 11 p.m.

The Staten Island Ferry is still New York's best bargain (50 cents roundtrip) with spectacular breezy views.

Bowling Green, at the foot of Broadway, is where Peter Minuit supposedly consummated the $24 deal that won him the Good Shopper Award of 1626. After years as a cattle market, and then a parade ground, it was leased to the city as a spot for public bowling. The fence that surrounds the area was built in 1771 and is a City Landmark. The **U.S. Custom House** (1907) on **Bowling Green** is one of New York's most opulent buildings. It shares a Beaux Arts heritage with the Metropolitan Museum of Art and is considered by some to be an even grander structure.

Fraunces Tavern *(54 Pearl Street,* ☎ *269-0144)* opened in 1763 and it was here that George Washington said farewell to his troops at the end of the Revolutionary War in 1783. The Tavern is now a restaurant open from Monday to Friday for breakfast, lunch and dinner with a very extensive and moderately-priced menu.

It is located at the corner of Pearl and Broad Streets. Broad Street was a canal during the Dutch period, which explains its unusual width. Walk up **Broad Street** to Number 8 and hold your breath: it's the **New York Stock Exchange**. A must-see (see "Priorities").

No matter what flavor portfolio you have, the original Custom House, which was later the Subtreasury Building, and is now **Federal Hall National Memorial** *(28 Wall Street)*, is a mini-Parthenon on the Acropolis of High Finance. This particular temple is where Washington took the oath as first President in 1789. The statue that's been marking the spot since 1883 is the one you see in all the pictures (he was actually sworn in on a second floor balcony). There's a free exhibition inside (Mon.–Fri., 9 a.m.–5 p.m., ☎ *825-6888)*.

Trinity Church sits on Broadway at the head of Wall Street almost as a conscience reminding the brokers to take stock. There's been a Trinity Church here since 1699, in one form or another. The doors to the church were modeled after the Ghiberti doors on the Baptistery in Florence (the south doors offer scenes of Manhattan's history). Sharing the church's fame is its cemetery, the oldest gravestone dates back to 1681, and the most famous are those of Alexander Hamilton and Robert Fulton.

South Street is where New York came into its own in the 1800s as the nation's preeminent port. In 1983 an 11-block landmarked setting called the **South Street Seaport Museum** was dedicated. The Seaport is a museum without walls. The several-block area has buildings that date from the early 19th-century and which housed merchants, sailmakers, riggers, printers, and grocers. Today there are elegant shops; you can eat pizza by the slice, oysters by the half-dozen, and pickles by the barrel; you can board the second-largest sailing ship in existence, watch someone build a big ship in a small bottle, and have some stationery made in a 19th-century print shop.

Pier 17 features a wrap-around, water's edge, multi-tiered deck: you've got the river right there, the tall-masted schooners tied up at Piers 15 and 16, the Wall Street skyline, the gorgeous **Brooklyn Bridge**, and—if the wind is right, an occasional whiff of the gorgeous **Fulton Fish Market**.

They also have a great collection of ships moored at the piers: schooners, tugboats, ferries, etc. There are walking tours, excursion boats, craft demonstrations, educational programs, and films. Stop at the **Visitors Center** *(207 Front Street,* ☎ *669-9400)* for complete information.

Children's Center of the Seaport *(167 John Street)* is a place for kids to drop in for hands-on exhibits, while the **Seaport Museum Boat Building** next door *(169 John Street)* lets them watch boats being assembled as they were in the good old days.

Best of all, there are two or three-hour cruises on the **Pioneer**, an 1885 schooner that will take you along lower Manhattan and pass the **Statue of Liberty**. Or you might elect an hour and a half ride on the **De Witt Clinton**, a replica of a turn-of-the-century steamboat. Call ☎ *669-9424* for hours and prices.

AGENDA NUDGE

P.S.: For sticklers, **City Hall** *is located in City Hall Park (Broadway and Murray Street). It has been called "an outstanding example of Federal period architecture...among the most beautiful buildings in America."* ☎ *788-4636.*

Agenda Shopping/Lower Manhattan

Syms

42 Trinity Place; ☎ *797-1199, 9 a.m.–6:30 p.m., Mon.–Fri.; 9 a.m.–8:30 p.m., Sat-Sun.*

Discount heaven for good quality, conservative clothes (Michael Jackson does not get his stuff here). The trick they use is to keep dropping the price until the garment sells. Lots of choices for him and her.

Century 21

22 Courtland Street; ☎ *227-9092, 7:45 a.m.–7 p.m., Mon.–Sat.*
A madhouse most of the time, but occasionally you can find extraordinary savings in this discount department store. They say they have designer originals—only God knows if that's true.

Fulton Market, The

South Street at Fulton; 8 a.m.–10 p.m., 7 days.
They have every kind of junk food ever dreamed of by man, as well as some specialty shops, fresh seafood, cafes, restaurants (13 in all), bakeries, confectioners, cheese shops, and on and on and on. The street level is devoted to retail food stalls. Sprinkled in (not necessarily in the best of taste) are souvenir shops. The second level is a mall for fast food.

Pier 17

South Street at Fulton; ☎ *669-9416, 9 a.m.–10 p.m., 7 days.*
Our favorite part of the seaport is Pier 17, a renovated pleasure pier filled with shops and restaurants and surrounded by the aforementioned deck with views of the East River traffic, the Brooklyn Bridge, and the Statue of Liberty that makes everything taste even better. One of our most memorable meals was a shared order of shopping-mall-generic chow mein (don't laugh: haven't you ever explored the wonderful world of gastronomic nostalgia?) which we savored while staring out at the skyline of Wall Street.

Agenda Best Bites/Lower Manhattan

Au Manderin $$$

2 W Financial Center/Winter Garden; ☎ *385-0313.*
Cuisine: Chinese. Avg. $40–$60.
Hours: Noon–9:30 p.m., 7 days.
A haute chinoise spot with a touch of California. Very pretty and very convenient if you're wandering the Wintergarden. Credit Cards: All major.

Pipeline

2 W Financial Center; ☎ *945-2755.*
Cuisine: American. Avg. $20–$40.
Hours: 11 a.m.–10 p.m., Mon.–Fri.; 11 a.m.–8 p.m., Sat.–Sun.
High tech surroundings as well as a "boffo" terrace in the warm weather. The food is first rate and it's a happening scene all the time. Credit Cards: All major.

Bridge Cafe $$

279 Water Street; ☎ *227-3344.*
Cuisine: American. Avg. $20–$40.
Hours: 11:45 a.m.–10 p.m., 7 days.

It used to be one of former Mayor Koch's favorite hangouts. It's tiny but packs a giant culinary wallop. Very sophisticated menu for the movers and shakers who drift over from City Hall and Wall Street. It's always a delectable surprise. Credit Cards: All major.

Ecco $$$
124 Chambers Street; ☎ 227-7074.
Cuisine: Italian. Avg. $40–$60.
Lunch: Noon–3 p.m., Mon.–Fri.
Dinner: 5 p.m.–midnight, Mon.–Fri.
The echo here is from the 19th century. A lush setting with mahogany, mirrors, a beautiful bar and an even more beautiful antipasto. Good, solid northern Italian cuisine that the Wall Street crowd puts their money on. Credit Cards: All major.

La Tour D'Or $$$
Bankers Trust Building, 16 Wall Street; ☎ 233-2780.
Cuisine: Continental. Avg. $40–$60.
Lunch: Noon–3 p.m., Mon.–Fri.
Dinner: 5–10 p.m., Mon.–Fri.
Do you want to have lunch in J. P. Morgan's old apartment? J.P. may be long gone but the memory of his money is represented in the prices here. Is it worth it? Yes! The view from the 31st floor extravaganza will make you forget the stocks you have to short-sell. Besides, how often do you get a chance to make a reservation at the Bankers Trust Building? Credit Cards: All major.

Fraunces Tavern Restaurant $$$
54 Pearl Street; ☎ 269-0144.
Cuisine: American. Avg. $40–$60.
Hours: Noon–9 p.m., Mon.–Fri.
Now we're talking the very beginning of the city. This is as close to Colonial New York as you're going to get. Downstairs is a pub with food to match—upstairs a museum and the room where Washington said farewell to his troops. A wonderful look at the 1700s without the help of Disney. Credit Cards: All major.

Upper Manhattan

N/S - The Cloisters to 86th Street
E/W - East River to Hudson River

Defining Upper Manhattan isn't easy. (For the people who live in SoHo, it's defined as any place above Houston Street.) But since this is a book for visitors, I've leaped zip codes and civic sensibilities in a single bound. The truth is, with the exceptions of forays to **Lincoln Center** and **Museum Mile**, visitors spend most of their time below 59th Street.

A funny thing happens to Manhattan on the way to 125th Street: it starts getting real skinny. Also, the East River turns right as Manhattan turns left. Enter the **Harlem River**. And, of course, **Harlem**. What most people don't realize, however, is that there are many Harlems: Black, Spanish, and Italian.

The Upper East Side, above 96th Street, develops a distinctly Latin beat as it bursts into **Spanish Harlem**. "El Barrio," unlike Madison Avenue in the seventies, is not a casual browser's delight. If traveling in this area, know exactly where you are going, and do not rely upon public transportation.

Spring for a cab (if the driver balks at taking you up there, remember that he's legally bound to take you anywhere within city limits).

The dividing line between Upper West Side Broadway and **Columbia University** Broadway is 110th Street, at which point New York becomes a college town. If you're in the neighborhood, by all means go in through Columbia's 116th Street and Broadway entrance for a look at the **Low Memorial Library** around which the campus was built.

Riverside Church, the **Cathedral Church of St. John the Divine**, and **Grant's Tomb**, are next on the agenda. To get your priorities in order: St. John's is, at present, the largest Gothic church in the world. Second only in floor space to St. Peter's in Rome, it will be, upon completion, the largest church of any kind in the world. Begun in 1892, the church is only about 2/3 complete—which means you may not want to hire the contractor, but by all means, go. It is splendid. Located at 112th Street and Amsterdam Avenue (☎ 316-7400), it's open daily from 7 a.m. to 5 p.m.

Equally memorable, but on a totally different scale, is **Riverside Church** at 122nd Street and Riverside Drive—its stone is carved to resemble the Cathedral at Chartres. Riverside has the world's largest carillon. You can hear it on Sundays before and after services, again at 3 p.m., and on Saturday at noon.

Q: Who's buried in Grant's Tomb—Not as simple as it sounds. A: General *and* Mrs. Grant. The **General Grant National Memorial** (*Riverside Drive at 122nd Street,* ☎ *666-1640*).

Harlem is defined geographically as going from 110th to 155th Streets and from river to river (skirting around **Morningside Heights**). But Harlem also borders on the Pacific Ocean, Canada and Mexico: it is the spiritual and cultural capital of Black America. It is from Harlem that signals are sent across the nation. Black pride. Black frustration. Black successes and setbacks.

Among the places to be covered on a Harlem tour is **Strivers' Row**, a string of handsome townhouses (some designed by Stanford White) between 138th and 139th Streets between Seventh and Eighth Avenues. The houses were intended for the upper white middle-class that never came. W.C. Handy, Eubie Blake, and many Black civic and professional leaders lived here.

The **Shomburg Center for Research in Black Culture** (*515 Malcolm X Boulevard, between 135th and 136th Streets,* ☎ *421-2200*) is a branch of the N.Y. Public Library with the world's largest collection of books, photographs, prints, personal papers, etc. documenting the history and literature of black people. Open Mon.–Wed., 12-8 p.m.; Thurs.–Sat., 10 a.m.–6 p.m.

There's probably no single street that signifies the "real" Harlem more than 125th Street. It is one of the strongest mental images we carry, and perhaps the most misleading. Back in the days when New York's Cafe Society trekked uptown to the **Cotton Club**, and the shows at the **Apollo Theater** featured the likes of Boos Smith, Billie Holiday, and Count Basie, 125th Street lit up Harlem.

Hopefully, you're hungry by this time. **Sylvia's** (*328 Lenox Avenue, near 127th Street,* ☎ *996-0660*) has been hailed as the Lutece of soul food. Go for the "smothered" chicken or ribs. NO credit cards, but the good news is you'll probably be able to get out for around $15 per person.

Harlem meets **Washington Heights** at **Trinity Cemetery** *(entrance on 153rd Street and Broadway)* where the Astors share eternity with the Van Burens, John James Audubon, and the author of the immortal, "'Twas the night before Christmas," Clement Clarke Moore.

The Cloisters in Ft. Tryon Park overlooks The Hudson River. It is a serene blend of meadows, woodland, chapels and sculpture.

The real attraction at the uppermost end of Manhattan is **The Cloisters**, a reconstruction of French and Spanish monastic cloisters located in **Fort Tryon Park**, property donated to the city by John D. Rockeller, Jr. One of the loveliest spots in the entire country (the Hudson River views are as glorious as the relics collected in Europe), the Cloisters houses the medieval holdings of the **Metropolitan Museum of Art**. The chapels were brought from Europe and rebuilt stone by stone in as idyllic a setting as one could find. (☎ *923-3700)* Suggested contribution. Tours are given every day at 3 p.m.

BOROUGHS

For an awesome view, take a cab to Brooklyn, then walk back to Manhattan across the majestic Brooklyn Bridge.

Unless you're in town to visit relatives, New York means Manhattan. It ain't necessarily so for those who live here, but the Bronx, Brooklyn, Queens, and Staten Island are not bursting at the seams with tourist attractions. For the locals the so-called "outer" boroughs are culturally rich outposts that offer nourishment to one and all, regardless of zip code.

In addition to sporting events (see page 237) that may lure you out of Manhattan, I've compiled a highly-selective list of places to go.

The Bronx

Bronx Zoo/Wildlife Conservation Park, The
> *Fordham Road and Bronx River Parkway;* ☎ *(718) 367-1010.*
> *Daily, 10 a.m.–5 p.m.; 5:30 p.m. on Sundays and holidays. Admission. By donation on Wed.*
> *IRT No. 2 train to Pelham Parkway station. Also Liberty Lines express bus from Madison Avenue (28th, 40th, 47th, 54th, and 84th streets). Call* ☎ *(718) 652-8400 for fare and schedules.*

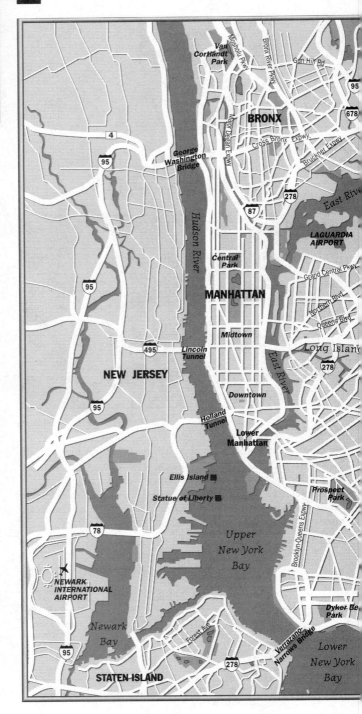

NY Boroughs

One of the most spectacular environments for wildlife in the world. Over 3000 animals and birds can be seen in simulated natural habitats. "Jungle World" is the newest indoor home for tropical Asian wildlife. Other exhibits include the World of Darkness (for nocturnal animals); Wild Asia, where an elevated monorail takes you through elephant, rhinoceros, and tiger country. All this plus one of the most original children's zoos in the country (an entrance fee is requested). The zoo also has snack bars and a restaurant.

New York Botanical Garden

Southern Boulevard, north of Fordham Road; ☎ (718) 817-8700.
Open daily, dawn to dusk. Admission by donation. Enid Haupt Conservatory is open 10 a.m.–5 p.m.
IND No. 4, CC or D trains to Bedford Park station, then No. 17 bus to Webster Avenue. Also Liberty Lines express bus from Madison Avenue (28th, 40th, 47th, 54th, and 84th streets). Call ☎ 881-1000 for fare and schedules.

A gorgeous 250 acres of azaleas, roses, herb gardens, pine and hemlock forests and the Bronx River waterfall. The star attraction is the Enid Haupt Conservatory—a Victorian crystal fantasy that has been landmarked. It has eleven glass pavilions with tropical jungles, deserts, palm courts, a fern forest, and special seasonal displays. For a snack or scenic lunch, there's the converted-into-a-restaurant Snuff Mill, an 18th century building used originally to grind snuff.

Poe Cottage

East Kingsbridge Road and the Grand Concourse; ☎ (718) 881-8900.
Sat., 10 a.m.–4 p.m.; Sun., 1 p.m.–5 p.m. Admission $2, children free.
IND CC or D train to Kingsbridge Road station.

A real treat for Edgar Allan Poe fans. The house has been preserved as a museum and guides lead visitors through the rooms.

Van Cortlandt Park (and Van Cortlandt Mansion)

246th Street and Broadway; ☎ (718) 543-3344.

Two square miles of park that was part of a Dutch land grant dating back to 1646. It has facilities for swimming, tennis, horseback riding, and picnicking. It's also the site of the Van Cortlandt Mansion (open Sat., 10 a.m.–3 p.m.; Sun., 11 a.m.–4 p.m.; Admission) which served as headquarters for British and American troops during the Revolution. Washington really slept here many times.

Brooklyn

Aquarium For Wildlife Conservation

Open daily 10 a.m.–4:45 p.m. Admission $7.75, adults, $3.50, children.
☎ (718) 265-3400.
IND F train to West 8th Street Station

Whales, sea turtles and eels swim fin to fin. There is also a pretty scary shark tank and, in summer, an outdoor dolphin show.

Brighton Beach

IND D or Q to Brighton Beach Station

It's only a short walk south from Coney Island to Brighton Beach which today has become known as "Little Odessa." The area, home to over 20,000 Russian immigrants, is crowded with people shopping at imported food stores or eating at exotic restaurants. You're always

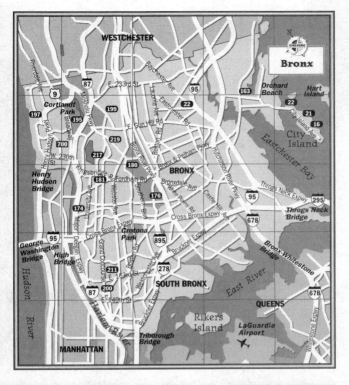

Places of Interest

163	Bartow Pell Mansion, Pelham Bay Park	F2
169	City Island	G2
174	Hall of Fame for Great Americans, 181 St & University Av	D4
176	Intl Wildlife Conservation Park/ Bronx Zoo, Fordham Rd & Bronx River Pkwy	E3
180	NY Botanical Garden	E3
181	Poe Cottage, E Kingsbridge Rd & Grand Concourse	D3
195	Van Cortlandt Mansion, Nr Bway & 246 St	D2
197	Wave Hill, Independence Av & 249 St	C2
199	Woodlawn Cemetery, Jerome & Bainbridge Avs	D2
200	Yankee Stadium, River Av & E 161 St	D5

Museums

211	Bronx Museum of the Arts, 165 St & Grand Concourse	D4
214	City Island Historical Nautical Museum, 190 Fordham St	G2
217	Lehman Art Gallery, Lehman College	D3
219	Museum of Bronx History, Bainbridge Av & E 208 St	D2
221	Museum of Migrating People, Baychester Av	E2
225	North Wind Undersea Institute, 610 City Island Av	G2

Foreign Currency Exchanges

700	Chemical Bank, 3775 Riverdale Av (718) 796-8411	D3

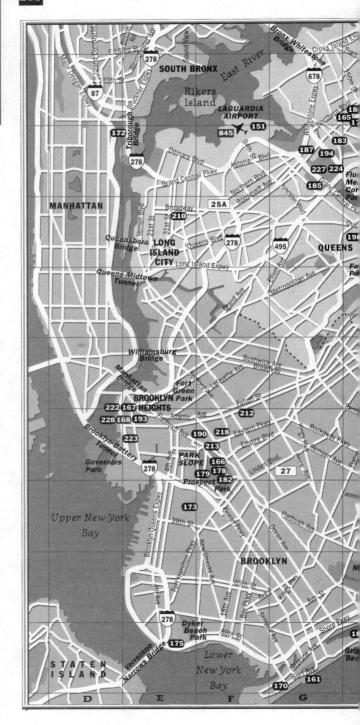

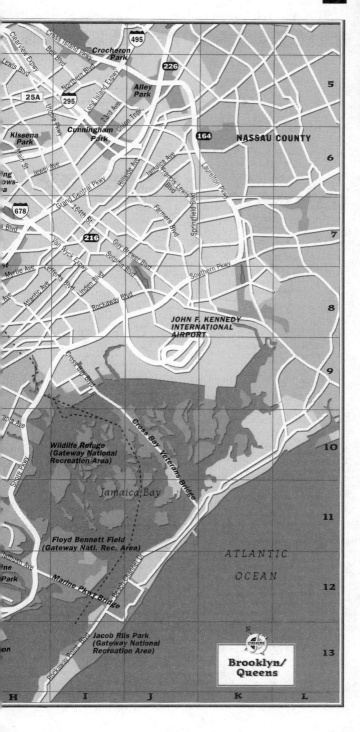

Brooklyn/
Queens

Brooklyn

Museums

212 Brooklyn Children's Museum,
145 Brooklyn Ave., Bkln F10

213 Brooklyn Museum, Eastern Pkwy
& Washington Av, Bkln F10

218 Muse Community Museum of Bklyn, 1530
Bedford Av, Bkln F10

222 National Maritime Historical Society,
Fulton Ferry Pk, Bkln D9

223 NYC Transit Museum
130 Livingston St, Bkln E10

228 Rotunda Gallery, Bklyn War Memorial,
Cadman Pl West, Bkln E10

Places of Interest

161 Aquarium for Wildlife Conservation, W 8
St & Surf Av, Bkln G13

166 Brooklyn Botanic Garden F10

167 Brooklyn Heights
Promenade, Bkln E10

168 Brooklyn Historical Society,
128 Pierrepont St, Bkln E10

170 Coney Island, Bkln G13

173 Green Wood Cemetery,
5 Av & 25 St, Bkln E11

175 Harbor Defense Museum,
Ft. Hamilton, Bkln E13

178 Lefferts Homestead,
Prospect Park, Bkln F10

179 Litchfield Villa,
Prospect Park, Bkln F10

182 Prospect Park Wildlife Conservation
Center/Prospect Park Zoo, Flatbush Av &
Empire Blvd., Bkln F10

188 Sheepshead Bay, Bkln H13

190 Soldiers' & Sailors' Arch,
Prospect Park, Bkln E10

193 Transit Exhibit, Boerum Pl
& Schermerhorn St, Bkln E10

Queens

Museums

210 American Museum of the Moving Image,
35 Av & 36 St, Qns E7

216 Jamaica Arts Center,
161-04 Jamaica Av, Qns I7

224 NY Hall of Science, Flushing Meadows-
Corona Park, Qns G6

226 Queens County Farm Museum,
73-50 Little Neck Pkwy,
Floral Pk, Qns J5

227 Queens Museum, Flushing
Meadows-Corona Park, Qns G6

Places of Interest

162 Aqueduct Race Track,
Ozone Park, Qns I8

164 Belmont Park Race Track,
Elmont, LI K6

165 Bowne House, Bowne St,
Flushing, Qns G5

172 Downing Memorial Stadium,
Randall's Island E6

177 Kingsland Homestead,
Flushing, Qns H5

183 Queens Botanical Garden,
Flushing, Qns H6

184 Queens Historical Society,
143-35 37 Av, Qns H5

185 Queens Wildlife Conservation
Center/Queens Zoo,
111 St & 56 Av, Qns G6

187 Shea Stadium, Flushing G6

194 USTA Natl Tennis Ctr, Flushing Meadows-
Corona Park, Qns G6

198 West Side Tennis Club,
Forest Hills, Qns H7

Transportation Terminals

150 Kennedy Intl Airport,
Jamaica, Qns J9

151 LaGuardia Airport,
Flushing, Qns F6

Foreign Currency Exchanges

700 American Express, JFK Intl Airport
American Airlines Terminal
(718) 656-5673 J9

720 Chemical Bank, 38-18 Bway
(718) 204-0952 G7

740 Chemical Bank, 107-36 71 Av
(718) 476-6600 H7

840 Thomas Cook Currency Services,
JFK Intl Airport Arrivals Bldg.
(718) 656-8444 J9

845 Thomas Cook Currency Services,
LaGuardia Airport
Delta-Northwest Terminal
(718) 533-0784 F6

only a pirogi's throw from a big bowl of borscht. If all you want is a snack, there's Mrs. Stahl's knishes at the corner of Brighton Beach and Coney Island Avenue.

Brooklyn Botanic Gardens

1000 Washington Avenue; ☎ (718) 622-4433.
Admission free. Hours change with the season, so call ahead. Closed Mondays.
IRT No. 2 or 3 train to Eastern Parkway/ Brooklyn Museum stop.

Fifty acres of gardens, flowers, trees, and new glass conservatories costing more than $25 million. The cherry blossoms that bloom in May are said to rival those in Washington, DC. If you're going to be here in the spring, call ahead for the exact time of bloom.

Brooklyn Children's Museum

145 Brooklyn Avenue; ☎ (718) 735-4400.
Suggested admission by donation. Mon., Wed., Fri.: 2 p.m.–5 p.m.; Thurs.: 2 p.m.–8 p.m.; Sat. & Sun.: 10 a.m.–5 p.m.
IRT No.3 train to Kingston Avenue. Walk 6 blocks north to St. Marks Place. Turn left and go down the block to the museum.
This was the world's first museum designed exclusively for children. Fossils, mounted mammals, prehistoric exhibits as well as technological and environmental displays. Most things can be touched.

Brooklyn Heights

IRT No. 2 or 3 train to Clark Street station.
One of the loveliest and most peaceful neighborhoods in all the city. Originally, it was an area for merchants to build their homes. Most of the brownstones and carriage houses are still as beautiful and elegant as they were when they were put up in the early 1800s. Clark Street leads down to The Esplanade (called "The Promenade" by residents) for a spectacular view of the Manhattan skyline across the East River.

Brooklyn Museum

200 Eastern Parkway; ☎ (718) 638-5000.
Mon., Wed.–Fri.: 10 a.m.–5 p.m.; Sat.: 11 a.m.–6 p.m.; Sun.: 1 p.m.–6 p.m. Suggested contribution by donation.
IRT No. 2 or 3 train to Eastern Parkway/ Brooklyn Museum stop.
It's the seventh largest art museum in the U.S. with an Egyptian collection that's considered to be one of the best in the world. Also known for its Japanese, Korean and Primitive African art. Chock-full of crafts from around the world. A great source for inexpensive gifts to take home.

Queens

American Museum of the Moving Image, The

35th Avenue at 36th St., Astoria; ☎ (718) 784-0077.
Open Mon.–Thurs., 1–4 p.m.; Sat., 10 a.m.–6 p.m.; Sun. until 6 p.m. Admission $7, children $4.
IND R train to Steinway St. Walk to 35th Avenue and turn right.
Fascinating exhibits that take you from the very beginning of film up to the present. There are two floors of costumes and memorabilia that predate the '40s. Most interesting of all, tapes that allow you to listen in as famous directors coached actors in their films.

Jamaica Bay Wildlife Refuge

Broadchannel West; ☎ *(718) 318-4340.*
Open daily from dawn to dusk. Admission free.
IND A train to Broadchannel station. Ask directions from there.
Some 2800 acres of land and 9000 acres of water are reserved for
nature walks, bird-watching and relaxation. There are more than 300
species of shore birds, water fowl and small mammals. There are also
guided tours on the weekends.

"I'm pretty well stocked, but you can leave me your card if you like."

Drawing by Woodman; ©1994, The New Yorker Magazine, Inc.

Staten Island

Jacques Marchais Center of Tibetan Art

338 Lighthouse Avenue, Richmond; ☎ *(718) 987-3478.*
Open Apr.–Nov.: Sat.–Sun. 1 p.m.–5 p.m.; Jun.–Aug.; Thurs.–Sun., 1–5
p.m.; closed Dec.–Mar. Admission $7, children $4.
Two stone buildings designed to look like a Tibetan monastery with
the largest collection of Tibetan art in the Western Hemisphere. The
center also features art from Japan, China, India and Southeast Asia.
There are gardens and a lotus pond for peaceful meditation.

Richmondtown Restoration

441 Clarke Avenue; ☎ *(718) 351-1611.*
Open Wed.–Fri., 10 a.m.–5 p.m.; Sat.–Sun., holidays, 1–5 p.m. Admission
$2.50.
From Staten Island Ferry station, take No. 113 bus to St. Patrick's Place.
Remarkably, this is an entire 96-acre historic village right in New York
City. It comprises 26 buildings dating from the 17th through the
19th century. Visitors can see demonstrations of early American
crafts.

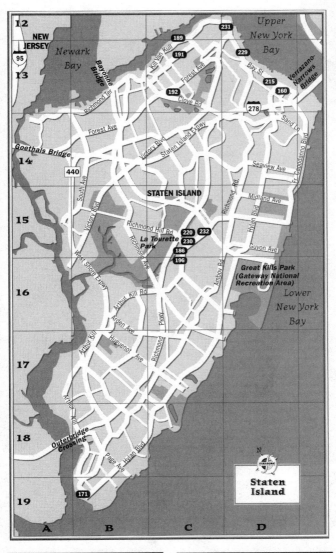

Museums

160	Alice Austen House & Garden, 2 Hylan Blvd.	**D13**
215	Garibaldi/Meucci Museum, 420 Tompkins Av	**D13**
220	Museum of Childhood, Bennett Hse, Richmondtown	**C15**
229	Staten Island Children's Museum, 914 Richmond Terrace	**D13**
230	Staten Island Historical Society Museum, Richmondtown	**C15**
231	Staten Island Institute of Arts & Sciences, 75 Stuyvesant Pl	**D12**
232	Tibetan Museum, Jacques Marchais Center, 338 Lighthouse Av	**C15**

Places of Interest

171	Conference House, Tottenville	**B19**
186	Richmondtown Restoration, Richmondtown	**C15**
189	Snug Harbor Cultural Center, New Brighton	**C13**
191	Staten Island Botanical Garden	**C13**
192	Staten Island Zoo, Barrett Park, Martling Av & Clove Rd	**C13**
196	Voorlezer's House, Richmondtown Restoration, Richmondtown	**C15**

Transportation Terminals

152	Newark Intl Airport, Newark, NJ	**A12**

NEW YORK SHOPPING AGENDA

The three floor wonderland of toys at F.A.O. Schwarz is guaranteed to entertain all ages.

The Best Around Town

Sometimes a pleasure and sometimes an adventure, shopping in New York has as many nuances as the glance you're given in the rearview mirror after asking a cabbie if he has change of twenty.

With shops reflecting the neighborhoods in which they're located, you'll find upscale goods on Fifth and Madison Avenues, and on 57th Street; bargains on the Lower East Side; avant-garde in SoHo and Greenwich Village; rock culture kitsch in the East Village, etc. But there are also museum shops, flea markets, auction houses and street vendors. (No, of course, you shouldn't buy watches on the street. But you might find a dynamite pair of earrings or gloves.) Also be aware of places that have "lost our lease" and are "going out of business." What most of them have lost is the second hundred years on their lease and are going out of business in the year 2085.

I've taken some favorites that didn't fall into one of my neighborhood roundups, and compiled the following agenda for the best shopping since the Indians took their $24 and ran.

Note: If you have items shipped back home, you can avoid the 8.75% N.Y.C. sales tax.

Antiques

As the savvy dealers say, they're not making antiques like they used to.

Sotheby's Auctions

1334 York Avenue at 72nd Street; ☎ *606-7000, 10 a.m.–5 p.m., 7 days.*

Christie's

502 Park Avenue at 59th Street; ☎ *546-1000, 9:30 a.m.–5:30 p.m., 7 days.*

Both of these auction houses have inexpensive sales held periodically (call to get dates) so that you can play the auction game without high anxiety.

Manhattan Arts & Antiques Center

1050 Second Avenue at 55 Street; ☎ *355-4400, 10:30 a.m.–6 p.m., Mon.–Sat.; Noon–6 p.m., Sun.*

A terrific antiques market in the European sense, everything is under one roof: a flock of dealers who carry everything from tiger teeth to Van Cleef tiaras.

Chelsea Antiques Building

110 W 25th Street (6th&7th Aves); ☎ *929-0909, 10 a.m.–6 p.m., 7 days.*
There are 12 floors filled with an antique browser's dreams. Collect-a-holics will find everything from jewels to junque. Some of the pieces are very serious museum quality. It's only a hop-skip-and a "charge" from the super Annex Flea Market, a block or so away (See Flea Markets, page 174).

A La Vielle Russie

781 Fifth Avenue; ☎ *752-1727, 10 a.m.–5:30 p.m., Mon.–Fri.; 11 a.m.–4 p.m., Sat.*

The ultimate in gorgeous glasnost: treasures from Mother Russia, including works by Faberge that are worth a czar's ransom.

Niall Smith Antiques

344 Bleecker Street & 96 Grand Street; ☎ *941-7354, Noon–6 p.m., Mon.–Sat.*

For anyone with a Biedermeier in his bonnet. Two shops filled with treasures collected over the years.

Lost City Arts

275 Lafayette Street; ☎ *941-8025, 10 a.m.–6 p.m., Mon.–Fri; Noon–6 p.m., Sat.–Sun.*

Filled with treasures discarded over the years: old street signs, gargoyles from building facades, manhole covers.

Back Pages Antiques

125 Greene Street; ☎ *460-5998, 10 a.m.–6 p.m., Mon.–Sat.; 1 p.m.–6 p.m., Sun.*

Want your own jukebox? They have them. All kinds of advertising art, pool tables and even Coke vending machines. Fun to browse through.

Henro

525 Broome Street; ☎ *343-0221, 11 a.m.–7 p.m., Mon.–Sat.; 11 a.m.–6 p.m., Sun.*

The couple who own Henro have been collecting American farmhouse furniture including children's furniture, for years. They have some really choice pieces.

Books

As the center of publishing in America, it's understandable why New York has the country's best selection of bookstores. It's easy to find something for every taste—even for those with no taste who haunt the x-rated bookstores on 42nd street.

Kitchen Arts & Letters

1435 Lexington Avenue; ☎ *876-5550, 10 a.m.–6 p.m., Mon.–Fri.; 11 a.m.–6:30 p.m., Sat.*

Nate Waxman has put together one of the largest collections of books on cooking, food, literature and art, a dedicated Foodie's favorite subject.

Barnes & Noble

Branches all over the City; ☎ *807-0099, Call for hours at individual stores.*

Discounted books, usually in great big wonderful superstores.

New York Bound

50 Rockefeller Plaza; ☎ *245-8503, 10 a.m.–6 p.m., Mon.–Sat.*

Books that are all about the city. Of course you're holding the best guide to NY in your hand but they have everything else anyone would want to know about my favorite metropolis.

Doubleday

724 Fifth Avenue (57th Street); ☎ *397-0550, 9 a.m.–midnight, 7 days.*

Very comprehensively stocked, but no discounts here. The good news is it's open until midnight for literary insomniacs.

Revolution Books

13 E 16th Street (Union Square); ☎ *691-3345, 10 a.m.–7 p.m., Mon.–Sat.; Noon–5 p.m., Sun.*

Stand up and be counted! Over 6000 titles that have to do with ferment and upheaval. It's the largest revolutionary bookstore in the U.S.A. If you feel a cause coming on head down to Union Square.

Strand Book Store

828 Broadway (12th Street); ☎ *473-1452, 9:30 a.m.–9:20 p.m., Mon.–Sat.; 11 a.m.–9:20 p.m., Sun.*

New York's answer to Foyle's in London. Musty, crusty, messy and totally incredible, should not be missed.

Argosy Book Store

116 E 59 Street; ☎ *753-4455, 9 a.m.–6 p.m., Mon.–Sat.; 10 a.m.–6 p.m., Sun.*

B. Dalton

666 Fifth Avenue; ☎ *247-1740, 8:30 a.m.–7 p.m., Mon.–Sat.; 12:30-6 p.m., Sun.*

Complete Traveller Bookstore

199 Madison Avenue (35th Street); ☎ *685-9007, 9 a.m.–6:30 p.m., Mon.–Sat.; 11 a.m.–5 p.m., Sun.*

Drama Bookshop

723 Seventh Avenue (48-49th Streets); ☎ *944-0595, 9:30 a.m.–7 p.m., Mon.–Fri.; Noon–5 p.m., Sun.*

Cameras and Electronics

Discounting may have become a national obsession but it has to be approached with lots of backup information when it comes to Camera and Electronics dealers. Always make a few comparisons before settling on the shop of your choice. Check *The New York Times* on Sundays for the latest prices.

47th Street Photo

67 W 47 Street; ☎ *921-1287 & 115 W 45 Street; 921-1287, 9:30 a.m.– 8 p.m., Mon.–Fri. Closed Sat.*

Usually trustworthy discounts by a less than charming group of salespeople.

Willoughby's Camera Store

110 W 32nd Street; ☎ *564-1600, 8:30 a.m.–8 p.m., Mon.–Fri.; 10 a.m.– 7 p.m., Sat-Sun.*

One of the largest selections you'll find. Prices are good but discounts may not be deep enough.

J & R Computer World

15 Park Row (at Wall Street); ☎ *238-9100, 9 a.m.–6:30 p.m., Mon.–Sat.; 11 a.m.–6 p.m., Sun.*

Not just for computers, although they carry a heroic selection, but also for cameras, TVs, personal stereos, etc. Terrific prices.

Clothing

Even more than its restaurants, New York's clothing stores reflect the neighborhoods in which they're located. There's the drop-dead chic of Fifth and Madison Avenues, the funk of the East Village, the off-beat elegance of SoHo and the open and close spectacle on Columbus.

If all this sounds too exhausting, you can always head for Bloomingdales, Barney's, Saks, Lord & Taylor, or Macy's to find designer boutiques (as well as snack shops and bathrooms) all under one roof.

Cockpit

595 Broadway; ☎ *925-5455, 11 a.m.–7 p.m., Mon.–Sat.; 12:30–6 p.m., Sun.*

We may not want to go off to war anymore but that doesn't mean we don't want to look that way. Flight Jackets, insignias, camouflage pants, flight boots for flying off into the blue yonder.

Chelsea Designers

128 W 23 Street; ☎ *255-8803, Noon–7 p.m., Mon.–Sat.; Noon–5 p.m., Sun.*

Elegant flowing designs for women made to drape in the most flattering way. Fabrics are crepe de chine silk, raw silk and wool. Everything rolls up into teeny, weeny little packets for effortless packing.

Gallery of Wearable Art

34 E. 67th Street; ☎ *425-5379, 10 a.m.–6 p.m., Tues.–Sat.*

You'll never see yourself coming and going in these one-of-a-kind little numbers. Collages, hand painting, and patchwork are all used to construct these masterpieces. They even have bridal gowns.

Addison on Madison

698 Madison Avenue; ☎ *308-2660, 10 a.m.–6:30 p.m., Mon.–Sat.*
Only shirts here and most of them are 100% cotton. The designs are button-down, French cuffs, or regular and the cotton comes from France.

S&W

287, 283, 165 W 26th Street; ☎ *924-6656, 10 a.m.–6:30 p.m., Mon.–Sat.; 11 a.m.–6 p.m., Sun.*
Designer clothes at a 40% discount, but since the prices are all in three figures, it still means serious dough. But, if you have to have that Armani blazer....

Shoofly

465 Amsterdam Avenue (82–83 Streets); ☎ *580-4390, 11 a.m.–7 p.m., Mon.–Sat.; Noon–6 p.m., Sun.*
Flights of Fancy shoes for the small set, also shoes for those Cinderellas whose tiny feet are still searching for their slippers.

Dollar Bills

32 E. 42nd Street (Grand Central Terminal); ☎ *867-0212, 10 a.m.–8 p.m., Mon.–Sat.*
Forget that this place looks like a tourist trap; inside there are Italian designer treasures for men, 40 to 50% off, lower than list. Some women's things too.

Nakazawa

132 Thompson Street (Prince Street); ☎ *505-7768, 11 a.m.–8 p.m., 7 days.*
Designer clothes with a decidedly Japanese accent done in plus sizes. Kimono style coats are Butterfly Beautiful.

"Hello...Book of World Records?"

Jewelry

In New York, a girl's best friend can be million-dollar diamonds or dollar rings. You'll find street vendors selling the latter practically right outside of posh diamond mines such as Harry Winston's. Then, there are the "have-I-got-a-bargain-for-you!" dealers in the "diamond district" *(47th Street; between Fifth and Sixth Avenues).*

Fred Leighton

773 Madison Avenue; ☎ *288-1872, 10 a.m.–6 p.m., Mon.–Sat.*
Show-stopping estate and antique jewels, alas, with prices that echo the quality. A favorite of ours for years.

H. Stern

645 5th Avenue; ☎ *688-0300, 10 a.m.–5:45 p.m., Mon.–Sat.*
Colored gemstones straight from the mines of Brazil, to be mounted in Sterns' elegant settings.

Fortunoff

681 5th Avenue; ☎ *758-6660, 10 a.m.–6 p.m., Mon.–Sat.*
Prices here are very attractive on mainstream type jewelry. Much better than department stores and neighborhood jewelers but not really discounted. You can get some good buys in the silver department on the 2nd floor.

Max Nass

118 E 28th Street (Park & Lexington); ☎ *679-8154, 9:30 a.m.–6 p.m., Mon.–Fri.; 9:30 a.m.–4 p.m., Sat.*
Handmade jewelry and also an antique collection that's very original. But their salespeople are really outrageous if you're lucky enough to find one.

Perfume and Cosmetics

Make-Up Center

150 W 53rd Street; ☎ *977-9494, 10 a.m.–6 p.m. Mon.–Wed; 10 a.m.–7 p.m. Thurs.; 10 a.m.–5 p.m. Sat.*
An unbelievable bargain! You get a private one-hour make-up lesson for $25.00, geared to your lifestyle or a special evening out. They do stage make-up and just plain "you" make-up. A lot less expensive than your shrink.

Il Makiage

107 E 60 Street; ☎ *371-3992, 9 a.m.–6 p.m. Mon.–Thurs.; 9 a.m.–3 p.m. Fri.*
The secrets of make-up application in a cozy non-threatening atmosphere. Even Cleopatra needed a little help at the beginning.

Boyd's

655 Madison Avenue; ☎ *838-6558, 9:30 a.m.–7:30 p.m., Mon.–Sat.; 9 a.m.–3 p.m., Fri.; 9:30 a.m.–6 p.m., Sun.*
If you can't find it here forget it. More make-up than Tammy Fay Baker could use up in a week. Perfume, hair accessories, combs, brushes and magnifying mirrors to scare you to death.

Revlon Store

767 Fifth Avenue; ☎ *486-8857, 9 a.m.–5 p.m., Mon.–Fri.*
This place used to be reserved for employees of the company, now it's for everyone who wants 60% off Revlon products.

Caswell-Massey

518 Lexington & 21 Fulton Street; ☎ *755-2254, 10 a.m.–6 p.m. Mon.–Fri.; 10 a.m.–5 p.m. Sat.*

They have house brands that reek of deja vu. The shops themselves are "old world" charming and a joy to browse in.

Food Shops

New York will give you a chance to sample some of the most extraordinary take-out goodies in the world.

Dean & DeLuca

(See page 133)

Balducci's

(See page 116)

Zabar's

(Seepage 103)

Gourmet Garage

453 Broome Street; ☎ *941-5850, 8 a.m.–8:30 p.m., 7 days.*

A small retail warehouse packed with some of the tastiest treats in the city. Trucks are always loading and unloading things like truffle oil, the most gorgeous veggies in the world and a cheese selection to make a grown Frenchman weep.

Vinegar Factory

431 E 91st Street; ☎ *987-0885, 7 a.m.–9 p.m., 7 days.*

The littlest Zabar, Eli, who also owns the outrageously expensive E.A.T. on Madison, has turned an old vinegar plant into a very chi chi market. It's known for its delectable brands and even has a chi chi cafe to match. The finest of fresh produce and patés. Great for picnic supplies.

"I'm from the calorie police, and I'd like a word with you."

For the Home

In a city where everyone is always eager for a new look, housewares, home furnishings and gifts are almost as important as plastic surgeons.

Wolfman-Gold & Good Co.

    117 Mercer Street; ☎ *431-1888.*
    (See page 128)

Takashimaya

    693 Fifth Avenue; ☎ *350-0100.*
    (See page 54)

Ad-Hoc Softwares

    410 W Broadway; ☎ *925-2652.*
    Part housewares, part hardware, it's the place for techie gadgets.

Felissimo

    10 West 56th Street; ☎ *247-5656, 10 a.m.–6 p.m., Mon.–Sat.*
    Four stories of beautiful objects to hold, touch and definitely buy.
    Jewelry, flowers, antiques, all displayed with an eye to the aesthetic.
    It's one of the best shows in town.

Geomancy

    337 E 9th Street; ☎ *777-2733, 12:30-7 p.m., Tues.–Sat.*
    The shop is filled with the best of Afghanistan, Italy, India, Japan and
    Zaire. There's sure to be something you'll want to own but that
    might mean an investment of from $5 to $4000.

D. Porthault

    18 E 69th Street; ☎ *688-1660, 10 a.m.–5 p.m., Tues.–Sat.*
    The rich and famous have been known to make a quick stop here to
    stock up on luscious linens (Sinatra, Streisand, etc.) No one gets
    short-sheeted here.

Mostly Bali

    324 E 9th Street; ☎ *777-9049, Noon–9 p.m., Tues.–Sat.*
    This is the place to say Bali, hi! If you can't jump on a freighter, it's
    the next best thing. Charming, whimsical animal carvings and masks,
    even a frog footstool. The prices are cheaper than trading beads.

Toys and Games

Big City Kite Co., Inc.

    1201 Lexington Avenue (81st Street); ☎ *472-2623.*
    (See page 79)

Enchanted Forest

    85 Mercer Street; ☎ *925-6677.*
    (See page 128)

F.A.O. Schwarz

    767 5th Avenue (58th Street); ☎ *644-9400.*
    (See page 49)

Penny Whistle Toys

    448 Columbus, 132 Spring Street; ☎ *925-2088.*
    (See page 94)

Forbidden Planet

    821 Broadway; ☎ *473-1576, 10 a.m.–8:30 p.m., 7 days.*
    For all the Cyber space nuts, outer space Nuts and sci-fi addicts no
    matter what their ages. Two floors filled with comics, posters, and
    Morphins to the next dimension.

"Wouldn't it be easier just to give the kids charge cards and let them buy what they want?"

Arts and Crafts

New Yorkers have made an art out of everything, even crossing the street against the light, but they also enjoy less dangerous forms of self expression.

Erica Wilson

> *717 Madison Avenue (63-64th Street);* ☎ *832-7290, 10 a.m.–6 p.m. Mon.–Sat.*
> H.Q. for superb needlework patterns and completed creations. She's the best in the city.

Pan American Phoenix

> *857 Lexington Avenue;* ☎ *570-0300, 10:30 a.m.–6:30 p.m. Mon.–Fri; 10:30 a.m.–6 p.m. Sat.*
> Toys, glassware, jewelry, pottery and wonderfully romantic Mexican wedding dresses.

Pearl Paint

> *308 Canal Street;* ☎ *(800) 221-6845 (see page 139)*

Sam Flax

> *425 Park Avenue;* ☎ *620-3060, 8:30 a.m.–6:30 p.m. Mon.–Sat.*
> Art supplies, drafting supplies and all the things that make an artist's heart go pit-pat.

Museum Shops

Before museum shops came along, museums were places to visit, enjoy, but resist the impulse to touch. The museums themselves finally understood what a wonderful bonus it would be for the visitor to take a bit of the museum home (if only a reproduction). Voila!—the museum shop was born. Today they've been expanded to include books, Christmas cards, crafts and gifts which swell the museum's coffers by millions each year.

(See Museum listings for hours.)

American Museum of Natural History, The
Central Park at 79th Street, New York, NY 10024; ☎ (212) 769-5100.

Asia Society, The
725 Park Avenue, New York, NY 10021; ☎ (212) 288-6400.

Brooklyn Museum
200 Eastern Parkway, Brooklyn, NY 11238; ☎ (718) 638-5000.

Cloisters Museum, The
Ft. Tryon Park, NY 10040; ☎ (212) 923-3700, ext. 158. Branch of the Metropolitan Museum of Art.

Cooper-Hewitt National Museum of Design, Smithsonian Institution
Fifth Avenue at 91st Street, NY 10128-9990; ☎ (212) 860-6868; FAX: 860-6909.

Guggenheim Museum
1071 Fifth Avenue (92nd Street), NY 10128; ☎ (212) 423-3500.

Guggenheim Museum SoHo, The
575 Broadway (Prince Street) NY 10012; ☎ (212) 423-3500.

International Center of Photography
Fifth Avenue at 94 Street, New York, NY 10128; ☎ (212) 860-1777.

Jewish Museum, The
1109 Fifth Avenue (92nd Street), NY 10128; ☎ (212) 423-3200.

Metropolitan Museum of Art, The
82nd Street & 5th Avenue, NY 10028; ☎ (212) 535-7710.

Museum of American Folk Art Book and Gift Shop
Two Lincoln Square, NY 10023; ☎ (212) 496-2966.

Museum of Modern Art Design Store, The
44 W 53rd Street, NY 10019; ☎ (212) 708-9700.

Museum of Television and Radio, The
25 W 53rd Street, NY 10019; ☎ (212) 621-8800.

Pierpont Morgan Library
29 E 36th Street, New York, NY; ☎ (212) 685-0008.

Snug Harbor Cultural Center
1000 Richmond Terrace, Staten Island, NY 10301; ☎ (718) 448-2500.

South Street Seaport Museum Shops
14 Fulton Street, or Cannon's Walk or 209 Water Street, NY 10041; ☎ (212) 669-9400.

Whitney Museum of American Art
945 Madison Avenue (75th Street), NY 10021; ☎ (212) 570-3676.

Flea Markets

Indoor and Outdoor

Shop till you drop, but this time it's the thrill of the hunt that makes flea markets more of a sport than a shopping experience. Foraging through tables filled with everything from discount lipsticks to depression glass (not depressing in the least), to Tiffany table lamps is the name of the game. Every Saturday and Sunday, New Yorkers crowd the markets looking for old dreams, new dreams and sometimes, nightmares. If you're here on a weekend, join the fun.

Antiques, Flea and Farmers Market
> *PS 183, 419 E 66th Street;* ☎ *(718) 897-5992, 10 a.m.–6 p.m. Sun.*

Green Flea/IS
> *44 Flea Market Columbus Avenue at 77 Street;* ☎ *(212) 721-0900/ 4952, 10 a.m.–6 p.m. Sun.*

Outdoors Annex Antiques Fair & Flea Market, The
> *25th Street at Avenue of the Americas;* ☎ *(212) 243-5343, 10 a.m.–6 p.m. Sat.–Sun.*

Greenmarket/Farmers Market
> *Union Square (Bdway at 17th Street);* ☎ *(212) 477-3220, 8 a.m.–6 p.m. Sat.–Sun.*

SoHo Antiques Fair and Flea Market
> *Broadway & Grand Street;* ☎ *(212) 682-2000, 10 a.m.–6 p.m. Sat.–Sun.*

Garage, The
> *112 W 25th Street; open Sat. & Sun. 9 a.m.–5 p.m., No Phone. (admission free) 2 floors, Indoors.*

Chelsea Antiques Building
> *110 W 25th Street,* ☎ *(924-3777) open daily, 10 a.m.–6 p.m.; (admission free) 12 floors, each with about a half dozen or so vendors, Indoors.*

Tin Door Antiques Fair
> *122 W 10th Street, open Sat. & Sun., No phone. 9 a.m.–5 p.m. (admission free) 2 floors.*

Tower Market
> *Broadway (West 4th & Great Jones Street) Sat. & Sun. 10 a.m.–7 p.m. Outdoors.*

RESTAURANTS

*The place to see and be seen, The River Cafe combines a dazzling
skyline view with American nouvelle cuisine.*

Introduction

New York is the eating capital of the world. There are some
25,000 restaurants that represent virtually all known cuisines and
can satisfy all palates and purses whether you have an appetite for
pate or pastrami, haute cuisine or hot dogs. There are more Szechuan restaurants per block than in Szechuan. There are better
Italian restaurants on Second Avenue than in many Italian
towns. Nowhere else on the entire planet will you find such a
dazzling variety of choices—both gastronomically, socially, and
economically.

I have profiled restaurants that I regard as quintessentially New
York: they are synonymous with the excellence, the glamour, the
pulse of the city. I hasten to add that these are not the only ones
that serve good food, nor is this list meant for New Yorkers trying to figure out which is the best French restaurant in the city.
Since this book isn't "The Backpacker's Guide to Gotham," I

presume a certain level of sophistication, or at the very least, adventure. (Neither is this "The Paranoid's Guide to NYC Restaurants"—so I'm not wasting your time telling you where not to go.) Instead, I'm drawing upon my years of experience writing about chefs and restaurants and travel to compile a primer for my hometown.

In addition to the restaurants featured, I have made suggestions on where to eat on a more casual, and often less expensive level in each of the neighborhoods covered in the book.

Prices

Dining out in New York is expensive. There's not much leeway around the $50–$60 per person (exclusive of wine, tax, and tip) figure that keeps cropping up at the "better" restaurants. But there is some: lunches are generally cheaper than dinners, and many restaurants have pre-theater dinners that are anywhere from one-third to one-half the usual price. Since the object of going to a restaurant is to have a wonderful time, I've never believed in choosing one I couldn't comfortably afford. Or afford to splurge on.

Credit cards

Unless otherwise noted, all restaurants profiled accept a variety of cards. Do not expect coffee shops or many of the small ethnic restaurants to take credit cards.

Le Bernardin   **$$$$**   ★ ★ ★

155 West 51st Street; ☎ *489-1515.*
Cuisine: French. Avg. $50–$100.
Lunch: Noon–2:30 p.m., Mon.–Sat.
Dinner: 5:30–10:30 p.m., Mon.–Sat.

The extraordinary success of this upscale fish house, and the reason it's had a ripple-effect on every chef in the city, was Gilbert Le Coze's knight-errant determination to find only the freshest and the best, his infallible sense of how, to cook each fish, and a palate that demands robust flavors. Sadly, Gilbert died several years ago, but his sister Maguy, who was always at his side, has returned to continue the LeCoze dedication to excellence. Today chef Eric Irpert, is as demanding as Gilbert used to be. Small wonder, he worked at both the fabled Tour D'argent and the trendy Jamin in Paris. No one who goes to Le Bernardin will ever say "Hmmm. This is good. It doesn't taste fishy." Well, nothing tastes fishy at Le Bernardin, but the fish who have given their all for the menu have very good taste.

So does the room. However, if permitted a minor caveat, it is so huge and impersonal (despite luxurious appointments) that it has the look of a hotel lobby. A grand hotel, to be sure, but a distinctly corporate image.

The carpaccio of tuna is pounded petal-thin and is sprinkled with chives and glossed with olive oil. Slivers of black bass (again served raw) are accompanied by basil and coriander leaves. Fashion-model thin "Pizza Bernardin" is decorated with teeny, tiny broiled shrimp.

RESTAURANTS

The main course showstopper was Paupiette of Black Bass and cabbage steamed to perfection and topped with a dab of Foie Gras.

Desserts border on the obsessive. Milk chocolate with a caramel meringue wrapped in a chocolate "purse" in a pool of vanilla sauce.

Bernardin's splendor in the bass can easily run to triple digits. Credit Cards: All major.

Bryant Park Grill $$ ★★

25 W 40th Street; (behind the New York Public Library); ☎ *840-6500.*
Cuisine: American. Avg. $20–$40.
Lunch: 11:30 a.m.–3:30 p.m.
Dinner: 5–10 p.m., 7 days.

New York had been hearing tales of a mythic restaurant that would bring a touch of the Paris "bois" to Bryant Park, for years. No one believed that the former seedy, druggy, pitiful little park would ever be anything but a place to avoid. Yes, Virginia, there is an occasional miracle, but this time it's not on 34th but on 42nd Street. Not only has Bryant Park been saved, greened and generally spiffed up but it has given birth to the Bryant Park Grill, an echo of the lush restaurants that are found in the parks of Europe. The grill is a handsome glass and steel pavilion whose windows open onto the park. Its roof garden in the summer is a more casual outdoor space with a separate seafood menu and a vista of the back of the Library and the park. There is also a terrace sprawling out from the pavilion with tables and traditional French rattan chairs. The scene is so charming you can almost hear Chevalier singing "Thank heaven for Little Parks."

The Grill room is Euro-elegant with lacquered walls and a slate floor. Brass is rubbed to a soft glow and the cut velvet banquettes make lingering over dessert a necessity. Atmosphere is everything at the Bryant Park Grill. One doesn't come for the food experience of the century. Still, if you're careful you can put together a well-meaning spread that will feed the body almost as well as the surroundings feed the soul. Grilled chicken or a clam roast or perhaps a decent Caesar Salad (with real anchovies). For an outdoor snack at the cafe, try one of their very good sandwiches that come with a crowd of french fries. Even the spicy guacamole and a drink are an event when you have them in such a romantic setting. I feel particularly at peace as I dream of an even better New York (once they finally finish the 42nd street renewal) over a succulent slice of brown-butter cake. It doesn't get much better than this. Credit Cards: All major.

Cafe Des Artistes $$$ ★★★

1 West 67th Street; ☎ *877-3500.*
Cuisine: Continental. Avg. $40–$60.
Lunch: Noon–3 p.m., Mon.–Fri.
Dinner: 5 p.m.–midnight, 7 days.

Cafe Des Artistes is located on a quintessential New York street on the ground floor of a building in which the duplex apartments are as legendary as the people who once dined at the restaurant: Valentino, Isadora Duncan, Noel Coward, Al Jolson. George Lang, restaurant consultant to the Planet Earth, took over in the mid-70s, careful to preserve the original Howard Chandler Christy murals of buxom beauties cavorting sans couture. One enters the dining room as

RESTAURANTS

though stepping into a luxurious country estate. Lots of wood, spot-lights bouncing off crystal and silver, carts overflowing with hors d'oeuvres and desserts.

Lang, Des Artistes' resident genius has created a menu that is in the most civilized terms, eclectic (this is not a classic French restaurant), dedicated to the finest ingredients. It's confident enough to avoid all that is terminally trendy. Among my favorite starters are salmon four ways (slices of dill-marinated gravlax, smoked salmon, perfectly poached salmon, and a hefty dollop of salmon tartar); "Snow White" anchovies with buffalo mozzarella and tomato; and home-cured brac-cioli with melon, parmigiana shavings and rosemary olive oil. The oys-ters are sweet and fresh, the charcuterie among the best I've had. Main courses run the gamut from pot au feu with marrow bones, braised beef with gingersnap gravy, roast baby chicken stuffed with fettucini, roast duck with brandied plums, and a wondrous steak tartar with pine nuts that is lightly toasted and curried.

Wines, salads, desserts, (The Ilona Tarte is fabled) and cheeses are selected with the same care as the bread and butter. Des Artistes def-initely celebrates the Yin and Lang of dining. Credit Cards: All major.

Carnegie Delicatessen $$ ★
854 Seventh Avenue (55th Street); ☎ *757-2245.*
Cuisine: Jewish. Avg. $20–$40.
Hours: 6 a.m.–4 a.m., 7 days.
You want the quintessential New York meal? Park your tush at the Carnegie. Eastern European Jewish "deli" is the city's major contri-bution to the culinary world and shouldn't be missed. True is true: Los Angeles corned beef or London salt beef simply don't cut the mustard. According to the Carnegie, the secret is the New York water in which briskets of beef are steamed after being injected with a solu-tion of salt, garlic, thyme, allspice, coriander and mustard seeds. Whatever.

Part of the Carnegie's charm is its total lack of charm. The noise and bright lights are almost as disconcerting as the wait staff, each of whom is convinced you don't know what the hell you're ordering and if you would only leave it to them. Never mind. It's not for nothing that Woody Allen shot *Broadway Danny Rose* here. The corned beef and pastrami are the best in town. A sandwich ($10.25) is piled high with three-quarters of a pound of meat. (If you're looking for an eco-nomical nosh to have in your suite at the Pierre, buy one sandwich and two extra slices of bread. You'll still be full.)

However, I advise on-site mastication because the Carnegie is as much a "sight" as a restaurant. Also, don't lull yourself into thinking that brunch is the answer, either. Just go and bite the brisket! Credit Cards: All major.

Daniel $$$$ ★★★
2 East 76th Street; ☎ *288-0033.*
Cuisine: French. Avg. $50–$100.
Lunch: Noon–2:15 p.m., Mon.–Sat.
Dinner: 6–11 p.m., Mon.–Sat.
Daniel Boulud was the chef of chefs at the very formidable Le Cirque until he decided to put the D for delicious into his own place, just a

croissant's throw from his old kitchen. There were rumblings all over the city; could Daniel, after mixing and stirring under the watchful, all-seeing eye of Sirio Maccioni (Le Cirque's owner) stir up his own storm. Well, Daniel has become the patron saint of the "nice guys finish last" set. Daniel not only finished first, he finished off any doubts about his heading a world-class restaurant.

The room itself is bland and undistinguished, a veritable sea of beige, but the menu and the celeb diners, more than make up for the dull decor. At any given time you can see Barbara Walters interviewing an artichoke or Girard Depardieu schmoozing in the back with Daniel. All his regulars from the "Big C" have followed the trail of champions that led to his new, "hot" French restaurant.

But happily, not too new, Daniel is a master of the classic not a plaything of nouvelle. And that's all to the good because the 90s have brought a desire for the familiar, not the unexpected.

Wonderful comforting things appear from the kitchen. A rich, mahogany pot-au-feu, poached foie gras in a heady duck broth with morels, and one of our personal favorites, a combo of Rillettes of duck, foie gras, rabbit, pork, squab and black truffles. This is definitely not food Mom used to dish up, except perhaps Daniel's mom. The other showstopper is his cod poached in a fennel perfumed broth with tomatoes, black olives and pesto. To end, just your run-of-the-mill strawberry mascarpone cake paired with an herbal tea ice cream, or, passion fruit sorbet with grapefruit custard in puff pastry.

Bring a lot of money, dinner with wine could reach three figures.
Credit Cards: All major.

Dawat **$$** ★★
210 East 58th Street (Second and Third Aves); ☎ *355-7555.*
Cuisine: Indian. Avg. $20–$40.
Lunch: 11:30 a.m.–3 p.m., 7 days.
Dinner: 5:30–11 p.m., 7 days.

The jewel in the crown of this peaceful pastel retreat is the omnipresence of Indian food guru, Madhur Jaffrey. Except for a very occasional whiff of curry and a few masks on the wall (no tented ceiling here), it's hard to tell you're in one of the city's best ethnic restaurants. Certainly, there is nothing to prepare you for the fact that you can dine like a maharajah at lunch for about $12.95—truly an astonishing bargain.

If you know your way around an Indian menu, you're likely to come upon a number of surprises in Jaffrey's signature dishes. For starters, try the shrimp flavored with garlic, mustard seeds and curry leaves; crisp spinach leaf and potato skin fritters; and the superb "snack cart" items including potato crisps and noodles in sweet, sour and hot chutneys. Favorite main dishes are fish (whatever is available that day) covered in fresh coriander chutney and steamed in a banana leaf; chicken cubes marinated in yogurt and ginger before roasting in a tandoor (clay oven); shrimp in coconut milk; and lamb in a spicy spinach puree.

Vegetarians will be in seventh heaven here, as well as aficionados of specialty breads (there are varieties of "nan" stuffed with ground lamb, or nuts and dried fruit, or onion and fresh coriander). Beer is the best beverage choice for everything. Desserts are best left to those poor souls who get excited over caramelized grated carrots, or sweet spongy cottage cheese dumplings. Credit Cards: All major.

Four Seasons, The   **$$$$**   ★★★

99 East 52nd Street (between Park and Lexington); ☎ *754-9494.*
Cuisine: American. Avg. $50–$100.
Lunch: Noon–2:30 p.m., Mon.–Fri.
Dinner: 5–9 p.m., Mon.–Fri.; 5–11 p.m., Sat.

If you put a gun to my head and demanded to know where to go if you had time for only one meal in New York, my answer would have to be The Four Seasons.

Like the Carnegie Deli, the Empire State Building, and Broadway, The Four Seasons could not exist anywhere else on earth. This is the quintessential New York restaurant. Period. And its celebrity and deserved success are not diminished one iota by the revelation (honk if you're surprised) that it does not always have the best food in town.

Once you accept that this is going to be an expensive evening (entrees alone are between $35 and $40 apiece) and stop comparing the kitchen to the culinary cathedrals of France, The Four Seasons will perform for you on more levels than "Les Mis."

As you walk up the staircase to the Grill Room, you can't help but marvel at the heroic space with burled French walnut walls, Mies van der Rohe chairs, Philip Johnson tufted banquettes, the tallest 20-foot ceilings in town, and landmark-worthy floor to ceiling windows curtained with swags of aluminum chain that are in constant motion.

The Grill Room, in more ways than one, means business. Even at night, you can smell lunch deals in the air like smoke hovering after the cease fire. The captain explained: "When we serve duck in the Pool Room, it is well cooked. In the Grill Room, it is rare." The Grill Room menu has choices like Carpaccio with Grana (cheese) and Arugula, and Baked Oysters with Golden Caviar. Everything is perfectly plated, and the wines by the glass are well-chosen.

However, if you're in a romantic mood and don't mind risking well-done duck, make a reservation in the Pool Room. You'll be ushered through a cavernous travertine-lined foyer which is a gallery for Picasso's 1919 stage curtain for the ballet, Le Tricorne.

The Pool Room's centerpiece is a white marble reflecting pool with full grown trees at each corner. Quite simply, the room is majestic. And always jammed. (Only card-carrying New Yorkers select the Grill Room over the Pool Room.) It's here that every table is a party, and no matter what you order, it's festive. The kitchen is known for its super savvy roasting and grilling. Menus change seasonally (i.e, the four seasons) and the wine list is not only a course in classic wine collecting, but it has some of the best (read: least expensive) prices you'll find in any restaurant.

A word about desserts. Actually two: Chocolate velvet. Credit Cards: All major.

Gotham Bar & Grill, The $$$ ★★★
12 East 12th Street; ☎ 620-4020.
Cuisine: American. Avg. $40–$60.
Lunch: Noon–2:30 p.m., Mon.–Fri;
Dinner: 5:30–11 p.m., Mon.–Sat.

The Gotham is guaranteed to raise your consciousness the moment you walk through the door. It is an award-winning riot of postmodern design. Platforms, risers, levels and angles litter the former warehouse space as though dropped by some divine architect. Parachute cloth chandeliers float like clouds above white linen covered tables. In the midst of all this urbanity, there's a mini-Statue of Liberty I could swear was lit by the static electricity of the Gotham's highly eclectic clientele.

Chef Alfred Portale once designed jewelry and he's carried his sculptural focus into the kitchen. Unlike today's fashionably flat painted platters, his food arrives at the table in 3D. There is not only drama, but height, to the salads. A creator rather than a follower of trends, he bursts with opinion: "food should be clever but delicious." The Gotham menu does. It preserves the best of French and Italian and translates it into pure Portale. The shellfish terrine is gorgeously Byzantine, a mosaic of prawns, scallops and lobster. Tomato salad has five or six different types of tomato, the veal carpaccio with curls of parmesan is brilliant, and the squab salad arrives with a peppery couscous and a curried vinaigrette that could drive you crazy. My hands-down favorite entree was sauteed black bass in red wine vinegar and port with shiitake mushrooms and leeks. But it was hard to choose, considering the dry-aged New York steak with crushed white peppercorns, marrow mustard custard (not our rhyme) and deep fried shallots.

Desserts are extravagant, wines are mainly American, and the tab will run about $60 per person. Credit Cards: All major.

Lutece $$$ ★★★
249 East 50th Street; ☎ 752-2225.
Cuisine: French. Avg. $50–$100.
Lunch: Noon–2 p.m., Mon.–Sat.

Dinner: 5:30–10 p.m., Mon.–Sat.

There is a widespread perception that Lutece is not merely one of the best French restaurants in New York, but one of the best in the entire country. Any criticism, in the past, centered around its not having kept up with the latest trends or its not having created them—rather like faulting a Rolls-Royce because it doesn't fly. Lutece used to be the capital of culinary deja vu, and Andre Soltner was the keeper of the flame. Recently, Soltner succumbed to the inevitable passage of time and decided to sell his beloved Lutece to a high profile chain. Enter Chef Eberhard Muller who has since answered the time-honored question, "What becomes a legend most?" He has walked a very narrow line, while celebrating the past and moving with dazzling conviction into the future. There is little doubt that Lutece will continue to be the yardstick with which fine French restaurants are measured.

Thankfully, there is nothing about a visit to Lutece that makes one feel intimidated. Not the decor which was recently updated and softened to rid it of its Paris in the 1950's look, the seamless service or the prices (comparatively speaking) will ruffle your Type-A personality: there is a prix fixe lunch and dinner tallies in at $60, or more if you select dishes with a surcharge.

Even though filling the toque of Andre Soltner is no easy trick, Chef Muller and Soltner both share a common border between Germany and Alsace. Who better would understand the food nuances of the region. Aside from that he also brings his exquisite interpretation of the classic fish repertoire that he developed while a chef at Le Bernardin.

The printed menu at Lutece is extensive, but I always hold out for the daily specials. Not that you can't be gastronomically paranoid and make it through on Lutece's whole roasted lobster in cognac butter or the duck breast with cherries and arugula or the sauteed skate in a tangy caper vinaigrette or, in fact anything that comes out of the Eberhard's kitchen.

Desserts are taken very seriously at Lutece. Apricots wrapped in phyllo, paired with a tropical sorbet or a fudgy chocolate torte surrounded by passionfruit. And with coffee, a big beautiful tray of cookies that have more than one bite in them.

After the last three-cheese pizza has been eaten, there will still be a Lutece. I hope! Credit Cards: All major.

March $$$$ ★ ★ ★
405 East 58th Street; ☎ (212) 838-9393.
Cuisine: Asian/American. Avg. $50–$100.
Dinner: 6–10 p.m., 7 days.

March not only feeds your body, but your soul as well. From the moment you step into this most romantic of townhouse settings, you're wrapped in March's security blanket of charm, elegance and a welcome just short of MacArthur returning to the Philippines.

Chef Wayne Nish and his partner Joseph Scalici are committed to a dining experience that includes one of the most creative menus around, a wine list (Scalici's personal territory) that has been constructed to showcase boutique vineyards and unexplored labels of 24-

carat quality. You're surrounded by Mozart sonatas, candlelight lamps, antiques, Limoge and a crackling fireplace. The chairs may be Biedermeier but the menu is pure Nish. He cooks with a palette of ingredients from all over the world, shopping in ethnic markets for new, offbeat flavors to heighten the drama of his invention. One of his favorite tricks is curing meat in soy sauce, lime juice and rice vinegar. His feeling for the subtle flavors of the East is no accident, Nish's real name is Nishimoto.

To start, there is always an hors d'oeuvre, a gift from the chef. Sometimes a perfect dumpling filled with veggies, sometimes a tiny souffle of spinach or squash, or a beggar's puree with lobster and black truffle, always surprising.

Next a glistening sashimi of yellowtail dressed with olive oil and soy sauce. Snow pea soup was bright enough for St. Patrick's day and velvety enough for Mel Torme. The house cured salmon wore it's créme freche and caviar as gloriously as it tasted. Entrees have unbeatable acts to follow, but somehow they do. Duck breast is pale, pink and melts on the tongue. Its paired with a crisp confettied leg and fruit chutneys. Nish's spin on meat and potatoes turns out to be ruby-red sliced aged sirloin with crispy caramelized shallots and garlic mashed potatoes so rich with butter and cream it has a Swiss bank account. If an end to all this has to come, let it come with March's warm walnut tart nestling next to homemade hazelnut ice cream or the bracing grapefruit sorbet in gin and coriander syrup.

When the season cooperates you can have your coffee and cognac in the tiny garden that the restaurant overlooks, but then, the fireplace won't be working. Maybe you can't have a perfect world, but March comes close! Credit Cards: All major.

Il Mulino   **$$$**   ★ ★ ★
86 W 83rd Street, between Sullivan and Thompson Streets; ☎ *(212) 673-3783.*
Cuisine: Italian. Avg. $40–$60.
Lunch: Noon–2:30 p.m., 7 days.
Dinner: 6–11:30 p.m., 7 days.
No sooner are you seated than the meal begins. A plate of homemade salami. A dish of breaded, perfectly sauteed sliced zucchini. A dynamite *bruschetta* (chopped tomato in a garlicky vinaigrette on toasted bread). And then a piece of Parmesan cheese scooped from a wheel larger than some Italian hill towns. All this to accompany generous drinks and a wine service that includes decanting all reds into enormous pitchers so they can really take a deep breath.

In the world according to Fernando Masci, the owner, there is always a wait while the kitchen prepares your dinner. "If you cut scallopine in the morning, it loses flavor." Everything at Il Mulino is *al dente*, including the pasta specials that Fernando himself prepares in the dining room.

Let Fernando talk you in to a pasta special to share as an appetizer. Whether fusilli with black truffles, *creme fraiche*, and champagne, or *pappardelle* with a peppery red sauce, you cannot go wrong. Veal and seafood entrees, assertively fresh, are standouts: a veal chop, thick as a dictionary but a lot more juicy, is boutonniered with a sprig of fresh sage; an elegantly thin, breaded chop served Abruzzi-style is topped with freshly chopped tomato and arugula; succulent scampi (flown in from Italy).

Desserts are stunners. An incredibly posh orange that has been luxuriating in a bath of cognac and Grand Marnier is brought to the table to be sectioned and dressed with slivers of marinated rind. You won't soon forget the fudgy splendor the chocolate cake. End it all with a glass of homemade grappa. Superlatives don't come cheap. Expect to leave many dollars behind. But you'll do it with a smile. Credit Cards: All major.

Osteria Del Circo $$$ ★★

120 W 55th Street; ☎ *265-3636.*
Cuisine: Italian. Avg. $40–$60.
Lunch: 11:20 a.m.–2:30 p.m., Mon.–Fri.
Dinner: 5–11 p.m., Mon.–Sat.
Ringling brothers would be impressed by another set of brothers, the Maccionis who have created a circus to be proud of. This one even serves food (Barnum & Bailey, eat your heart out!) They come to the food scene naturally since their father Sirio the famous ringmaster of Le Cirque has obviously spread the restaurateur genes around to the rest of the family. Even his wife Egi, who rolls a mean ravioli, has gotten into the new act.

The result of all this family solidarity is a wonderful, warm, relaxed restaurant that is always in a playful mood. There are bright colored banners suspended from the ceiling, sculpted monkeys climbing up and down poles, and metal circus figures that twirl. So does everyone's heads as they try to take in the decor. It's useless really, you enter sensory overload as soon as you step across the threshold.

The menu is loaded with Egi's favorite family repertoire which must have given the Maccioni boys the strength to open this vibrating celebration of La Dolce Vita. Egi's Zuppa ala Frantoiana is a purée of 30 different veggies (would anyone dare to count). The soup is rich enough for a meal but everything else on the menu looks so wonderful, the only thing to do is eat on. Another Egi-ism is the sage ravioli browned in butter. The gnocchi with walnuts and tomatoes make you forget you ever heard of cholesterol. The small pizzas are as thin as Twiggy and covered with a spicy prosciutto and tomato blanket. The desserts are center ring perfect. Bomboloncini (Italian jelly doughnuts) filled with chocolate, raspberry and vanilla custard come with a tiny clown sitting on the plate. A cup of cappuccino is in reality a chocolate cup filled with creme. Perhaps reality is the wrong word to use at "Circo." What a shame Fellini isn't around to capture it all on film. On the other hand perhaps he already has. Credit Cards: All major.

Oyster Bar $$$ ★★

Grand Central Station, Lower Level (42nd Street and Vanderbilt Avenue);
☎ *490-6650.*
Cuisine: Fishhouse. Avg. $40–$60.
Hours: 11:30 a.m.–9:30 p.m., 7 days.
Since the Oyster Bar opened in 1913, nearly every President of the U.S. has eaten here: Jack Kennedy even had a kind word for the New England Clam Chowder. (Harry Truman played it safe with a piece of

plain broiled fish.) Diamond Jim Brady always joked with the waiters, promising a $50 tip if he failed to identify his favorite Wellfleet oysters—even while blindfolded. Although Jim never lost, he tipped the $50 anyway. That's how good the food is here.

The menu is printed daily after the buyer comes back from the Fulton Fish Market. The guys here are very proud of the fact they were the first to serve Mako shark after the release of *Jaws:* it made them feel they were fighting back! Reading the menu is an encyclopedic experience that no fish lover should miss. Among the most famous dishes are the oyster pan roast and oyster stew, both creamy and soup-plated with the former a mite creamier and even spicier. You can sit at the enormous counter (perfect for travelers on their own) and watch them being made. She-crab soup, and bouillabaisse are exemplary starters as well. The quality of the fish being as impeccable as it is, I'd suggest the luxury of the Truman approach: it's likely to be a while before a piece of plain fish will taste as good. Besides, then you won't feel as guilty trying one of the desserts: banana cream pie, coconut layer cake, caramel nut sundae—to name a few million calories. Credit Cards: All major.

Palm $$$ ★★
837 *Second Avenue;* ☎ *687-2953.*
Cuisine: Steakhouse. Avg. $40–$60.
Hours: Noon–11:30 p.m., Mon.–Sat.
Here's the deal: the Palm doesn't take reservations and frankly, I wouldn't believe them if they did. Listen, these guys don't even have a menu. You have to ask the "don't-ask-me" waiter and hope to pry from his sealed lips some hint of what's cooking. Only if he knows that you already know will he fess up about the veal, fish, and Italian specialties. But don't let this minor victory go to your head. Just try to get him to tell you what it costs! And yet, people line up for tables, even though the Palm has clones all over the country. Why? The reason is that they serve BIG food.

Everything about the Palm is larger than life, including the check. However, in all fairness, they are merely fulfilling one of the fantasies that card-carrying carnivores have about New York steakhouses. Some want them plush and quiet, with deference paid to the thickness of the steak and the size of the martini. But those who gravitate toward the mayhem and madness of the Palm are looking for the Great American Clubhouse Experience. As a meeting place for newspaper people who use hushed tones only at funerals, the room is noisy, smokey, and filled with sawdust on the floor. Still run by the grandchildren of the original owners, the operation spilled over across the street to a mirror image of itself at Palm Too.

For your first visit, don't order anything but steak or lobster. On a good night, they are cooked to perfection. The lobsters look like mutants and weigh in at four pounds. They run about $55. The size of the steaks would give a terradactyl pause. Since you have to cross the Palm with so much silver, think seriously about sharing. No matter what the waiter says, there's plenty of food if you split a sirloin and go halvies on the onion rings and potatoes, both of which can be super-crunchy and greaseless on that same good night. Most people opt for the cottage fries, but the hash browns are better. The tab somehow always comes out close to $60 per person, even if you share. Credit Cards: All major.

Patria   **$$$**   ★ ★ ★

250 Park Avenue South (20th Street); ☎ *777-6211.*
Cuisine: South American. Avg. $40–$60.
Lunch: Noon–2:45 p.m., Mon.–Fri.
Dinner: 6–10:45 p.m., 7 days.

Douglas Rodriguez may not be a "Latin from Manhattan" but he's definitely *the* Latin in the Manhattan restaurant scene today. Patria is one of the most scintillating new places for foodies who crave Neuvo Latino cuisine (and who among us can't relate to that). If Nuevo Latino hasn't come to your neighborhood yet, it's New World, Cuban-based cuisine which Rodriguez takes and molds into his own nontraditional combinations of flavors and textures. He uses products from Ecuador, Peru, Cuba and Miami, and combines them for his own very special signature dishes. The food at Patria is not shockingly hot, it's just wonderfully spicy and totally original.

If Carmen Miranda herself were in the kitchen plating the food it couldn't be more vivid or colorful. Even the plates are huge colored glass circles topped with as many tints and textures as Rodriguez can come up with. The usual reaction to the presentation is open-mouthed wonderment. The space itself is just as heroic, sprawling over two floors. It's usually packed and vibrating with sound. Every-time a plate is set in front of a diner, there is an ohhh or aaaa, or just a gasp. No one can react to these technicolor presentations silently.

I tried out the Oysters Suarez which were layered with spinach, plantain, manchigo cheese and a hot horseradish salsa. They were fiery and sensational. The Cuban style Tamal was filled with lobster and saffron crab escabeche. Serano ham was served (are you ready) with foie gras lily marmalade. The combinations are almost interplanetary! The dish that really stopped the music here was the sugar cane tuna—a loin slice of tuna the size of Texas impaled on a stalk of sugarcane, served atop a bed of chayote. I couldn't help noticing the reactions of people who didn't know their mashed potatoes were going to be blue (this is an antique variety of spud). Dropped jaws, once again.

Dessert was a match for the rest of the fireworks on the menu. My finale was a mammoth chocolate cream-filled cigar with spiced bread ice cream. Patricia also has a terrific collection of imported exotic sodas that might be just the answer to whether red or white is appropriate with blue potatoes. Credit Cards: All major.

Petrossian   **$$$$**   ★ ★

182 West 58th Street; ☎ *245-2214.*
Cuisine: French. Avg. $50–$100.
Lunch: 1:30–3 p.m., 7 days.
Dinner: 5:30–11:30 p.m., 7 days.

The room is filled with palms, marble, pink lights, fluted champagne glasses, burled wood, flowers, etched Erte mirrors, and even the chandelier from Mme. Lanvin's bedroom. It is pure fantasy, a colorized version of an Art Deco set from an Astaire-Rogers film. Waiters have not merely been coached, they have been choreographed to ensure that everyone gets million dollar service. Well, let's face it: if you're going to have a $110 appetizer, you might as well do it right.

The Royal Gourmet is a neat little presentation of 30 grams (just over an ounce) each of beluga, sevruga, and ossetra caviar. Your $110 also includes toast and temporary custody of a tiny gold paddle (the Petrossians say that silver imparts a taste to the caviar). Period. Maybe a wedge of lemon. But forget about onions, eggs or sour cream. These guys play for keeps: they claim to have first dibs on the best of the Caspian crop and aren't about to let you junk it up.

Since Petrossian is a restaurant that also retails its own products (caviar, foie gras, and smoked salmon), I continued sampling the house brands. Work! Work! Work! I had a salad with shavings of the best foie gras I've ever tasted piled high atop beans and lettuce. Slices of smoked salmon were sheer velvet perfection: part of the secret of its success was the "secret" wood used for smoking.

Chef P.G. Gustafsson has brought the rest of the menu into the nineties—very light sauces with delicate flavors. The emphasis here is on combinations and contrasts: crisp potato galettes layered with smoked salmon; warm foie gras on a chestnut pancake. Roast baby pheasant arrives with a cranberry sauce as light in taste as color. The lobster and sweetbread napoleon has a whisper-soft balsamic vinegar sauce.

For light eaters, there are prix fixe lunches and pre- and after-theater menus. Otherwise, the sky's the limit. However, caviar prices are significantly lower here than in some other restaurants, and the quality is impeccable. Credit Cards: All major.

"Oh, for pity's sake! Put it on your American Express card and blow your top when you get the bill."

Drawing by F.B. Modell; ©1968, The New Yorker Magazine, Inc.

Rainbow Room, The   **$$$**   ★★★

30 Rockefeller Plaza; ☎ *632-5100.*
Cuisine: American. Avg. $40–$60.
Dinner: 5–11 p.m., Tues.–Sat.

You've heard about "restaurant as theatre." Well, The Rainbow Room goes them one better: it is the restaurant as a movie. From the moment you enter the fabulous marble lobby at 30 Rock, you know this is going to be an extraordinary experience. Step onto the special express elevator to the 65th floor (the ultimate in gastronomic foreplay). Step off into the dramatic glass and rosewood columned chamber where you're guided along by young cutie-pies in page-boy suits (don't let Betty Friedan near this place or she'll have a fit!). A few steps up to the two-story multi-tiered room with a 32-foot revolving dance floor and you are ready to check your skepticism with the maitre d'. The Latin band is playing "Guantanamera" and you surrender unconditionally. There is no way not to love this room, unless you are related by blood to the grinch who stole Christmas.

The party line is that The Rainbow Room is a restoration of the 1934 original. Waiters in two-tone cutaways. Silver lame tablecloths. Busboys with gleaming silver bowls spoon fresh ice into water goblets. Without your even noticing it, one band has been replaced by another. Suddenly, the sounds of Gershwin and Porter. The flash of Baked Alaska's flaming in the aisles. A cigarette girl with plenty of leg and a little pink hat (Is her name Trixie?) hips her way around the room. The twinkle of city lights outside the windows competes with the laughter at ringside tables.

But man does not live by glitz alone. Rumor has it that you have come here to eat. The menu, by design, is as retro as the decor. Alligator pear. Oysters Rockefeller. (Perhaps that's the cigarette girl's name.)

Begin with champagne, otherwise you'll never forgive yourself. Head directly into the "Shellfish Extravaganza": an overwhelming display of oysters, clams, mussels, lobster, shrimp and crab with proper sauces for each. Given my druthers, I'd stay with champagne and open the time capsule for lobster thermidor, the MGM of fish courses. Whoever heard of cholesterol in the forties.

The frozen praline souffle with hot chocolate sauce will produce more guilt than Kafka, that is, if you're strong enough to pass up Baked Alaska lit with the eternal flame of culinary nostalgia. Even if you have to take back all your empty beer cans and save up the deposit money, be sure to fly somewhere over The Rainbow Room. It is a joy. Credit Cards: All major.

Serendipity 3   **$$**   ★
225 East 60th Street; ☎ *838-3531.*
Cuisine: American. Avg. $20–$40.
Hours: 11:30 a.m.–midnight, Mon.–Fri; 11:30 a.m.–2 a.m., Sat.–Sun.
If the Mad Hatter held his tea party in New York, this is where it would be. Half wonderland and half boutique, everything blends into a topsy-turvy environment that is totally unique. The word "serendipity" means the art of finding the pleasantly unexpected by chance. That's exactly what happens when you step through the door and find yourself surrounded with boutique items such as Hebrew eye-charts, and stuffed animals cute enough to make Noah think twice. But you're afraid to linger because who knows what treats await inside. After all, this is the place Cher had her *Moonstruck* party, Barbra Streisand sang "Happy Birthday" to her mother, and Andy Warhol once sketched at a back table.

The gorgeous back room is white brick, with a white tin ceiling, white oak tables and chairs. The most expensive of the Tiffany lamps, now valued at $750,000, still illuminates the banana splits with all the high drama of Garbo's key light. When you're not looking up at the lamps, or hunting for celebs around the room, there's much food for thought. The environmental kitsch is translated into birthday party cuisine. The signature "frozen hot chocolate" is presented in a swimming pool size bowl. The foot-long hot dogs (they originated here) take up half the table. Burgers are festooned with red caviar and sour cream, and cappuccino is brought into the fourth dimension with a huge bonnet of whipped cream topped with a mound of shaved chocolate. Like a hyperactive kid, the menu careens from comfort food (Shepherd's pie, cheese omelets, French toast) to Zen Hash (brown rice and veggies), a ricotta cheese sandwich with lemon curd dressing, and a frozen apricot smush. You gotta love these guys! Credit Cards: All major.

Sign of the Dove, The $$$ ★★
1110 Third Avenue; ☎ 861-8080.
Cuisine: American. Avg. $40–$60.
Lunch: Noon–2:30 p.m., Mon.–Sat.
Dinner: 5:30–11 p.m., 7 days.
The Sign of the Dove, with its graceful arches, brick walls, skylit ceilings has always been a beautiful setting. Now, thanks to chef Andrew D'Amico, it is a wonderful restaurant.

D'Amico is not a self-indulgent chef, he is too good an editor. Instead of tuna, he uses skate in a salad nicoise. Sauteed sweetbreads are paired with Chinese sausage and yu-choy (a bok choy green reminiscent of both broccoli and mustard greens). Pan-seared tuna (read: cooked on the outside, raw inside) has a sweet, fresh taste off which to play the accompanying taramasalata. However, I lost my heart to a Maine lobster and oyster pan roast that was in the same league as Bernardin's shellfish fricassee. D'Amico produced a creamy sauce with just enough chili to warm the roof of your mouth rather than snap at your tongue. Main courses featured a shellfish stew with saffron; grilled swordfish with caramelized scallions and lobster butter; veal medallions with braised endive, chanterelles, and wild rice pancake. Sea scallops luxuriated in a thyme and olive oil broth surrounding a tian of eggplant, tomato and zucchini. Again, an assertively spiced sauce.

The dinner menu includes an excellent cheese service with which to finish off a wine selected from the truly first-rate list. Desserts are neither slivers of nonsweets nor plated as if presenting jewelry to be worn. The real food concept continues: tarte tatin with cinnamon ice cream, orange creme brulee tart, and a superb sleeve of dark chocolate filled with white chocolate in a raspberry coulis.

Those addicted to love in the afternoon will adore a prix fixe lunch that includes dessert and coffee. At the very least, stop in while you're "doing" Third Avenue for a drink and one of the terrific snacks served at the bar. Credit Cards: All major.

"21" $$$ ★★
21 West 53rd Street; ☎ 582-7200.
Cuisine: American. Avg. $40–$60.
Lunch: Noon–2 p.m., Mon.–Fri.
Dinner: 5:30–10 p.m., Mon.–Fri.; 5:30–11:15 p.m., Sat.–Sun.
In the wine cellar at "21", in the private reserve section, there's a bottle of Dom Perignon '59 with Joan Crawford's name on it. Aristotle Onassis left behind a bottle of Pommard '62. The ceiling in the

downstairs dining room is littered with toys: baseball bats, ballet slippers, NFL helmets, plane models, trucks, and boats. (You know you've "arrived" in New York when The "21" Club accepts your contribution to the ceiling.) A brass plaque identifies "Bogie's Corner" where Bogart and Bacall fell in love. Let's face it, you need a machete to cut through the nostalgia in this joint: it's that thick. It's that wonderful!

Once inside, it's as though you've wandered onto the set of "Lifestyles of the Rich and Hungry." Young men wearing suits that cost more than your mortgage payments discuss the stocks they've been buying; elegantly turned out middle-aged women network, trading names of plastic surgeons and estrogen creams with equal facility; and then you spot a movie star. Is this a place or what?

The fact that they happen to serve food at this pit stop for millionaires is real nice. Not the best food in the world, but think of it as an admission charge and it won't hurt a bit. I love "21." It's a major New York institution, and even though its values are as suspect as those of Willy Loman, "attention must be paid." The ingredients here are as impeccable as a blue-chip stock. The cuisine is "men's food" or more accurately, "old kid's food." Actually, "rich, old kid's food" when you think of the "21" burger costing $24.50.

For the record, the "in" dishes are the infamous burger (save your money), a nicely-spiced chicken curry that isn't on the menu and chicken hash (talk about retro food!). For the ladies who lunch, cobb salad. If you can, do "21" for lunch rather than dinner. The "floor show" is infinitely better. Credit Cards: All major.

Union Square Cafe $$$ ★★★

21 East 16th Street; ☎ *243-4020.*
Cuisine: American. Avg. $40–$60.
Lunch: Noon–2:15 p.m., Mon.–Sat.
Dinner: 6–11:15 p.m., Mon.–Sat.

This is the Yuppie "21." A big, open, friendly, comfortable place for the soon-to-be rich and famous. A lunchtime hangout for downtown publishers and the uptown art crowd, this is not a place for the starry-eyed. You'd need a supercomputer to tally up the combined SAT scores of these dudes. Owner Danny Meyer is a bright as a penny reflection of his clientele. He wants the best and isn't prepared to settle for anything less.

The room buzzes with groups of people discussing foreign rights or best seller lists. Lots of suits. Very intense talk about jobs and futures and whether to order sheeps-milk cheese ravioli with black peppercorns and sage butter or the risotto with duck livers, pancetta, and sweet red onions. Arugula gnocchi is served with a spicy garlic-and-Pecorino cream sauce. Food here is nothing if not hearty. But that's not all it is. Chef Michael Romano's menu is eclectic enough to encompass a bit of French and some all-American despite its Italian nill-town influence. Among the main courses, grilled marinated fillet mignon of tuna (a chunk of tuna seared on the outside but sushilike inside) is a standout.

Side orders are especially appealing: hot garlic potato chips; mashed turnips with crispy shallots; sauteed spinach with lemon. Top desserts include a ginger *creme brulee*, and a hot apple tart with *creme fraiche*. Discuss your wine selection with Danny—he roams from table to table. As usual, we're in the $50 per head ballpark, plus wine and tip. However, Union Square Cafe is one of a handful of restaurants whose chef creates a cross-cultural cuisine that is more than original—it's delicious. Credit Cards: All major.

AGENDA PREDICTION

The fabled Le Cirque restaurant which has always been included in my "quintessential" N.Y. restaurant choices has closed temporarily and will re-open as part of the Villard Houses at the New York Palace Hotel (see Hotels). The opening will take place after we've gone to press. My "culinary connection" informs me that Le Cirque will add 2000 to its world famous name and return in an even more dazzling form.

ROOMS WITH A VIEW
or
When is a restaurant not a restaurant?

I have a number of favorite restaurants I always suggest to visitors that go far beyond the question of food. Not that some of those listed wouldn't rate inclusion on any "best restaurant" list, but their locations are extraordinary enough to warrant being highlighted in a special category.

Boathouse Cafe $$ ★★
(Open March–October) Central Park Lake, East Park Drive at 73rd Street;
☎ *517-2233.*
Cuisine: American. Avg. $20–$40.
Lunch: 11 a.m.–4 p.m., 7 days.
Dinner: 5:30–10:30 p.m., 7 days.
Picture this; you're right smack in the middle of Manhattan, you can hear car horns in the distance and overhead a traffic reporting helicopter is circling ominously. But you're sitting at the edge of a mirror-top lake, gazing out at rowers crossing the water lazily in the lavender twilight. Ok,—where are you?

The Loeb Boathouse in Central Park was built overlooking the lake in 1954, and ever since it's been one of the best ways to spend a summer afternoon in this chaotic city. Aside from renting out boats (and even a gondola, complete with gondolier, yet), there is a cafe that's a magical spot to have a light meal and drink in the view. They serve a very basic northern Italian menu which probably will not linger in your memory, but the setting certainly will. The weather doesn't have to be perfect either, because they have indoor seating with the same view. My favorite time at the Boathouse is just as the sun sets and the lights come on in the skyscrapers that ring the park. And then, there's always the first star to wish upon. That wish is likely to be a return trip to this idyllic spot. Credit Cards: All major.

Crab House, The $$ ★
Chelsea Pier Complex, 23rd Street & Hudson River; ☎ *835-2722.*
Cuisine: Fishhouse. Avg. $20–$40.
Dinner: 4–10 p.m., 7 days.

True, the Crab House is part of a chain of seafood houses that serves nondescript food, true you can only dare to order the simplest of grills or sandwiches but holy mackerel, the view is awesome! Shaped like a lighthouse, its back porch hangs over the river and if you're lucky enough to bribe someone for an outside table, you'll have tears in your eyes at sunset. They don't take reservations, but you should have none about going anyway! Credit Cards: All major.

Hudson River Club, The $$$ ★ ★

250 Vesey Street (No. 4 World Financial Center); ☎ *(212) 786-1500.*
Cuisine: American. Avg. $40–$60.
Lunch: 11:20 a.m.–2:30 p.m., Mon.–Fri.
Dinner: 5–9:30 p.m., 7 days.

Located in the newest and most attractive part of the city, and in the same building with the illuminated palm trees and marble floors of the glorious Winter Garden, the Hudson River Club is not merely a culinary convenience: the food here is first-rate, despite its "high-concept" of focusing on Hudson River Valley cuisine. The kitchen here is not only filled with enthusiasm and talent, the often-exquisite plating stands up to the competition. All this as one gazes at an unobstructed view of New York harbor, the Statue of Liberty, and Ellis Island. The room itself is wood-paneled with leaded glass doors tinted gold to match Wall Streeters' favorite color. For starters, there are roasted oysters on a bed of peppercorns that have a briny, slightly spicy taste; or a cone-shaped blue-crab-and-potato-fritter coated in crusty almonds and set afloat in a rich tomato sauce. A brilliant lobster consomme is all the more intense for not having any cream. Main courses include filet of salmon, with an assertive parsley-dill sauce and "woven" potatoes and an extraordinary shank of veal with citrus and sage. Desserts are equally spectacular: for sheer taste, the individual lemon meringue pie; for sheer architecture, the deliciously silly tower of chocolate. Credit Cards: All major.

River Cafe, The $$$ ★ ★

1 Water St., Brooklyn; ☎ *(718) 522-5200.*
Cuisine: American. Avg. $40–$60.
Lunch: Noon–2:30 p.m., Mon.–Fri.
Dinner: 6–11 p.m., 7 days.

This would be a dynamite restaurant no matter where it was located, but it happens to be located on a barge underneath the Brooklyn side of the Brooklyn Bridge. A dazzling sea-level view of the lower Manhattan skyline coupled with the soft sound of a piano bar compete for your attention with the imaginative menu and equally arresting presentations. Who wins? You do. The food is as provocative as the cityscape. Cumin-flavored lamb sausage is accompanied by a goat cheese fondue; a tuna carpaccio and salmon tartare with a warm vegetable salad and black olive cream; and salmon cured in the same spices used to make pastrami, are only a few of the starters. Main courses include grilled swordfish or polenta, seared duck livers, rack of lamb in a chestnut crust with sweet potato puree. Desserts are every bit as scenic as the view and sweeten the reality of a taxi back to Manhattan. Credit Cards: All major.

Sea Grill, The $$$ ★ ★ ★

19 West 49th Street (Rockefeller Plaza); ☎ *246-9201.*

Cuisine: Fishhouse. Avg. $40–$60.
Lunch: 11:30 a.m.–2:30 p.m., Mon.–Sat.
Dinner: 5:30–11 p.m., Mon.–Sat.

Marble, brass, and cherrywood accents add to the luxury liner luxury that makes the Sea Grill one of the city's poshest rooms. The added bonus here is that its glass walls look out onto the Rockefeller Plaza skating rink (perhaps for a glimpse of Brian Boitano whizzing by) and the luminously gilded statue of Prometheus. This is one of those quintessential New York settings. In the fall and winter, especially when the giant Christmas tree is up, there's probably no finer location in which to capture the seasonal excitement of the city. In the spring and summer when there are tables outside, the changing colors of the waters in the fountain surrounding Prometheus provide a light show worthy of the Music Hall. Chef Ed Brown has brought his considerable talent with the fish side of the menu to a new plateau here. Not that carnivores have been overlooked but Chef Brown has a reputation of pushing the fish "envelope" just a little bit further than most. In the course of a single tasting, I luxuriated in a thick, rich, chowder, I demolished the crab cake with stone-ground mustard, and went on without taking a breath to the succulent sugarcane shrimp impaled on a rosemary branch. Dessert, of course. No one can turn down the dense chocolate steamed pudding or the Bailey's caramel flan wrapped in phyllo. The view may be great but the Chef at the Sea Grill is more than a match for it. Credit Cards: All major.

Tavern on the Green $$$ ★★
Central Park at 67th Street; ☎ 873-3200.
Cuisine: American. Avg. $40–$60.
Lunch: 11:30 a.m.–3:30 p.m., Mon.–Fri.
Dinner: 5–10 p.m., 7 days.

Imagine Catherine the Great's hunting lodge as done by Disney. Sitting in the Crystal Room at Tavern on the Green in the middle of Central Park is like being inside a kaleidoscope and looking out. Twinkling lights illuminate the trees, and the city's most extravagant patio is filled with garden party furniture and a dance band. Magic time. Tavern is a multimedia carnival in which it seems, every table has someone to whom the wait staff sings "Happy Birthday." This is the place to which grandmothers love to be taken, and guys named Vito bring their dates when they come into "the city." This is New York's party palace, more flashbulbs going off than at a disco opening, a restaurant in which everyone eats the bread—with lots of butter, and the waiters are trained to check ID's before serving alcoholic beverages. Incredibly, the food IQ at Tavern, has taken a definite leap forward recently. In the past, steam tables and lackadaisical cuisine were the order of the day here. Today, their new chef Patrick Clark, has brought a touch of the south to this land of "Continental Ho-Hum." Upgrading the menu is on the front burner here. Lobster and corn chowder, grilled pork porterhouse with mashed sweet potatoes and, shut my mouth, ribs and all the fixins. And that's only for starters. Holy gourmet! What is there for all those guys named Vito to eat? Credit Cards: All major.

Windows on the World $$$ ★★★
One World Trade Center; 107th floor; ☎ 524-7000.

RESTAURANTS

Cuisine: American. Avg. $40–$60.
Lunch: Noon–1:30 p.m., Mon.–Fri.
Dinner: 5 p.m.–10 p.m., 7 days.

They tend to refer to it as the "new Windows" because of the catastrophic terrorist bombing of the World Trade Center which closed the original Windows for over three years. Thank heavens it's not too new. In fact with the exception of the hip young bar area anyone who adored the feeling of sitting on the clouds above New York, in the old Windows, will still feel right at home. But clouds have no luxurious chairs to sink back into, no smiling waiter to make certain your wine glass is full, and certainly don't come complete with a menu that includes specialties from all over the world. However, after all is eaten and done, to borrow a thought from William S, the view's the thing.

The dining room is set at different levels in a terraced pattern so everyone can see the breathtaking vistas of the city. It's not unusual for people to stroll from window to window between courses to get different views as New York spreads itself out below. The Statue of Liberty looks souvenir-sized from the 107th floor. My favorite time here is sunset. If you play your reservation right you can see the city lights come on, daylight vanish and the moon come into view. Considering the spectacular setting, the substantial prices seem almost reasonable.

The views from the plates are almost as astonishing as the ones outside. To begin a golden-brown caramelized softshell crab drizzled with a curry sauce or a giant Portabello mushroom, big enough to hide an elf, stuffed with snails in a fragrant green garlic butter. Squab comes roasted in a thick salt crust that makes the meat fall from the bone and almost melt on your fork. For sheer drama, the whole Veal shank enclosed in parchment and roasted with herbs and Mexican seasonings is an art form in itself. Desserts continue the visual pyrotechnics with crisp beggars purses filled with fruits and melted chocolate, crunchy rice pudding croquettes, warm and creamy on the inside, or an apple tempting enough for Snow White, covered in phyllo and partnered with Apple Jack ice cream.

There is a separate space for even more serious foodies and oenophiles (grapies), called Celler in the Sky. Same view but a jewel-box approach to food is coupled with rare wines at even rarer prices. Despite it's name, the Celler has a raised floor to give the illusion of actually floating out over New York Harbor. No matter which room you choose, don't miss a visit to Windows. The experience will make you feel you're sitting on top of the world! Credit Cards: All major.

World Yacht Cruises   ★

Pier 81, W. 41st Street and the Hudson River; ☎ *630-8100. Call for sailing information.*
Cuisine: American.
Brunch: $40.00
Dinner: Mon.–Fri—$65.00; Sat. $79.00

Don't ask any questions. Just go. Like taking the bateaux mouches in Paris, and a gondola ride in Venice, you have to see New York from the water or else you just haven't seen New York. It is an unforgettable spectacle as you leave the pier and head downtown, circling the tip of Manhattan and going up the East Side to 42nd Street, passing the

Seaport, the Empire State Building and the Chrysler Building (they comprise what we call "the Gershwin view") and almost up to the UN before turning back to snuggle close to the Statue of Liberty before docking. You will have seen the very best of the skyline from the very best vantage point. Now, make no mistake about it: this is not a Circle Line cruise. This is a yacht. People are dressed to the nines. I counted three bottles of Dom Perignon passing me in the aisle as I sat down. Dinner was an acceptable meal, albeit dangerously reminiscent of business-class airline food. But who cares? The dining room had large picture windows, starched linen napery, and enough silver and china to make you feel first class for the entire cruise. Between courses you can polish the dance floor as the orchestra plays, or else go up on deck for a stroll. The staff is friendly, service is thoughtful and you'd have to be a real malcontent not to have a good time. I've lived in New York all my life and found the evening totally exhilarating.

Agenda/Best Hotel Dining Rooms

New York is experiencing a great Renaissance in hotel dining. In the past, the hotel dining room was to be avoided like a bad case of the shingles, but today the city is enjoying some of the best cuisine around, tucked away in its Grand Hotels.

Monkey Bar, The $$$ ★ ★
Hotel Elysée; 60 East 54th Street; ☎ 838-2600.
Cuisine: American. Avg. $40–$60.
Lunch: Noon–2:30 p.m., Mon.–Fri.
Dinner: 6–11 p.m., 7 days.
The monkey business that goes on here, in this fab bastion of deco decor is delicious fun, and that's no bananas. Chef John Schenk has created a menu that is international in flavor. Everything from couscous to collards turn up along with some of the best soups in town. The roast cod with the creamiest of mashed potatoes is what I personally go ape for. Credit Cards: All major.

Les Celebrites $$$$
Essex House; 155 W 58th Street; ☎ 484-5113.
Cuisine: French. Avg. $50–$100.
Dinner: 6–10 p.m., Mon.–Sat.
Chef Christian Delouvrier's fabulous talent has made Les Celebrities the hottest hotel dining room in town. The room itself is a jewel-like setting for the paintings by celebrities (Van Johnson, Peggy Lee, James Dean), hence the name. Les Celebrites fairly glows with deep colors and elegant decor. A room for a celebration or the start of an affair. The food matches the atmosphere in luxurious use of truffles, foie gras and Delouvier's creativity. No one leaves without knowing they've dined in a "great" restaurant. Try the honey lacquered duck with vegetable fricassee and fig puree. Credit Cards: All major.

Fifty Seven Fifty Seven $$$ ★ ★ ★
The Four Seasons Hotel; 57 East 57 Street; ☎ 758-5700.
Cuisine: American. Avg. $40–$60.
Lunch: 11:30 a.m.–2 p.m., 7 days.
Dinner: 6–10 p.m., 7 days.
A very classic American grill in the opulent surroundings of the Four Seasons Hotel, with an innovative American menu to match. Susan Weaver is a chef for all seasons, not just four, as she turns out seasonal

specialties using the best, most natural ingredients she can find. Great lusty crab cakes, creamy roast carrot soup with chestnuts, one of the best cobb salads I've ever had, a meltingly tender lamb shank with velvety mashed potatoes. Bruno Feldeisen, Fifty Seven, Fifty Seven's world-famous pastry chef contributes an orange risotto cake and a most unusual, crunchy, Banana cream pie. His ice creams are unbelievable, just don't expect "57" flavors. Credit Cards: All major.

Le Regience $$$ ★

Hotel Plaza Athénéé; 37 E 64th Street; ☎ *606-4647.*
Cuisine: French. Avg. $40–$60.
Lunch: Noon–2:30 p.m.
Dinner: 6–9:30 p.m., 7 days.

Pale blue clouds painted on the ceiling and gilded chairs, all the signs point to either dining with Louis the IV or your favorite Francophile. The food is as classic as the surroundings. For heavens sake, they're still serving coquilles St. Jacques and I'm loving it. No cutting edge here, just a dependable mousse au chocolate when you really need one. Credit Cards: All major.

Marks $$$ ★

The Mark Hotel; 25 East 77th Street; ☎ *879-1864.*
Cuisine: American. Avg. $40–$60.
Lunch: 11:30 a.m.–2 p.m., 7 days.
Dinner: 6:30–10:30 p.m., 7 days.

This is a "sink-down-into-the-tufted-banquets" kind of room. Wall to wall comfort with Edwardian overtones and a domed ceiling for an extra touch of British Pizzazz. You can count on them for a tasty salmon tartar, a very comforting braised beef with julienne of veggies and even a top-drawer hamburger at lunch. Credit Cards: All major.

Kokachin $$$

Omni Berkshire Place; 21 E 52nd Street; ☎ *753-5800.*
Cuisine: Asian. Avg. $40–$60.
Lunch: 11:30 a.m.–2 p.m., Mon.–Fri.
Dinner: 5:30–9:30 p.m., 7 days.

Elka Gilmore was the talk of San Francisco when she opened Elka's to showcase her exotic Asian repetoire. It was a smart move for the Omni Berkshire to lure the brilliant Elka to their new hotel where she now dazzles the New York Foodies with her "fusion" fantasies. Everything that arrives at the table is presented with an elegance and artistry as well as inscrutable subtlety. A crabmeat and asparagus napoleon was showered with lemongrass, rack of lamb is dressed in a tamarind glaze, paired with a sweet onion tart. A tiny Japanese bento box overflows with tiny delicacies from the sea. Every plate a picture, every bite exquisite. Credit Cards: All major.

Cafe Pierre $$$ ★★

Hotel Pierre; 61st Street/Fifth Avenue; ☎ *838-8000.*
Cuisine: French. Avg. $40–$60.
Lunch: Noon–2:30 p.m., 7 days.
Dinner: 6–11 p.m., 7 days.

Bertrand Vernejoul, the chef at the Cafe Pierre has a daunting ghost in his kitchen. August Escoffier was the very first chef to mix it up at the Pierre and Vernejoul definitely has a hard act to follow, (since he last potted around with the best of them in Lyon and Paris) even umpteen years later. Chef Vernejoul is most definitely up to the task with his risotto of wild mushrooms, rack of lamb in an herb crust and a stunning black and white chocolate mousse. There is even good old chicken pot pie on the menu, but here it's capped with a flaky puff-pastry. The elegant room is a soothing sliver of gray with bronze inlaid marble and Italian mirrors. There are silks and satins rounding out a very European atmosphere. Credit Cards: All major.

Fantino   **$$$**   ★

The Ritz Carlson; 112 Central Park South; ☎ *757-1900.*
Cuisine: Mediterranean. Avg. $40–$60.
Lunch: Noon–2 p.m., Mon.–Fri.
Dinner: 5:30–11 p.m., Tues.–Sat.

Luscious is the first word that comes to mind as you look into the peach and mauve environment of Fantino. The warmth from the fire-places is echoed by the staff and the creative spin on continental cui-sine of Chef Stephen Cummings. It's served up on extraordinary china designed by Gianni Versace. Everything at Fantino is designed to feed the spirit as well as the body, but they manage to more than satisfy both. Cummings, who comes to the Ritz via Manchester and then Canberra Australia has updated the menu from the "Italian Craze" that hit New York like an exploding cannoli during the 80s. Today a sleeker, more Mediterranean choice has been made. Mussels are sauteed in a passionfruit butter, lamb chops wear a coat of goat cheese, trimmed off with a spicy ratatouille. One of my favorites on the menu is red snapper on a bed of ripe tomatoes and spicy capers. Alongside is a saffron risotto croquette. A napoleon of raspberries ends dinner on a French note. Credit Cards: All major.

44   **$$$**   ★★

The Royalton; 44 West 44th Street; ☎ *944-8844.*
Cuisine: American. Avg. $40–$60.
Lunch: Noon–3 p.m., 7 days.
Dinner: 6–10:45 p.m., 7 days.

Talk about power lunching. As you wait to be seated, editors whiz by, supermodels slink through and Broadway stars twinkle. You know you've sliced through that cutting edge and are privy to New York at its trendiest. The setting is clearly minimal so as not to compete with the fireworks. The filet of salmon is crisper than the conversation and it comes with dates. The Roesti potatoes with bacon and shallots are definitely rich folks' "soul food." They are also famous for their bath-rooms. I'll say no more!!! Credit Cards: All major.

Lepinasse   **$$$**   ★★★

The St. Regis; 55th Street at Fifth Avenue; ☎ *753-4500.*
Cuisine: Continental. Avg. $50–$100.
Lunch: 11:45 a.m.–1:45 p.m.
Dinner: 5:30–9:45 p.m., Mon.–Sat.

This baronial dining room at the St. Regis is filled with dramatic flower arrangements, lighting that would flatter Frankenstein and the masterful presence of Gray Kunz. Even though this world class chef rarely has time for table chit-chat, his dedication to excellence is everywhere. Also the decidedly oriental influences he uses to their most brilliant advantage make his food mysterious and exotic; goose liver covered in a crunchy taw-root crust dressed with mango, ginger and line or for dessert, a quince soup with white chocolate ice cream. Do not go to Lespinasse if you're in the mood for meat and potatoes! Credit Cards: All major.

Agenda/Best Teas in the City

Now that hard liquor has gone the way of the Edsel, and the zillion coffee bars that have sprung up around town serve as waiting rooms for caffeine junkies, the "tea and sympathy" crowd are crooking their "pinkies" and sipping Oolong or Earl Gray as if there was no tomorrow. Maybe our British roots are beginning to show, no matter the reason, New York has become a "Tea for Two" town.

AGENDA TEA-FORMATION

Tea is served from 3 p.m. to 6 p.m. There are usually no reservations required. Most of the tea choices on my agenda serve a full English tea (sandwiches, scones, clotted cream, and pastries. I find that tea before theater replaces dinner and doesn't cost anywhere as much. It also leaves a window of opportunity for a snack apres the show.

Hotel Pierre   **$$$**   ★★★
62nd Street and Fifth Avenue; ☎ *838-8000.*
$26. pp.
Tea is served at the Pierre in the opulent Rotunda, an oval room off the lobby that is a fairytale come to life. Full tea is served, but if coffee is your drug of choice, they have a separate rare coffee menu. Credit Cards: All major.

Four Seasons, The   **$$$**   ★★★
57 East 57th Street; ☎ *758-5700.*
$26. pp.
The lobby lounge, which is tucked into a quiet corner of the hotel's dramatic lobby, serves tea that includes 11 selections and a three tiered tray loaded with tea goodies. Credit Cards: All major.

Carlyle, The   **$$$**   ★★
Madison at 76th Street; ☎ *744-1600.*
$22.50 pp.
Lots of red velvet, love seats, pink fabrics and roses. This small, theatrical little room might have come from a Harem, in fact it almost did. Its style was copied from Tophapi Palace. Tea couldn't be sipped in a more exotic atmosphere. Credit Cards: All major.

Plaza, The   **$$$**   ★★★
Fifth Avenue at 59th Street; ☎ *759-3000.*
$23. pp.
Tea at the **Palm Court** is as close to the European Grand Hotel as we're going to get in the city. There are soft violins in the background, huge potted palms, marble topped tables, and only a few "mittle-europa" touches by Ivana Trump. Best of all, it takes you back to a much better century. Credit Cards: All major.

Lowell, The   ★★
28 East 63rd Street; ☎ *838-1400.*
$21.50 pp.
The Pembroke Room is a vision of Victorian charm. Chintz is everywhere. Shades of Lady Wyndemere, ruffles and flourishes are the

order of the day. A perfect escape from the maddening Madison Avenue crowd. Credit Cards: All major.

Anglers & Writers ★

420 Hudson Street; ☎ *675-0810.*
$10–$15.

Books and country charm make this a relaxing place for a quiet cuppa and a slice of homemade lemon cake. Credit Cards: All major.

Regency Hotel, The ★

540 Park Avenue; ☎ *759-4100.*
$22.

THE LIBRARY. The snuggest, book-lined room is tucked into a corner of the Regency, a hotel not known for it's warmth. They've more than made up their usual "chill" with this perfect spot for tea. The Library also gives chapter and verse in snacks all day long. Credit Cards: All major.

Tea & Sympathy ★★

108 Greenwich Avenue; ☎ *807-8329.*
$10–$20.

Very authentic Brit tea room, possibly because it's owned by a very authentic Brit who takes her tea very seriously. Each table gets its own cake stand that overflows with sandwiches, scones, cakes and the ever-present clotted cream. Her teas are unique, ranging from mango to licorice (lots more mundane varieties as well). Credit Cards: Cash only.

Takashimaya ★★★

693 Fifth Avenue (54th Street); ☎ *350-0100.*
$10–$20.

The Tea Box Cafe downstairs, is an exquisite spot for a spot of tea. They serve both American and Japanese varieties and a jewel-like assortment of Japanese sweets. As with the rest of the store, this place is not to be overlooked. Credit Cards: All major.

Parlor at Cafe des Artistes, The ★★

1 W. 67th Street; ☎ *877-3500.*
$5–$20.

Just across the lobby from the beautiful Cafe Des Artistes there sits a tiny outpost that's filled with all the trappings of a coffee house in Old Vienna. Even if tea is your drink of choice they still serve up extravagant cakes and pastries as well as hors d'oeuvres and drinks. Is that the Merry Widow in the corner? Credit Cards: All major.

Agenda/"Hot" Breakfasts

Everyone's heard of the New York "Power Breakfast" by now, but it's still fun to be an observer on what has become the most important meal of the day. Today, the smoke-filled back rooms for making deals have been replaced by resplendent arenas where yogurt and fruit, or bran muffins are the bargaining chips. Reservations are a must. Breakfast hours are 7–11 a.m.

Plaza, The ★★★

768 Fifth Avenue; ☎ *546-5310.*
$15–$35.

The Edwardian Room is a baronial space with a view of Central Park and an aura of wealth and elegance that makes it the most beautiful place to breakfast in New York. Aside from that, more deals are made

RESTAURANTS

here on any given morning than Monty Hall could have dreamed of. Credit Cards: All major.

Regency Hotel, The   ★★★
540 Park Avenue; ☎ *759-4100.*
$15–$35.
If historical facts are of interest before you make a breakfast reservation, the Regency was the hotel where the "Power Breakfast" was born. Our theory is that since the Regency is a favorite with the L.A. set, and everyone knows they get up as soon as the California sun rises, business is conducted in the early A.M. When they unpacked their pastel cashmere sweaters, they unpacked this bizarre custom as well. God help us. Credit Cards: All major.

Peninsula, The   ★★★
700 Fifth Avenue (55th Street); ☎ *247-2200.*
$15–$35.
Breakfast here is in Belle Epoque splendor, overlooking Fifth Avenue. The restaurant, Adrienne, which in the evening is a beautiful bastion of continental cuisine, is packed with Hong Kong traders, lots of Japanese investors and random L.A. types who couldn't get a reservation at the Regency. Credit Cards: All major.

The following is our agenda for less powerful but far more relaxed breakfasts around town.

Cafe Botanica   ★★
Essex House, 160 Central Park South; ☎ *484-5120.*
$15–$35.
The view of the park here is just about the best way to start the day. Everything here is bright and airy, the wicker and brass adds to the gardenlike grace of this room. All this, and very good oatmeal. Credit Cards: All major.

Mayrose $ ★★
920 Broadway (21st Street); ☎ *533-3663.*
$10–$15.
Buckwheat pancakes and fresh berries in a part of town that's not known for farmhouse breakfasts. Credit Cards: All major.

Pink Teacup, The $ ★★
42 Grove Street; ☎ *807-6755.*
$10–$20.
Grits, eggs over easy, the kind of home-cured bacon that tastes of hickory and fresh biscuits. Shut our mouths, but you may not be able to do the same here. Credit Cards: All major.

Good Enough To Eat $ ★
483 Amsterdam Avenue (83rd Street); ☎ *496-0163.*
$10–$20.
Some people think you can get the best breakfast in town here. GETE is committed to the freshest, most countrified food they can serve, scrambled eggs with dill, biscuits with fruit-flavored butter and waffles that float off your plate. Credit Cards: All major.

Veselka $ ★
144 2nd Avenue (9th Street); ☎ *228-9682.*
$5–$10.
Start the day with a crisp order of blintzes and sour cream. You want to talk stick-to-your-ribs! They may slow you down a little but it's a

great way to arm yourself for a typical New York day. Credit Cards: Cash only.

Friend of a Farmer $ ★

77 Irving Place (18 & 19 Streets); ☎ 477-2188.
$10–$20.
Yummy muffins and homemade breads and jams in a pretty farmhouse setting. Credit Cards: All major.

Four Seasons, The $$$ ★★★

57 East 57 Street; ☎ 758-5000.
$20–$35.
Despite feeling there is an echo in the room, Fifty Seven Fifty Seven has one of the most electric power breakfasts in the city. Execs with a sweet tooth line up at dawn for Chef Weaver's lemon ricotta pancakes. These are award-winning pancakes, not the stuff that comes courtesy of an Aunt Jemimah box! East also meets west 57th street with a classical Japanese breakfast. An inscrutable way to start the day. Credit Cards: All major.

© 1994 H. L. SCHWADRON

"We've got to unload some of this stuff.
How do you say 'leftovers' in French?"

Dining in the Theater District

I've always felt that pre-theater dining should have some definite ground rules: first, elegant dining deserves enough time to savor the experience fully, not with one eye on the clock and the other waving your credit card frantically at the waiter. Second, if you're going to the theater, the play's the thing (who said that?) and not the heartburn that seems to be creeping up past your program. I suggest that you schedule your visit to a "four star" gastronomic wonder for another evening and pick one of the terrific, more casual choices I've put together for pre-or-post theater nourishment.

Barbetta   **$$$**   ★ ★ ★
321 West 46th Street; ☎ *246-9171.*
Cuisine: Italian. Avg. $40–$60.
Lunch: Noon–2 p.m., Tues.–Sat.
Dinner: 5–11:30 p.m., Tues.–Sat.
It's been around for years and is still a family-run restaurant. Located
on the ground floor of a lovely old townhouse, the food is solid Ital-
ian fare with no real surprises. But the pastas are comforting and the
risottos first rate. A bonus in the summer is an exquisite tiny garden
in the back. Credit Cards: All major.

Becco   **$$**   ★ ★
355 West 46th Street; ☎ *397-7597.*
Cuisine: Italian. Avg. $20–$40.
Lunch: Noon–3 p.m., Mon.–Sat.
Dinner: 5 p.m.–midnight, Mon.–Sat.; noon–10 p.m., Sun.
Great antipasto that makes the perfect dinner before the theater. The
rest of the menu is devoted to the kind of Italian specialties everyone
loves, hearty, peasant fare that's served up with a bottomless spoon.
Credit Cards: All major.

Carmine's   **$$**   ★
200 West 44th Street; ☎ *221-3800.*
Cuisine: Italian. Avg. $20–$40.
Hours: 11:30 a.m.–11 p.m., 7 days.
This is one of the new-wave Italian "family-style" restaurants with
platters made up for the table. Carmine's is big, raucous and always a
lot of fun. I think you should probably wait till after the show for this
one, so that you're assured of living long enough to see the finale.
Credit Cards: All major.

Frico   **$$**   ★ ★
402 W 43rd Street; ☎ *564-7272.*
Cuisine: Italian. Avg. $20–$40.
Lunch: Noon–3 p.m., Mon.–Fri.
Dinner: 4:30 p.m.–midnight, 7 days.
The same great guys who brought you Becco have opened up Frico
which specializes in food of the Friuli region of Italy. Most of the
dishes are based on corn so Frico turns out some of the best polenta
in the city. The name of the restaurant refers to a delectable torte
stuffed with sausage and cheese, perfect for an after-theatre snack and
a brisk walk. Frico is terrifico. Credit Cards: All major.

44   **$$$**   ★ ★
Royalton Hotel; 44 West 44th Street; ☎ *944-8844.*
Cuisine: American. Avg. $40–$60.
Lunch: Noon–3 p.m., 7 days.
Dinner: 6–10:45 p.m., 7 days.
Perfect for pre-theater because the menu is filled with fascinating
appetizers you can put together for a light dinner. If you're ready to
push the envelope further there are also fascinating entrees and des-
serts. Watch out for shooting stars, everyone drops into 44 eventually.
Credit Cards: All major.

Jewel of India   **$$**   ★ ★
15 West 44th Street; ☎ *869-5544.*
Cuisine: Indian. Avg. $20–$40.
Lunch: Noon–3 p.m., 7 days.

Dinner: 5:30–11 p.m., 7 days.

Brass, mother-of-pearl, and dressy silk tapestries in a room that smells of sandalwood spice. If you're in the mood for a curry with the fringe on top, you're in the right place. Credit Cards: All major.

Joe Allen $$ ★ ★

326 West 46th Street; ☎ 581-6464.
Cuisine: American. Avg. $20–$40.
Hours: Noon–midnight, 7 days.

Twenty years ago, a bartender at P.J. Clarke's was bitten by the Broadway bug and went west, to 46th Street. He wanted to open a place where actors, dancers, and the backstage crews could afford to come for a burger and a beer. Today everyone comes to Joe Allen for his burgers and black bean soup and his unbelievable brownie in fudge sauce. Credit Cards: All major.

Lotfi's $$ ★

358 West 46th Street; ☎ 582-5850.
Cuisine: Moroccan. Avg. $20–$40.
Dinner: 4:30–11 p.m., Mon.–Sat.

A Moroccan bazaar couldn't smell more fragrant than Lotfi's. The aromas from the kitchen would break even the Sheik of Arabi's heart. Stuffed phyllo with chicken livers and lamb melts on the tongue. The humus is rich and tart, the lamb tajine studded with prunes and toasted almonds. Casbah cuisine at its best. Credit Cards: All major.

Ollie's $ ★

200 B. West 44th Street; ☎ 921-5988.
Cuisine: Chinese. Avg. $10–$25.
Hours: 11 a.m.–midnight, 7 days.

Crowded, noisy, Hong Kong style barbecue joint. They have great ribs, pork and best of all soup bowls the size of Chicago filled with broth, wanton, pork and noodles. What could be better before "Miss Saigon?" Credit Cards: All major.

Orso $$ ★ ★ ★

322 West 46th Street; ☎ 489-7212.
Cuisine: Italian. Avg. $20–$40.
Hours: Noon–11:45 p.m., 7 days.

"Hot," "In," bursting at the seams with wonderfully light Italian food and some of the real heavyweights in the theater. Always actors, producers, agents, shoveling in the pastas, the soups and the paper-thin tiny pizzas that are the real stars here. If you want to make the "Broadway scene," this is most of it. Credit Cards: All major.

Virgil's Real Barbecue $$ ★ ★

152 West 44th Street; ☎ 921-9494.
Cuisine: BBQ. Avg. $20–$40.
Hours: 11:30 a.m.–11 p.m., 7 days.

Carnivore alert! This is the new top spot in the theater district to pull up a rib and pig-out. This is not a place for nouvelle cuisine, this is a place for Texas brisket, golden brown chicken and pulled pork sandwiches. Each plate is heaped with mashed potatoes, or dirty rice or if you're a fanatic, collards. If you're still hungry, there are hush puppies and birch beer. Smoking is definitely permitted but only for the meats. Credit Cards: All major.

Soup Kitchen International $ ★

259A W 55th Street; ☎ *757-7730.*
Lunch: 11 a.m.–3 p.m. Avg. $5–$10.

If you prefer pressure instead of croutons with your soup, then a visit to the infamous "Soup Nazi" should be on your agenda for a stressful slurp before your mateneé. Famous for wonderful soup, more punishment than any self respecting Dominatrix would administer, and the attention of the writers for NBC's *Seinfeld*. Al Yeganeh has more than a soupcon of drill sergeant in him. Credit Cards: Cash only.

MUSEUMS

The Metropolitan Museum of Art is the largest art museum in the Western Hemisphere. It spans four blocks.

Even if you break out in a nasty rash at the thought of spending endless hours marching up and down, staring at pictures and trying to look as absorbed as that couple next to you, even if you'd rather be at Barney's or Bloomingdales, and even if museums are usually the last thing to appear on a tight travel agenda, go! New York's museums are as much a part of the fabric of the city as Broadway, The Skyline or Central Park. The endless banquet that the city's museums offer may be too much for a single visit, but a taste of one or two will prove to be just as memorable as the Empire State Building.

Alternative Museum

594 Broadway; ☎ *966-4444.*
Sun.–Thurs. 10 a.m.–5:45 p.m.; Fri.–Sat. 10 a.m.–8:45 p.m., Admission by contribution.
Specializing in political and sociopolitical art. It exhibits "the works of emerging and mid-career artists who have been underrecognized and disenfranchised because of ideology, race, gender, or economic inequality." The Alternative Museum is a lot more fun than it's brochure would have you believe.

American Crafts Museum

40 West 53rd Street; ☎ *956-3535.*
Tues., 10 a.m.–8 p.m.; Wed.–Sun., 10 a.m.–5 p.m.; Admission $5, children $2.50.

This very engaging collection comes from craftspeople all over the world. They work in every conceivable medium and the results are usually fanciful and full of whimsical charm.

American Museum of the Moving Image, The

35th Avenue at 36th St., Astoria, Queens; ☎ *(718) 784-0077.*
Open Mon.–Fri., 11 a.m.–5 p.m.; Sat.–Sun., 11 a.m.–6 p.m. Admission $7, children $4. IND R train to Steinway Street, Walk to 35th Avenue and turn right.

Fascinating exhibits that take you from the very beginning of film up to the present. There are two floors of costumes and memorabilia that predate the forties, a projection imaging machine so that you appear to be wearing a costume from a classic such as *Gone With the Wind*, and most offbeat of all, tapes that allow you to listen in as famous directors coached actors in their films.

The American Museum of Natural History houses 34 million items ranging from reassembled dinosaur skeletons to the fabled Star of India 563 carat sapphire.

American Museum of Natural History, The

79th Street and Central Park West; ☎ *769-5100.*

Actually occupies the entire area from 77th to 81st Streets and Central Park West to Columbus Avenue. The *Guinness Book of World Records* cites it as the world's largest museum: "it comprises 19 interconnected buildings with 23 acres of floor space." It has also been described as a "colossus", and "an architectural hodge-podge." Whichever, it cannot be overlooked.

From the life-sized display of a herd of wild elephants to a 94-foot long diving whale to an actual 34-ton meteorite to the fossilized skeletons of reconstructed dinosaurs to the fabulous Star of India 563-carat sapphire, the American offers a dazzling kaleidoscopic view of the inhabitants of the peoples of Asia, Mexico, and pre-Colonial America. You can peek into a tepee, hear songs of Africa, and go island hopping in the Pacific. The Hall of the South American Peoples is a new permanent exhibition focusing on the 12,000 -year cultural history of the peoples of the Andean Highlands and Amazon Basin.

Naturemax Theater, The
☎ *769-5700.*
Hours are Sun.–Tues., 10 a.m. –5:45 p.m., Fri., and Sat. 10 a.m.–8:45 p.m. Admission $7 adults, $5 children. The gift shop often has interesting jewelry and artifacts. Call for schedules. Admission, Museum plus ticket, $12 adults, $6.50 children.
The museum has the city's largest indoor movie screen: four stories high and 66 feet wide. Programs take you on journeys around the world. The main entrance to the museum is on Central Park West, although the "carriage" entrance on 77th Street allows entry without walking up steps.

Hayden Planetarium
81st Street near Central Park West; ☎ *769-5920.*
Long before there were men on the moon, there were kids in outer space at the Astronomy Department of the Museum. Happily, the Planetarium with its distinctive copper dome, has lost none of its magic despite our newly-acquired sophistication. Sky Theater is where a projector illuminates the inside of the dome with the night sky to show everything from the birth of the planets to cosmic illusions. If you're looking for a close encounter of a psychedelic kind, the Planetarium hosts a laser show on Friday and Saturday evenings that is coupled to a dynamite sound system. Be sure to see the items on display at the gift shop if you need something for the kids back home. Admission.

Asia Society, The
725 Park Avenue (70th and Park); ☎ *288-6400.*
Open Tuesday thru Saturday from 11 a.m.–6 p.m., Sundays from noon till 5 p.m. Admission $3.00.
You'll find exhibits here including a core collection given by John D. Rockefeller III, photographic essays on Asian life, art from Aboriginal Australia, and Japanese arts. A highly manageable gallery.

Brooklyn Museum
200 Eastern Parkway; ☎ *(718) 638-5000).*
Open Wednesday to Sunday, 10 a.m.–5 p.m. Suggested contribution. IRT No. 2 or 3 train to Eastern Parkway/Brooklyn Museum stop.
It's the seventh largest art museum in the United States, with an Egyptian collection that's considered to be one of the best in the world. Also known for its Japanese, Korean, and Primitive African Art. There are rooms from a typical 17th century Brooklyn house that have been reconstructed, and the sculpture garden has artifacts and relics from "lost New York." And the museum's gift shop, chock full of crafts from around the world, is a great source of inexpensive gifts to take home.

Children's Museum of Manhattan, The
212 West 83rd Street (between Broadway and Amsterdam Avenue); ☎ *721-1223.*
Open Mon.–Tues., 10 a.m.–5 p.m.; Wed., 10 a.m.–8 p.m., Fri.–Sun., 10 a.m.–5 p.m. Admission $5.
It is dedicated to self-discovery and participation for toddlers to teen-agers. Four floors of exhibit and activity centers including a Brainato-

rium and a Nature and Pet Care Center. Guides explain, answer questions, and conduct workshops. There are hands-on exhibits plus puppeteers, storytellers, musicians, and artists who show and tell at the same time. The museum's gift shop lets you take away some of the fun you've been seeing.

Cloisters, The

Open Tuesday thru Sunday, 9:30 a.m.–5 p.m. Admission $8 adults, children free. Tours are given every day at 3 p.m. (☎ 923-3700).

A reconstruction of French and Spanish monastic cloisters located in Fort Tryon Park, property donated to the city by John D. Rockefeller, Jr. One of the loveliest spots in the entire country (the Hudson River views are as glorious as the relics collected in Europe), the Cloisters houses the medieval holdings of the Metropolitan Museum of Art. The chapels were brought from Europe and rebuilt stone by stone in as idyllic a setting as one could find. Among the highlights here are the Unicorn Tapestries—a series of seven tapestries that are stunningly realistic.

Cooper-Height Museum, The

2 East 91st Street; ☎ 860-6868.
Open Tues., 10 a.m.–9 p.m.; Wed.–Sat., 10 a.m.–5 p.m.; Sun., Noon–5 p.m. Admission $3 adults, $1.50 children.

It is the Smithsonian Institution's National Museum of Design, located since 1976 in Andrew Carnegie's landmark mansion. Philanthropist Peter Cooper's granddaughters, founded the collection that today spans 3000 years of design history and includes drawings, prints, textiles, furniture, metal- and woodworks, ceramics, glass and wallpaper. The museum shop here is one of the best in the City. Designs in gifts for the home are dedicated to the excellence found in the museum's permanent collection.

The Ellis Island Immigration Museum tells the moving story of the more than 12 million immigrants who entered the U.S. between 1892-1954.

Ellis Island Immigration Museum

It can be reached with the Circle Line ferry, 7 days a week 9:30 a.m.–3:30 p.m., ☎ 883-1986. (Admission is included in Ferry ride tickets. See the Statue of Liberty).

Twelve million people passed through Ellis Island between the 1890s and 1954. For a truly moving experience, walk through the same rooms they did, you can almost hear the din of the endless lines of human beings who came to America to change their lives or follow a dream. Part of the exhibit includes The American Immigrant Wall of Honor; the largest wall of names in the world. We dare you not to have a lump in your throat.

El Museo del Barrio

1230 Fifth Avenue (at 104th Street); ☎ *831-7272.*
Open Wednesday thru Sunday, 11 a.m.–5 p.m. Admission $4 adults, $2 children.
Devoted to the art and culture of Puerto Rico and South America. Barrio is a term for the Hispanic ghetto that shares space in what was once exclusively black Harlem. The museum is for many Hispanic New Yorkers, a major cultural bond with their heritage. For others, it is an opportunity to expand their appreciation of these cultures via lectures, films, concerts and exhibits.

Frick Collection, The

1 East 70th Street; ☎ *288-0700.*
Open Tuesday thru Saturday, 10 a.m.–6 p.m.; Sunday, 1–6 p.m. Admission $5 adults, children $3 (not admitted under 10).
Everyone loves it because the Frick does its best not to let you know it's a museum. The block-long mansion is in the style of Louis the Something-or-Other, a chateau you might expect to come upon in the French countryside rather than on Fifth. The charade here is that you're simply wandering through the Frick Mansion in which Henry Clay Frick, steel magnate, robber baron, partner of Andrew Carnegie, sequestered his Duveen-selected art collection rather than expose it to the pollution of Pittsburgh.

The Frick, then, is a double-whammy treat. Not only do you get to see how the mega-rich lived, but what they lived with: Mrs. Frick's living room is fully outfitted with eye-popping furniture as well as an El Greco here and a couple of Titians there. Everything all wrapped up in one gorgeous, not-to-be missed package.

Solomon R. Guggenheim Museum, The

1071 Fifth Avenue (88th Street); ☎ *423-3500.*
(See page 13.)

Guggenheim Museum SoHo, The

575 Broadway (at Prince); ☎ *423-3500.*
Open Sun., Wed., Thurs., Fri., 11 a.m.–6 p.m. Sat., 11 a.m.–8 p.m. Admission $6, $4 children.
The look of the SoHo branch of the Guggenheim is a far cry from its big brother on 5th Avenue. This annex is in a red brick, landmarked, cast-iron ornamented building, dating back to the 1800s. There's 30,000 square feet of exhibition space so that the Guggie could stretch a bit.

International Center of Photography

1130 Fifth Avenue (at 94th Street); ☎ *860-1777.*
Open Tues., 11 a.m.–8 p.m.; Wed.–Fri., 11 a.m.–6 p.m.; Sat.–Sun., 11 a.m. to 6 p.m. Admission $4 adults, $2.50 children.
The Center, a must for shutterbugs, changes exhibits to focus either on a photographer or a type of photograph. You'll find programs and

workshops on everything you've always wanted to know from aesthetics to technique, from the 19th century to now, and from masters like Cartier-Bresson to emerging talents. The gift shop has posters, books, and catalogs.

Intrepid Sea-Air-Space Museum

Pier 86, West 46th Street and Twelfth Avenue; ☎ *245-0072.*
Open Wed.–Sun., 10 a.m.–5 p.m. Admission $10 adults, $5 children.
It is housed in a World War II aircraft carrier that served in the Pacific. "Sea, air, space" is the motto of this museum with planes parked on deck and items from our history in space on display. If ever there was a kid's dream come true, this is it.

Jewish Museum, The

1109 Fifth Avenue (at 92nd Street); ☎ *423-3200.*
Open Sun.–Thurs., 11 a.m.–5:45 p.m. Admission $7, children $5.
This museum under the aegis of the Jewish Theological Seminary of America, houses the most extensive collection of judaica in the world, ranging from coins and medals to books, manuscripts, ceremonial objects, folk art, and a permanent exhibit focusing on Biblical archaeology. Both contemporary and historical themes are highlighted in a variety of educational programs. Modern artists such as Jasper Johns, Louise Nevelson, Modigliani, Chagall, and Lipchitz, have all been represented here. Special exhibits cover the range of Jewish experience.

Lower East Side Tenement Museum

97 Orchard Street; ☎ *431-0233.*
Open Tues.–Fri., 11 a.m.–5 p.m.; Sun., 11 a.m.–6 p.m. Admission by donation. Free on Tuesday.
Built in 1864, 97 Orchard St., represents the daily way of life for the millions of immigrants from Europe who poured into the Lower East Side at the turn of the century. It was not unusual for 10 or 12 people to sleep in each room at 97 Orchard. Tours are conducted so that the public can understand what people endured to come to America.

Metropolitan Museum of Art, The

82nd Street and 5th Avenue; ☎ *879-5500*
(See page 14).

Museum for African Art, The

593 Broadway; ☎ *966-1313.*
Open Tues.–Fri., 10:30 a.m.–5:30 p.m., Sat.–Sun., Noon–6 p.m. Admission $5 adults, $2.50 children.
This fascinating museum is in SoHo not far from the downtown branch of the Guggenheim. African Art, history and culture are explored with a focus on sub-Saharan African culture. Its collections include sculpture, costumes, masks and architectural designs. The shop here showcases carvings, fabrics and jewelry.

Museum of American Folk Art, The

☎ *977-7170.*
Open Tues.–Sun., 11:30 a.m.–7:30 p.m. Admission is free.
It's alive and well and living (for the next few years) at 2 Lincoln Square, where its Eve and Morris Feld Gallery is housed in a state-of-the-art space. Included in this fabulous collection are works that date from the mid-18th century, when American artists were usually self-taught and came from a crafts tradition. The museum, dedicated to

preserving this rich folk heritage, is the perfect place to stop on your way to events at Lincoln Center. While admission is free, a modest contribution is greatly appreciated. The museum's gift shop next door is filled with handmade crafts, toys, and decorative objects as well as a wonderful collection of folk-art books.

Museum of the City of New York, The

Fifth Avenue at 103rd Street; ☎ *534-1672.*
Open Wed.–Sun. 10 a.m.–5 p.m. Admission $5 adults, $3 children.
Originally located in Gracie Mansion, moved in 1930 because the mansion wasn't fireproof. It says something about New York's regard for politicians that the mansion was declared fit as a fiddle for use as the official residence of the Mayor. So it has remained ever since. Meanwhile, back at the museum you'll find as loving a collection of New York memorabilia as anyone has ever gathered. There are models and dioramas chronicling the city's growth from its beginnings as a Dutch outpost in the New World. Laced with theatrical mementos, taped city sounds, historical paintings and period rooms, it's the perfect place to wander before setting forth. Check with the desk about their walking tours.

Museum of Modern Art, The

11 West 53rd Street; ☎ *708-9480.*
Open Thurs., Noon–8:30 p.m.; Fri.–Tues., Noon–8:30 p.m. Closed Wednesday. For film listings, call 708-9490. Admission $8 adults, $5 children.
For devotees of 20th-century art, MOMA is a must—despite recent renovations intended to make the museum more accessible but which, in fact, take away much of its former intimacy. MOMA may have lost some muscle with the transfer of Picasso's *Guernica* to the Prado in Spain, but its collection of Picasso paintings and sculpture is the best to be seen this side of the Atlantic. In addition, MOMA is home to some of Matisse's most exquisite interiors; some of the most exciting Gaugins, Vuillards, Toulouse-Lautrecs, Chagalls, Miros, and Giacometis to be found anywhere. There is an extensive display of the constructivist movement led by Mondrian and Malevitch and a collection of surrealistic masterpieces that includes some of Magritte's eeriest paintings. Not to be missed is the "meditation corner" with Monet's fabulous triptych *Water Lilies.*

You'll find U.S. masterpieces that are bigger than life and, on a smaller scale, a treasure trove of drawings and prints by Johns, Rauschenberg, Stella, and the elders Picasso, Munch, and Toulouse-Lautrec. The photography gallery paints its own picture of 20th-century America, as does an extraordinary film library (there are daily showings at no extra charge).

A voracious collector, MOMA also keeps track of modern furniture, utensils, and architecture, and even has some of the craziest cars ever designed. The sculpture garden displays works by Rodin, Matisse, and Newman in an idyllic setting. Even the bookstore is great, with its selection of books, cards and souvenirs. But the real shopper's delight is found down the block at the **Museum Design Store** *(44 West 53rd Street).* A big, bright new MOMA shop that's almost two stories high with award-winning designs for home, office, nursery, and game room. Everything from Barcelona chairs to key chains and worth a visit just to keep up with the newest consumer goodies from all over the world.

Museum of Television and Radio, The

Located at 25 West 52nd Street; ☎ *621-6800.*
Open Thurs., Noon–8 p.m.; Tues.–Sun., noon–6 p.m.; Closed Mon.
Admission $5 adults, $3 children.

They have a collection of seven thousand radio and ten thousand television broadcasts spanning a sixty-year period. These tapes are available to the public via broadcast consoles at which you can enjoy anything from your favorite episode of "I Love Lucy" to one of FDR's fireside chats.

National Museum of the American Indian /Smithsonian Institution

One Bowling Green; ☎ *825-6700.*
Open 7 days, 10 a.m.–5 p.m. Admission is free.

The museum celebrates the heritage and the culture of the native people of the Western Hemisphere. Brand new, and housed in what used to be the U.S. Custom House, one of the most beautiful representations of Beaux Arts architecture in the city, it has over 20,000 square feet of exhibition space to display it's more than one million artifacts. The Museum is part of the Smithsonian in Washington where they are planning an even larger exhibit space to open in the year 2000.

South Street Seaport Museum

12 Fulton Street; ☎ *669-9400.*
(See page 15.)

Whitney Museum of American Art, The

Open Wed.–Sun., 11 a.m.–6 p.m., ☎ *570-3676. Admission $8 adults, $6 children.*

Like the Guggenheim, is housed in a building that competes for attention with the art on display. Designed by Marcel Breuer of Bauhaus (and Breuer chair) fame, the Whitney looks, at first glance, upside down. Its three tiers of concrete seem to defy gravity as they cantilever out over the street.

Founded by Gertrude Vanderbilt Whitney in 1931 (her personal collection serves as the museum's core), the Whitney moved into its new home in 1996, by which time it was established as the preeminent address for 20th-century American art: Hopper, Nevelson, Johns, Rauschenberg, Calder, Warhol, et al. The focus and exhibit spaces here are quite unique, not to be confused with MOMA. A cafe looks out onto the sculpture garden, and the lobby shop sells prints and books. Their showcase for gifts is at The Store Next Door (easy to find). They have a totally unique collection of jewelry, scarves, crafts and cards, etc. However, this is not a place to pinch pennies.

Police Museum

Police Academy, 235 East 20th Street.
By appointment (☎ *477-9753), 9 a.m.–3 p.m. Free.*

"Stick-em-up" was heard in New York even when it was named New Amsterdam. They have a complete collection of brass knuckles and ivory nightsticks and other knick-knacs of the trade. Who says "crime doesn't pay?"

AGENDA FOR GALLERIES

Art lovers will find a variety of galleries to suit every taste.

Gallery hopping in New York is one of the city's favorite spectator sports. They open, they close, they move, but they always add the most adventurous spices to the art scene here. The Gallery agenda is listed by area so that you can include at least one or two if you're dining or shopping nearby. (Gallery hours vary—call in advance.)

Upper East Side

(59th to 90th Streets)

Acquarella Galleries
   18 East 79th Street; ☎ *734-6300.*
   20th century master paintings and drawings.

Art of the Past
   1242 Madison (89th Street); ☎ *860-7070.*
   Bronzes, stone sculptures, Tibetan temple art.

Avanti Galleries
   22 East 72nd Street; ☎ *628-3377.*
   Specializes in Post World War II artists.

Carus Gallery
872 Madison (71st Street); ☎ 879-4660.
20th century avant-garde works.

CDS Gallery
76 East 79th Street; ☎ 772-9555.
Arts from the Americas, Europe and Australia.

Eastlake Gallery
1078 Madison; ☎ 772-8810.
Old Masters, Impressionists, and 20th Century Modern.

Barry Friedman
851 Madison (70th Street); ☎ 794-8950.
European avant-garde paintings from the 20s and 30s.

Hirschl & Adler Galleries
21 E 70th Street; ☎ 535-8810.
851 Madison; ☎ 744-6700.
19th and 20th century American decorative arts and modern artists.

Jaro Art Galleries
955 Madison (75th Street); ☎ 734-5475.
Specializing in Yugoslav Naive artists.

Jordon-Volpe Gallery
958 Madison (75th Street); ☎ 570-9500.
American Impressionist and Modern painting.

Mary-Anne Martin Fine Art
23 E 73rd Street; ☎ 288-2213.
Latin American art.

Frank J. Miele Gallery
1262 Madison; ☎ 876-5775.
Contemporary artists working as 19th century folk artists.

Gerald Peters Gallery
177 E 78th Street; ☎ 628-9760.
American art from the 19th and 20th century.

Sindin Galleries
956 Madison (75th Street); ☎ 288-7902.
Contemporary art/Picasso, Miro, Rivera, Zuniga, etc.

Wildenstein & Company
19 E 64th Street; ☎ 879-0500.
Varied, known by every serious collector and museum in the world.

Midtown

Associated American Artists
20 W 57th Street; ☎ 399-5510.
The best in prints and works on paper.

J. N. Bartfield Gallery
30 West 57th Street; ☎ 245-8890.
Western art (oils, watercolors, bronzes, drawing)

Grace Borgenicht Gallery
724 Fifth (56th Street); ☎ 247-2111.
Contemporary American artists.

Marisa del Re Gallery
41 E 57th Street; ☎ 688-1843.
Modern and Contemporary artists.

Andre Emmerich
41 E 57th Street; ☎ *752-0124.*
Contemporary American and European Art.

James Goodman Gallery
41 E 57th Street; ☎ *593-3737.*
Paintings and sculptures by Botero, Calder, de Kooning, Picasso, etc.

Sidney Janis Gallery
110 W 57th Street; ☎ *586-0110.*
20th century European and American masters.

Kennedy Galleries
730 Fifth (56th Street); ☎ *541-9600.*
Specializing in 18th, 19th and 20th century American Art for over 100 years.

Jan Krugier
41 E 57th Street; ☎ *755-7288.*
European and American masters.

Lladro Art Gallery
43 W 57th Street; ☎ *838-9341.*
Contemporary artists from Spain.

Marlborough
40 W 57th Street; ☎ *541-4900.*
19th and 20th century American and European masters.

O'Hara Gallery
41 W 57th Street; ☎ *355-3330.*
Impressionist masters.

Pace Prints
32 E 57th Street; ☎ *421-3237.*
Prints of Contemporary, Modern and Old Master artists.

Paulina Rieloff Gallery
200 Lexington (32nd Street); ☎ *683-1228.*
Specializes in South American artists.

Sacks Fine Art
50 W 57th Street; ☎ *333-7755.*
American paintings after late 19th and 20th century.

Viridian Gallery
24 W 57th Street; ☎ *245-2882.*
Abstract Art.

Zabriskie Gallery
724 Fifth Avenue (50th Street); ☎ *307-7430.*
Contemporary photographs, paintings and drawings.

SoHo/TriBeCa

Brooke Alexander
59 Wooster; ☎ *925-4338.*
Contemporary paintings, drawings and sculpture.

Mary Boone
417 W Broadway; ☎ *431-1818.*
Contemporary American and European paintings.

Frank Bustamente Gallery
560 Broadway; 226-2108.
Contemporary German, Polish, Scandinavian and American Art.

Leo Castelli
420 W Broadway; ☎ *431-5160.*
580 Broadway; ☎ *431-6279.*
Showcase for new movements in Abstract Expressionism, Pop art, Minimalism, and conceptualism.

Condesto/Lawler Gallery
524 Broadway; ☎ *219-1283.*
Abstract and figurative work in all media.

Fred Dorfman
123 Watts Street; ☎ *966-4611.*
New artists showcased.

Four Color Images, Gallery of Comic Art
524 Broadway; ☎ *431-4234.*
Original contemporary comic book and trading card art.

O.K. Harris
383 W Broadway; ☎ *431-3600.*
Opened in 1969, they feature paintings, sculpture, and photography. They are the oldest gallery in SoHo.

Sally Hawkins Gallery
448 W Broadway; ☎ *477-5699.*
Art as jewelry and post-Modern emerging artists.

Max Protetch
560 Broadway; ☎ *966-5454.*
Architectural, painting, drawing and sculpture artists.

Stephen Rosenberg Gallery
115 Wooster; ☎ *431-4838.*
American and European contemporary painting.

Scott Alan Gallery
270 Lafayette Street; ☎ *266-5145.*
Contemporary art from Mexico and Spain.

Tony Shafrazi Gallery
119 Wooster Street; ☎ *274-9300.*
Contemporary American and European paintings and sculptures.

Sonnabend Gallery
420 W Broadway; ☎ *966-6160.*
Contemporary European and American art.

AGENDA ENTERTAINMENT

The Winter Garden Theater has been the stage for many long-running Broadway plays including "Cats."

All the world's a stage in New York City. Theater, music, opera, dance, movies, museums, television, comedy clubs—and even sports arenas entertain a city with nearly as many performers as there are people in the audience. New York is the world champ for "things to do."

Here's where you need a finely tuned agenda. The days of picking up cancellations for a big Broadway hit just before curtain time are over. The same holds true for ringside seats at sporting events, or in cabarets where your favorite jazz is being played. Consult a copy of the Sunday *New York Times* (Arts & Leisure Section), or *Time Out, The New Yorker* or *New York Magazine* as far in advance of your trip as possible. Call NYC/On Stage (☎ *768-1818*) for information on theater, music and dance events. (Toll-free from out-of-state, ☎ *(800) STAGE-NY.*) Decide what you want to see and either write for tickets or use one of the electronic reservation systems (Ticketmaster, ☎ *307-*

4100) to be certain you have seats for the event and time that you want. If you're going to be staying at a large hotel, consider calling the concierge for some pre-arrival help in getting the reservations you desire.

Theater

The Great White Way (Broadway) is still a collage of huge electrified signs, theater marquees and movie posters.

Broadway

The star-studded stages that make up the "Great White Way" are located in a small section of the city between 41st and 53rd Streets, between Sixth and Eighth Avenues. Many theaters have been given landmark status to protect them from New York's ongoing demolition fever. The heart and soul of the area is Schubert Alley, a private connecting street between 44th and 45th Streets. You can almost smell the greasepaint as you stroll through.

Everybody wants to give their regards to Broadway. But that's not as simple as it sounds. The plays that are surefire hits are sold out months in advance. And then there's the price of a ticket to a Broadway show. We've already broken the $60.00 mark for an orchestra seat, and have even gone into three figures for a few imports from London. Still, there are ways to lower the ante, and your blood pressure, at the same time.

Shakespeare In The Park

Delacorte Theater

Central Park, 81st Street & Central Park West, ☎ *598-7100, 861-7277.* For anyone visiting New York during the summer months, these open-air productions are almost as much fun as the Old Globe used to be. Tickets are free, but the lines are as long as some of the soliloquies, and begin forming well in advance of the 1 p.m. box-office

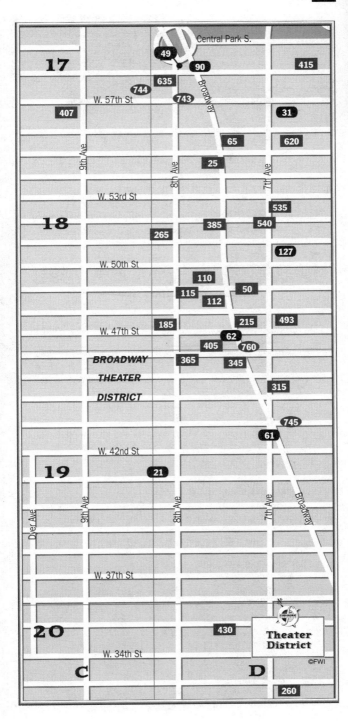

AGENDA ENTERTAINMENT

Museums

| 90 | City Gallery, 2 Columbus Circle | D17 |
| 127 | Whitney Museum of American Art, at Equitable Center: 787 Seventh Av | D18 |

Places of Interest

31	Carnegie Hall, 154 W 57 St.	D18
49	NY Convention & Visitors Bureau, Executive Offices and Information Center, 2 Columbus Circle	D17
61	Times Square, Bway from W 42 to 47 Sts	D19
62	TKTS, W 47 & Bway	D19

Transportation Terminals

| 21 | Port Authority Bus Terminal, 8 Av & W 42 St. | C19 |

Foreign Currency Exchange

743	Chemical Bank, 970 Eighth Av 935-9935	D18
744	Chemical Bank, 969 Eighth Av 974-1594	D17
745	Chemical Bank, 1501 Bway 719-2180	D19
760	Chequepoint USA, 1568 Bway 869-6281	D18

opening. Most New Yorkers make a "happening" out of it and bring a blanket, a bird and a bottle to ease the waiting. Performers here include "big" names eager for a chance to tread the boards with the Bard. Casts are almost always top notch.

ECONOMY AGENDA

Half-Price Theater Tickets

TKTS

If you don't mind standing on line for an hour or so, you can usually buy tickets (cash or traveler's checks only) to shows that are not entirely sold out for half the normal price, plus a $1.50 service charge, however, some are only discounted 25% so be sure to ask first. Tickets are available on the same day as the performance, but aside from a few sold out hits, the selection is surprisingly large. The line moves briskly and if you arrive about half an hour before the booth opens you'll be able to wrap things up within 45 minutes. (The TKTS line is an experience in itself with everyone chatting back and forth about what's really hot and what they've already seen. You're surrounded by countless critics, helping you make a choice.)

TKTS

47th Street and Broadway, ☎ 768-1818.
Mon.–Sat: 3 p.m.–8 p.m. for evening performances on the same day.
Mon & Wed: 12 p.m.–2 p.m. for matinee performances same day.
Sun: 2 p.m.–8 p.m. for both matinee and evening, same day.

TKTS

Two World Trade Center, ☎ 768-1818.
Mon.–Sat: 11 a.m.–5:30 p.m. for all performances, same day. Except, tickets for Wed, Sat, and Sun matinees may be purchased the day before. Tickets for Sunday evening are also sold on Saturday. Aside from the hours being more civilized, lines are generally shorter here, and of course, indoors, to protect you from the elements (both weather and Times Square "hoopla.")

Twofers

Twofers allow you to go to the box office in advance of performance date and buy tickets at half-price (two-for-the-price-of-one). The obvious advantage is that you can plan ahead, although twofers are not always available for the show of your dreams. Twofers may be picked up at the **New York Convention and Visitor's Bureau** *(2 Columbus Circle, or 158 West 42nd Street)*. You can also write in advance to **Hit Shows**, *300 West 42nd Street, N. Y., N.Y. 10036* and enclose a self-addressed stamped envelope. They'll put you on their mailing list. Twofers are also found in hotel lobbies, and some shops and restaurants.

Off Broadway

Because Off-Broadway productions are cheaper to mount and the pay scale is far lower than Broadway, plays are produced here that wouldn't otherwise see the light of day. Some of the most exciting productions of past seasons have originated Off-Broadway. This is where producers can afford to take chances that could never be risked on the starstruck "Great White Way."

Off-Broadway began in Greenwich Village, at the Provincetown Playhouse, where Eugene O'Neil was the resident playwright. Even today most of the Off-Broadway action is in the Village: at the Lortel, the Cherry Lane, the Sullivan Street Playhouse (where "The Fantastics" has been playing for over 35 years), Circle in the Square Downtown, Playwrights' Horizon, etc.

Some of the best-known repertory groups are **Circle Repertory** *(99 Seventh Avenue)*, **Negro Ensemble Company** *(424 West 55th Street)*, **Hudson Guild** *(441 West 26th Street)*, **The Manhattan Theater Club** *(City Center, 131 West 55th Street)*, and the **AMAS Repertory Theater** *(1 East 104th Street)*.

©1994 HENRY MARTIN

*"You know, this would make an excellent
screen play or Broadway musical."*

Perhaps the two most famous Off-Broadway theaters are:

Public Theater
425 Lafayette Street, ☎ 598-7150.
Under the brilliant leadership of its founder Joe Papp, this six-theater complex has launched such hits as "A Chorus Line," and "Cuba and his Teddy Bear" with Robert De Niro. Both of them wound up on Broadway as do many of the workshop productions originating at the

Public. Today the Public Theater maintains the same excitement it did while Papp was alive. Ticket prices are between $20 to $25, but 25% of the seats are held for sale before the performances at one-half of the ticket price. It's called "Quiktix," and tickets may be purchased from 6 p.m. before evening performances, and 1 p.m. prior to matinees.

Other Off-Broadway theaters have sprung up all over town, most notably on 42nd Street between Ninth and Tenth Avenues, which is now called "Theater Row," and is home to companies such as Playwrights Horizons.

Off-Off Broadway

Welcome to the world of experimental theater. Performers here usually work for the credits on their resumes, and in the hopes they can attract an agent to see them on stage. Playwrights who would never be given a chance elsewhere can see their work mounted. One of the most respected of all the stages here is **Cafe La Mama Experimental Theater Club** where Harvey Fierstein first presented "Torch Song Trilogy." **The Ridiculous Theatrical Company** *(100 7th Avenue South)* offers satires and theater of the absurd (☎ *239-6200*).

Music

Saved from the wrecker's ball and restored to its former glory, Carnegie Hall has the best acoustics in the city.

The New York music scene is perhaps the most exciting in the world. The opportunities for musicians to study with top professionals or play in concert halls, ballet theaters, opera houses, and on Broadway are unique. From New York street musicians to chamber-music groups to the New York Philharmonic itself, visitors to the city can treat their ears to the best in sound.

As an added bonus, the lure for musicians to appear before a New York audience is strong enough to bring symphonic orchestras from all over the world. The musical calendar in New York is far more active than those for the other arts. Check the Sunday *New York Times* and you'll find more ads for music than theater.

For recorded information about music and dance events, call **NYC/On Stage** (☎ 768-1818). Toll-free from out-of-state, ☎ 800/STAGE-NY.

Until recently reduced price tickets to music and dance events were available at the TKTS/Bryant Park booth at 42nd Street and Sixth Avenue but it closed and at press time there were no discounted tickets for the music scene in the city. Hopefully this silly decision is just temporary.

Concert Halls

Alice Tully Hall

Lincoln Center, 65th Street and Broadway; ☎ 876-5000.
Located in the Juilliard School, this intimate recital hall has acoustics that best highlight chamber music groups. The Chamber Music Society of Lincoln Center has made it their home.

Avery Fisher Hall

Lincoln Center, 65th Street and Broadway; ☎ 875-5013.
Home of the New York Philharmonic under the baton of Kurt Masur. Season runs Sept.-May. One of the most important orchestras in the world, the New York Philharmonic goes back some 150 years, the longest running musical hit in town. One of the best bargains around is a reduced priced ticket to a Philharmonic open rehearsal. Call ☎ 875-5000 for the rehearsal schedule. During July and August, when the Philharmonic is not in residence, the Mostly Mozart Festival fills the hall.

Brooklyn Academy of Music (BAM)

30 Lafayette Street, Brooklyn; ☎ (718) 636-4100.
This is the oldest musical center in the country. Four separate theaters include a large concert hall for symphony orchestra series, Ballet companies and chamber music. The season runs from fall through the spring.

Carnegie Hall

881 Seventh Avenue (57th Street); ☎ 247-7800.
Saved from the wrecker's ball and restored to its former glory, the acoustics here are still the best in the city. Orchestras from all over the world want to appear on the stage that presented Tchaikovsky, Toscanini and Rachmaninoff.

Town Hall

123 West 43rd Street; ☎ 840-2824
Before Lincoln Center, Town Hall was one of the few concert halls available for recitals and chamber ensembles. Prices here are far less expensive than Lincoln Center.

Tisch Center for the Arts

1395 Lexington Avenue (92nd Street Y); ☎ 996-1100.
There is almost always some musical event going on here drawing the best and most famous soloists in the world. You can write ahead for the schedule of events.

Opera

Probably no area of music in New York has seen such radical changes in the past few years as the opera. Once an art form that was the lapdog of the rich, opera has been redefined as theater where the actors sing and the composers come from the Hall of Fame rather than Tin Pan Alley. The person at the eye of the local operatic hurricane is Beverly Sills who, while director of the New York City Opera, stood up and challenged the Met as the premier company in the city. Located at the **New York State Theater**, right across the plaza at Lincoln Center from the Metropolitan Opera House, the feisty Brooklyn-born coloratura was determined to take new, exciting paths. Not that the Met has been resting on its laurels. This is the place to hear Pavarotti, Domingo, Te Kanawa, and some of the ritziest intermission chat in town. The friendly rivalry between the two opera companies has turned New York into an opera lover's delight.

Amato Opera

319 Bowery (at 2nd Street); ☎ *228-8200.*

Opera for the "man in the street." That may not be politically correct but it sums up the philosophy of this wonderfully energetic little company that has clung to life for years bringing opera at affordable prices to New York. They do all the Italian favorites and they've been selling out since 1948.

Metropolitan Opera House

Lincoln Center, Broadway and 64th Street; ☎ *362-6000.*

Tickets range from $25 to $140, depending on the day of the week and location. However, the budget approach is to arrive at least two hours before curtain and buy standing room for about $25.00. For a real bargain attend one of the free concerts given by the Met in Central Park during the summer. The season is September through May.

New York City Opera

Lincoln Center, New York State Theater, Broadway and 63rd Street; ☎ *870-5570.*

Ticket prices are about half of the Met's. Try to send for seats before you arrive. The season is July through November.

Dance

Of all the performing arts, dance has undergone the most dramatic renaissance in recent years. It used to be that the dance audience in New York comprised Manhattan matrons at obligatory performances of *Swan Lake*, and the *Nutcracker Suite*.

Stand back! The dance scene in New York, nourished by Broadway, opera ballets, and ballet companies such as those founded by Twyla Tharp, Robert Joffrey, Alvin Ailey, and Arthur Mitchell (Dance Theater of Harlem) exploded. Whether you prefer modern, classical, or ethnic, the scene here is vital enough to ensure more choices than you'll have time for.

American Ballet Theatre

Lincoln Center, Metropolitan Opera House, Broadway & 64th Street; ☎ *362-6000.*

The ABT is in the forefront of presenting new ballets, both modern and classical in style. It also has the distinction of having attracted most of the greats who defected from Russia: Nureyev, Makarova, and Baryshnikov himself. The season is May–July.

Drawing by B. Petty; ©1965, 1993, The New Yorker Magazine, Inc.

Brooklyn Academy of Music (BAM)

30 Lafayette Street, Brooklyn; ☎ *(718) 636-4100.*
Dance events go on all year round. The Martha Graham Company usually makes a stop here as well as Jose Limon, and Twyla Tharp.

City Center, The

131 West 55 Street; ☎ *581-1212, 581-7907.*
Home to various dance companies including the Joffrey Ballet, Dance Theater of Harlem, and Alvin Ailey.

Joyce Theater

175 8th Avenue (19th Street); ☎ *242-0800.*
A new dance space that's part of the revitalization of the Chelsea area. The Joyce is home to the Eliot Feld Ballet. Other companies from around the country make stops here.

New York City Ballet

Lincoln Center, New York State Theater, Broadway and 63rd Street;
☎ *870-5570.*
The great George Balanchine was the guiding force behind the New York City Ballet until the day he died. Both he and Jerome Robbins created ballets that are classics in the repertoire, and are repeated over and over again. If you are visiting in December, write in advance for tickets to the "Nutcracker." It's a real dazzler. The seasons are May-June, Nov.–Feb.

Movies

New Yorkers love the movies. All kinds of movies: old, new, cult, classic, and documentary. Many visitors find New York the perfect place to catch up on those small but perfect gems that never make it to the local mall. **Check the newspapers for schedules**. Plan on arriving early since movie houses around town usually have lines before show time. Most first-run houses charge $8 to $8.50 admission, and almost that much for the popcorn.

Places for film buffs to explore include:

Museum of Modern Art, The
> *11 West 53rd Street;* ☎ *708-9400.*
> Included in the price of admission to the museum is a ticket to a screening of a film from MOMA's vast collection of classics. There are two separate theaters. The showings are in the afternoon and evening. (See Museums, page 213.)

Museum of the Moving Image, The
> *35th Avenue at 36th St., Astoria, Queens;* ☎ *(718) 784-4520.*
> Films are often shown here and movie buffs should call for information. (See Museums, page 208.)

Public Theater
> *425 Lafayette Street;* ☎ *598-7171.*
> The Little Theater, part of the Public Theater complex, shows golden oldies and classics almost every weekend afternoon. Admission.

Whitney Museum, The
> *945 Madison Avenue (75th Street);* ☎ *570-3676.*
> The Whitney is used as a showcase for new American filmmakers. Film shown here may be too avant-garde or experimental for regular release. Museum admission fee entitles you to see the film. (See Museums, page 214.)

Television Shows

Free tickets are available from the Visitors and Convention Bureau *(2 Columbus Circle),* ☎ *(800) NYC-VISIT.* If you want to see some of your favorite shows that originate in New York, write ahead to

CBS
> *Ticket Division, 524 West 57th Street, NY, NY 10019.*

NBC
> *30 Rockefeller Plaza, NY, NY 10012.*

ABC
> *Guest Relations, 36A W. 66 Street, NY, NY 10023.*

Museum of Television & Radio, The
> *25 West 52nd Street;* ☎ *621-6800.*
> A modest suggested contribution allows you to recapture the golden age of radio and television. Their archive of American TV and radio broadcasts are available for replay. Pull up one of the consoles and enjoy.

The Club Scene

Any bartender in the city with a singing brother-in-law is a potential Billy Rose and the seedy corner pub, a hot new cabaret. (The mortality rate, as you can imagine, is high.) Before even thinking twice about going to a club, check sources: the *New York Times* (Friday and Sunday), *New York* magazine, the *Village Voice*, or *The New Yorker*. You'll find out who's appearing while you're in town, and at what times.

Always call ahead. Do you need a reservation? Is there a cover charge? Is there a minimum in addition to the cover charge? If they serve food, what kind and at what time? Obviously, you're not expecting a gourmet experience when going to a club, but it's often helpful to know that you can skip dinner, go to the theater, and have a light supper just before the jazz gets hot.

(For opening and closing hours call ahead, they change too frequently to rely on.)

Jazz

B. Smith's
777 Eighth Avenue (47th Street); ☎ *247-2222.*
Chic, split-level restaurant with a rooftop cafe for jazz keeps crowds coming late into the night.

Birdland
2745 Broadway (105th); ☎ *749-2228.*
Upper West Side jazz at its best. Restaurant keeps body and soul together with American and Cajun specialties.

Blue Note
131 West 3rd Street; ☎ *475-8592.*
Deco setting for "le jazz hot." Jazz brunches on weekends.

Bradley's
70 University Place; ☎ *228-6440.*
Intimate wood-panelled room for musicians, neighborhood regulars, and you.

Cafe at the Sign of the Dove
1110 Third Avenue (65th Street); ☎ *861-8080.*
Handsome space next to the restaurants for hor d'oeuvres and jazz.

Chicago B.L.U.E.S.
73 8th Avenue (13th Street); ☎ *924-9755.*
One of the new blues strongholds in the city. Top drawer musicians jam here even when they feel in the Pink.

Knickerbocker Bar & Grill
33 University Place; ☎ *228-8490.*
Burgers, beer, and bassists make this one of the most popular stops in town. Also has a jazz pianist on tap.

Knitting Factory

74 Leonard Street; ☎ *219-3055.*

Funky groups in a funky room make as much noise as possible. It all works to the listener's advantage.

Michael's Pub

211 East 55th Street; ☎ *758-2272.*

This place was put on the map by Woody Allen who usually sits in with the group on Monday nights to exercise his clarinet. Even if he doesn't show up, there are top jazz acts with whom to drown your sorrow.

Red Blazer Too

349 West 46th Street; ☎ *262-3112.*

Dixieland and a look into the past are the highlights in this theater-district club. Lots of nostalgia and toe-tapping for a somewhat more mature crowd.

Sweet Basil

88 Seventh Avenue South (Bleecker Street); ☎ *242-1785.*

Jazz in a mini-greenhouse setting. Plants, white brick walls and some of the town's best jazz groups.

Tavern on the Green—Chestnut Room

Central Park West at 67th Street; ☎ *873-3200.*

A showcase for jazz performers from all over the world in a gorgeous room. There's an after theater menu.

Village Vanguard

178 Seventh Avenue (11th Street); ☎ *255-4037.*

This cellar club is more than 52-years-old and should be designated a jazz museum. The room still echoes with the sounds of John Coltrane, Miles Davis, and Charlie Mingus.

Zinno

126 West 13th Street; ☎ *924-5182.*

Italian food and all that jazz. Almost sounds too good to be true.

Cabarets and Comedy Clubs

Algonquin Hotel—Oak Room

59 West 44th Street; ☎ *840-6800.*

You can't get any more sophisticated than Michael Feinstein or Julie Wilson who have performed here. Veddy upper crust place to be for singers and jazz.

Cafe Carlyle

Carlyle Hotel; Madison Avenue at 76th Street; ☎ *744-1600.*

This is where Bobby Short has been singing the most romantic songs ever written for more years than anyone can remember.

Caroline's

1626 Broadway (49th Street); ☎ *757-4100.*

Some of the brightest comedy acts in town compete for your attention. In the good old days, Pee Wee Herman was one of their showstoppers.

Catch A Rising Star

253 W. 28th Street; ☎ *539-4493.*

They're back! It was always a showcase for the newest comedy stars-to-be. They launched all the greats including Robin Williams.

Chez Josephine
414 West 42nd Street (off Ninth Avenue); ☎ *594-1925.*
Une hommage to the legendary Josephine Baker by one of her sons. Has become a very "in" spot for pre- and post-theater dinner with a middle-of-the-room piano.

Chicago City Limits
1105 1st Avenue; ☎ *888-5233.*
Like the Second City in Chicago, this is drill team group improvisation. The audience throws out suggestions and the group fires away.

Dangerfield's
1118 First Avenue (61st Street); ☎ *593-1650.*
Rodney doesn't perform here regularly but his enthusiasm for giving new comics a break is contagious.

Danny's Skylight Room
Grand Sea Palace; 346 West 46th Street; ☎ *265-8130.*
An unlikely place for great singers and smooth music. Served up with snacks in the back of a Thai restaurant. Only in New York!

Duplex, The
61 Christopher Street; ☎ *255-5438.*
Joan Rivers and Woody Allen were some of the new acts who broke-in here. A Greenwich Village comedy hall of fame.

Improvisation
433 West 34th Street; ☎ *279-3446.*
This is the place that sets the standard for all other comedy clubs. Practically every "big" name comedy performer started here.

Nell's
224 West 14th Street; ☎ *675-1567.*
Victorian elegance mingled with jazz and a very dressy crowd. You can dance all night (didn't Eliza say that?)

Rainbow & Stars
GE Building, 30 Rockefeller Plaza; ☎ *632-5000.*
Same smashing views as the Rainbow Room (see "Restaurants") but this time seen from an elegant cabaret, featuring name performers from Broadway and Hollywood.

S.O.B.'s
204 Varick Street (Houston Street); ☎ *243-4940.*
Mardi Gras-like atmosphere in a big room that echoes the samba and other Sounds of Brazil. There are tastes of Brazil to round out the experience.

Stand-Up New York
236 West 78th Street; ☎ *595-0850.*
A new kid on the comedy block that's found a home on the Upper West Side. Political Comedy Night on Mondays is a neighborhood favorite. Abbe Hoffman (of 1960's student unrest fame) made his club debut here.

West End Cafe
2911 Broadway; ☎ *316-4916.*
Home of the "Beat Generation" in the 1950's is now a Columbia University hangout that gets straight A's for comedy. Draws from the best of the improvisational groups.

Tramps

51 W. 21st Street; ☎ *727-7788.*

The rock and roll bands are drawn to Tramps with the determination of a swarm of musical bees to the grooviest flower around. It's a mega "cool" atmosphere to chill out in.

Country/Western/Folk

Cottonwood Cafe

415 Bleecker Street; ☎ *924-6271.*

Village Tex-Mex food coupled with country and western music. Good ole-boy atmosphere.

Denim & Diamonds

511 Lexington Avenue (48th Street); ☎ *371-1600.*

Barbecue and some of the biggest stars of country music appear here. They also give dancing lessons so you can doe-se-doe with the best of them.

Rodeo Bar

375 Third Avenue; ☎ *683-6500.*

Barbecue coupled with down home country performers make it a top spot for toe-tappers.

Dance Clubs and Nightclubs

Au Bar

41 East 58th Street; ☎ *308-9455.*

As of this writing, THE place to see and be seen. Eurochic at its most demanding. People wait months for a reservation at this disco/dinner club. Be prepared for the dressiest crowd in town.

CBGB

315 Bowery (Bleecker Street); ☎ *473-7743.*

Punk with a capital P. Weird haircuts. Clothes that look as though they've been in an air raid. Always a great sound at this disco for the punk headliners who play here.

China Club

2130 Broadway (75th Street); ☎ *877-1166.*

China blue walls, Chinese wall hangings (and assorted dragons) make this one of the more exotic places to dance and listen to music. A favorite of those in the business, top music stars often drop in and jam.

Crane Club

408 Amsterdam Avenue (78-79 Streets); ☎ *877-3097.*

Hot, hot hot!. The Upper West Side's first really serious club. Wall-to-wall Armani suits and Donna Karan outfits. There's a DJ, food from around the corner at Wilson's, and by 11:30 p.m., enough white wine has been poured to float the bond market.

Limelight

47 West 20th Street; ☎ *807-7850.*

If you're into outrageous, what could be better than a 19th century church turned disco. Stained-glass windows, chapels, and the original church pews surround a crowd of up to 2000. Who said never on Sunday?

Nell's

246 West 14th Street; ☎ *675-1567.*

Uh oh. Doorman discretion on who gets into this ultra chic, ultra "in" dance and supper club. Victorian overstuffed sofas and gilt mirrors give it a British men's club look. Attracts a veddy dressy crowd.

Palladium, The

126 East 14th Street; ☎ *473-7171.*

Opened by the owners of the fabled Studio 54. A huge space crammed with multi-image T.V. screens and 2001 lighting effects.

Rainbow Room, The

30 Rockefeller Center; ☎ *632-5000.*
Do not miss it! See "Restaurants."

Roxy, The

515 West 18th Street; ☎ *645-5156.*
They have the world's largest dance floor (18,000 sq. feet) and they use it for rollerskating to disco as well as regular dancing. They also have a voo-doo night on Thursday's. Pretty unbelievable stuff!!

Tatu

151 East 50th Street; ☎ *753-1144.*
Very theatrical, glamorous atmosphere. Unlike most dance clubs, the food here is not just something to pick at until the next set.

Roseland

239 West 52nd Street; ☎ *247-0200.*
What becomes a legend most? Ballroom dancing is alive and well and polishing the parquet in the same place it's been for 65 years. A great place to carry out your Fred and Ginger fantasies.

Tunnel, The

220 Twelfth Avenue; ☎ *695-7292.*
Not since *Phantom of the Opera* has there been such a spooky environment in which to have fun. It's a huge vaulted chamber that leads off into nothingness (and abandoned train tracks). Think of 15,000 square feet of tunnel with a dance floor to match. Attracts everyone from punkies to Via Veneto lookalikes.

Webster Hall

125 E 11th Street (3rd & 4th Avenues); ☎ *353-1600.*
Five floors, of vibrating, ear-splitting and thoroughly invigorating disco diversion. The Hoi, the Polloi and the just plain weird mix and mingle to a very "cool" sound.

Bars

The bar scene in New York is all things to all people. There are bars for shots of whiskey, bars for singles, bars for lingering over a martini. As a matter of fact, there is a bar almost everywhere you turn around.

Algonquin Lobby Bar

Algonquin Hotel; 59 West 44th Street; ☎ *840-6800.*
If there's a Brit show in town, you'll find members of the cast sitting here. Definitely not for the disco crowd, very sedate, reeks with atmosphere from a bygone era. (see "Hotels").

Bemelmans Bar

Carlyle Hotel; Madison Avenue at 76th Street; ☎ *744-1600.*

A small and cozy very upscale bar named for the Bemelmans murals that decorate the walls.

Fanelli's

94 Prince Street; ☎ *226-9412, 9 a.m.–2 p.m., 7 days.*
It's been around for 125 years or more and the neighborhood still isn't bored with it.

Hard Rock Cafe

221 West 57th Street; ☎ *489-6565.*
"I can't hear you! What did you say-" Bring ear muffs! (See "Restaurants.")

Joe Allen's

326 West 46th Street; ☎ *581-6464.*
A show-biz hangout with a bar that must attract almost everyone appearing on Broadway. (See "Restaurants.")

Chumley's

86 Bedford Street (Grove & Barrow); ☎ *675-4449, 4:30 p.m.–1 a.m., 7 days.*
Unnumbered door, speakeasy ambiance and a true original left over from the 20s. It's a village landmark and so are the burgers.

Lincoln Tavern, The

51 W 64th Street; ☎ *721-8271, 11:30 a.m.–1 a.m., 7 days.*
Attention Martini Mavens
The featured drink on their menu is called the Solid Glass Martini. A wide-mouthed martini glass contains a cube of vodka or gin with a lemon or olive frozen in the center. It comes with extra spirits on the side to act as anti-freeze. Imagine, a martini popsicle.

McSorley's Old Ale House

15 East 17th Street; ☎ *473-9148, 11 a.m.–1 a.m., 7 days.*
New York's oldest bar. Reeks atmosphere and college kids.

Monkey Bar

Elysee Hotel; 60 East 54th Street; ☎ *838-2600.*
Way back in the 30s the Monkey Bar was considered the cat's meow by most of the celebs of the day. At cocktail time you could lift your glass with Talulah Bankhead, Tennessee Williams, or Helen Hayes. It was just waiting to be up-dated, glitzed and polished to its splendid style today. It's the "hottest" bar in town because: Monkey see, Monkey do. (See "Hotels.")

Morgans Bar

Morgans Hotel, 237 Madison (37th Street); ☎ *726-7600.*
Words like eerie, smoky, basement, mysterious, DARK, make this "glitter Ghetto" the new in bar in town. (See "Hotels.")

Oak Bar

Plaza Hotel; Fifth Avenue at 59th Street; ☎ *759-3000.*
This is the one many New Yorkers think is the best hotel bar in town. Jam packed most of the time but worth the crush if you get near a window. (See "Hotels.")

P.J. Clarke's

915 Third Avenue (55th Street); ☎ *355-8857, Noon-4 a.m., 7 days.*
If you had to pick one New York bar for New York atmosphere, this is it.

Penn.-Top Bar

The Peninsula Hotel, 55th and 5th Avenue; ☎ *247-2200.*

Glass all around, way up on the 23rd floor, and almost eye-to-eye with the lights of the city. In the summer you can sip your Negroni outdoors. (See "Hotels.")

Pete's Tavern

129 East 18th Street; ☎ *473-7676, 11:30 a.m.–11 p.m., 7 days.*

Pete's was doing business back in 1864. O. Henry was a regular. Still a popular haunt for writers and struggling actors.

Prince Street Bar

125 Prince Street; ☎ *228-8130, 11:30 a.m.–11 p.m., 7 days.*

This SoHo spot is a favorite with art dealers and shoppers alike. Lots of kitsch to go with the food and drink.

Ritz Carlton Hotel, The

112 Central Park South (59th Street); ☎ *664-7700.*

Very comfortable bar, presided over by the magnificent Norman, one of the best bartenders in town. He mixes a world-class martini as he brings back the lost art of bar talk. (See "Hotels.")

Rainbow Promenade

30 Rockefeller Plaza (65th floor); ☎ *632-5000.*

You've left your tap shoes home and rather than tripping the light fantastic you would prefer to sip it. Well, right outside the Rainbow Room is a fab little bar with the same dynamite view. You can even have a "little meal" as you gaze at the lights. (See "Restaurants.")

Sardi's

234 West 44th Street; ☎ *221-8440, 11 a.m.–midnight, Mon.–Sat.*

This legendary bar in the theater district should be a must on your agenda, however, the legendary restaurant attached to it should be avoided like the plague.

White Horse Tavern

566 Hudson Street (11th Street); ☎ *243-9260, 11 a.m.–2 a.m., 7 days.*

A landmark pub thanks to Dylan Thomas.

Windows on the World, The Greatest Bar on Earth

One World Trade Center; ☎ *524-7000 (See Restaurants).*

Having a drink at an altitude of 107 floors can really give it a kick. But that's nothing compared to the kick of the new Windows on the World bar. Divided into areas it has dancing, little nooks and crannies for a private drink and food stations where sushi, shabu, shabu and oysters are prepared. It's casual, fun and it doesn't cost the price of the Taj Mahal to see the stupendous view. (See "Restaurants.")

Microbreweries

To be a card-carrying member of the '90s you have to tap into the new microbrewery pub scene that's been fermenting in the city for a while. The following are the foamiest, yeastiest and tastiest micros in town. So, roll out the barrel!

Tiphoon Brewery

221 East 54th Street; ☎ *754-9006.*

Westside Brewing Co.

340 Amsterdam Avenue (76 Street); ☎ *721-2161.*

A.S. Gordon's Brewing Co.
> *212 W 79th Street;* ☎ *579-9777.*

Park Slope Brewing
> *356 6th Avenue (5th Street), Brooklyn;* ☎ *(718) 788-1756.*

Zip City Brewing Co.
> *3 W 18th Street;* ☎ *366-6333.*

Bayamo
> *704 Broadway (Washington Place);* ☎ *475-5151.*

Neptune Brewery
> *88 10th Avenue (15th Street);* ☎ *229-2129.*

Chelsea Brewing
> *Pier 59 (West Street at 18th);* ☎ *336-6440.*

Hansen's Time Square Brewery
> *160 W 42nd Street;* ☎ *398-1234.*

Yorkville Brewery
> *1359 First Avenue (73rd Street);* ☎ *517-2739.*

Heartland Brewery
> *35 Union Square West (16th Street);* ☎ *645-3400.*

"It was so depressing. When I go to the theatre, I want to be entertained."

Drawing by Bruce Eric Kaplan; ©1994, The New Yorker Magazine, Inc.

SPORTS

Shea Stadium in Queens is home of the New York Mets and also hosts many concerts throughout the year.

Aside from the daily decathlon most New Yorkers participate in just trying to get across town, New York is a sports lover's dream come true.

Spectator Sports

Baseball

New York's two clubs that seem to make endless "do or die" pennant races every year are the Mets and the Yankees (until Steinbrenner decides to move them to Mars). The baseball season runs from April through October with enough home games scheduled to ensure most visitors a chance to say, "Take me out to the ballgame."

The **Yankees**, of course, date back to the golden years of baseball when teams were made up of legendary superstars such as Joe DiMaggio and Mickey Mantle. The Yankees' home base is **Yankee Stadium** in the Bronx, ☎ 293-6000. Tickets can be purchased at the stadium or through Ticketron outlets. The stadium can be reached by subway: either the IRT No. 4 train to 161st Street station; or the IND D or CC to 161st Street station.

The **Mets**, who were born much later than the Yankees, have captured New Yorker's hearts as the "underdogs" fighting their way to the top of the heap. They appear at **Shea Stadium** in Queens, ☎ *(718) 507-8499*. The stadium can be reached by the IRT No. 7 Flushing Line to Willets Point, Shea Stadium station.

Football

In the "nothing is ever simple in New York" tradition, both of New York's football teams, the **NY Jets** and the **NY Giants** are based in New Jersey at the **Meadowlands Sports Complex**, ☎ *(201) 935-8888*. Not people to hold a grudge, New York football fans trek across the river loyally. The football season is from September through January. The best way to reach the Meadowlands, if you're not driving, is to take a bus from the Port Authority Bus Terminal, *Eighth Avenue at 42nd Street*, ☎ *564-8484*.

Basketball

The home team is the **NY Knickerbockers** (the Knicks) who play at **Madison Square Garden**. The season runs from October to April. College basketball tournaments are also held at the Garden in November and March. Madison Square Garden *(32nd Street and Seventh Avenue*, ☎ *465-6744)* is easily reached by subway or bus.

Boxing

The stellar attraction for New Yorkers is the **Golden Gloves Amateur Tournament** usually held in March of each year. But there are also bouts that go on a couple of times a month, usually on a Thursday. Madison Square Garden *(32nd Street and Seventh Avenue*, ☎ *465-6744)*.

Hockey

One thing you have to say about the **Islanders** and the **Rangers**, New York's hockey jockeys, is that they never skate on thin ice. The Rangers do their figure eights at **Madison Square Garden**, *(32nd & Seventh Avenue*, ☎ *465-6744)*. The Islanders team up on the ice at the **Nassau Coliseum**, Hempstead Turnpike, Uniondale, NY, *(☎ (516) 587-9222)*.

Tennis

The **U.S. Open Tennis Championships** is the superstar event of the year. Originally played in Forest Hills, it has been moved to the *National Tennis Center in Flushing Meadows, Queens, (☎ (718) 760-6200)*. It takes place in September and most of the "greats" of the game appear along with numerous celebrities.

Horseracing

Thoroughbred racing is one of the most popular spectator sports in New York and attracts hordes of people on a regular basis.

Aqueduct, *in Ozone Park, Queens, (☎ (718) 641-4700)* is the largest thoroughbred track in the country. It can be reached by subway: just "take the A train" (IND line) to the Aqueduct stop. The season runs from October through April.

Belmont Park Racetrack *(☎ (718) 641-4700) in Elmont, NY on Long Island* has its season from May-Oct. This is where the last race of the "Triple Crown", the Belmont Stakes is run. Music concerts often take place after the races. Belmont can be reached by the Long Island Railroad. A day at the races can also be arranged by contacting the **New York Racing Association** *(☎ (718) 641-4700)* for directions and racing schedules.

Thoroughbred harness racing is held at **Yonkers Raceway** in *Westchester County,* ☎ *(914) 968-4200* (just outside the city limits), and also at the *Meadowlands in East Rutherford, New Jersey,* ☎ *(201) 935-8500*. Both of these can be reached by bus from the Port Authority Bus Terminal, *Eighth Avenue at 42 Street,* ☎ *564-8484.*

Participant Sports

If you have fidgety feet, the city is alive with activities that run the gamut from jogging to skiing.

Bicycling

There are bike rental stores sprinkled throughout the city that can be found in the New York Yellow Pages, but for a central location that can't be beat, the **Loeb Boathouse in Central Park** *(☎ 517-2233)* has bikes at an hourly or daily rate. Mar.–Nov., 10 a.m.–5 p.m., 7 days.

Golf

Chelsea Sports Complex
> *23rd Street & the Hudson River,* ☎ *336-6000.*
> *Hours: 6 a.m.–11 p.m., Mon.–Fri.; 8 a.m.–9 p.m., Sat.–Sun.*
> Both an indoor and outdoor driving range as well as instructions are provided. There's even a club house and Pro shop.

Ice Skating (Indoor)

At **Sky Rink** *(☎ 336-6000; 6 a.m.–11 p.m., Mon.–Fri.; 8 a.m.–9 p.m., Sat-Sun. Included in admission to sports complex)* there's skating year round. It's part of the new Chelsea Sports Complex (see Chelsea, page 110) located at 23rd Street and the Hudson River. You can skate and gaze out at the serene Hudson River all at the same time. It's also used by the Pros for their practice time.

Ice Skating (Outdoor)

For sheer drama and romance, the skating rink at **Rockefeller Center** *(Fifth Avenue at 50th Street,* ☎ *332-7654), $8.50 adults, $6.75 children, $4 skate rental. 9 a.m.–10 p.m., Mon.–Fri.; 8:30 a.m.–midnight, Sat.–Sun.*, would make Nancy Kerrigan twirl for joy. You can skate in this incredible setting from October-April. The picture postcard time to be here is over the holidays with the giant Christmas tree in the background. Skates are available for rental.

Central Park has its own skating rink that's a bit more casual and relaxed. **Wollman Rink** at *63rd and the East Drive* is open from November-April. Rental skates are also available here.

Horseback Riding

You won't have to give your kingdom for a horse at the **Claremont Riding Academy**, *175 West 89th Street,* ☎ *724-5100, 6:30 a.m.–10 p.m., Mon.–Fri.; 8 a.m.–5 p.m. Sat.–Sun*. You can rent one from them for about $33 an hour, and a reservation is required. The bridal paths in Central Park are just a few blocks away.

Rollerblading

Blades West
> *120 West 72nd Street;* ☎ *787-3911.*
> Weekday and weekend rentals.

EXCURSIONS

Hyde Park is full of Roosevelt family memorabilia, and the library houses FDR's presidential papers.

That's a New Yorker for you. No sooner do you get here than I'm telling you how to get out. The reason is that the northeast corridor of this country offers everything from restorations to roulette. I've suggested some of the most popular destinations for day trips, places frequented by visitors and New Yorkers alike.

This is probably the only time during your trip to New York that a car might come in handy. Check with the desk at your hotel about rental agencies.

New York

The Hudson River Valley

Kykuit—Pocantico Hills, Tarrytown, New York. The Rockefellers called this home until Nelson's death in 1979. The name is the Dutch word for "lookout," because it stands on a cliff overlooking the Hudson. The setting is magnificent. Nelson bequeathed it, in his will, to the National Trust for Historic Preservation, and now you can see this 40-room beaux arts villa in all its glory, including more than 70 works by Calder, Brancusi and Moore. Best of all it can be reached from New York City by boat from May through October. Admission. ☎ *(914) 631-9491*. Call for boat schedules.

The Sleepy Hollow Restorations include Washington Irving's home "*Sunnyside*." The house is filled with memorabilia belonging to Irving. If "The Headless Horseman" was your favorite ghost story, then you probably would love to explore the area where Rip Van Winkle took a nap.

Two miles away on Route 9 is **Philipsburg Manor** near Tarrytown. It was built by a Dutch family in the 1700's who chose to root for the British in the Revolution and subsequently lost their home and land. Everything has been perfectly preserved including a grist mill attached to the house.

Van Cortlandt Manor farther up on Route 9 is close to the town of Croton-on-Hudson. This is a far more extensive restoration than Philipsburg. There's an 18th-century Dutch manor house, a tavern, gardens, fruit orchards, etc. In addition to tours of the house and gardens there are also craft demonstrations.

All three Sleepy Hollow Restorations are about an hour and a half drive from New York City and have an admission fee. Call ☎ *(914) 631-8200* for driving instructions.

Hyde Park was the Roosevelt family home since 1867. FDR was born there in 1882 and returned frequently during his presidential years. It's full of family memorabilia and the library houses FDR's presidential papers. He and Eleanor are buried in the rose garden. Admission. For hours and driving instructions call ☎ *(914) 229-9115*.

West Point is a wonderful day trip that has the added advantage of being accessible by boat. The **Hudson River day line** leaves from Pier 81 *(West 41st Street,* ☎ *630-8120)* at 9:30 a.m. and returns at 6:30 p.m. You sail up the **Hudson River**, under the **George Washington Bridge**, alongside the Palisades (cliffs) of New Jersey, and past some really beautiful scenery. When you get off at **West Point**, there's a sightseeing bus that meets the boat and drives you to the U.S. Military Academy. The museum, chapels, and the monuments are in the midst of 4417 cadets who train at the Academy from which Eisenhower and MacArthur graduated. Military parades are held during the year. For West Point information and schedules call ☎ *(914) 938-3507*. If you plan to visit by car, they will also give you driving instructions.

Nyack is the perfect example of a Hudson River village that came into its own around the turn of the century. Large Victorian houses were built to overlook the river, and the town became a favorite for prosperous New Yorkers who were captivated by the charm of Nyack's setting. (Helen Hayes lived there.) Today, its streets are filled with antique and crafts shops. Artist Edward Hopper was born in Nyack and his boyhood home (Hopper House) is now an art gallery and museum. There are also street fairs held in mid-May, mid-July and mid-October. Call the **Nyack Chamber of Commerce** *(*☎ *(914) 353-2221)* for information and driving instructions.

Long Island

East Hampton

The North Shore of Long Island has become *the* summer destination for New Yorkers to play, be chic, and rub elbows with writers, film-makers and other movers and shakers from the city. The most popular of the summer colonies are the Hamptons (East, South, and West). The Hamptons are still one of the hottest, trendiest, summer scenes.

These tiny 19th century villages can hardly hold all the restaurants, antique shops, craft shops, and boutiques that are crammed into its charming streets and lanes. One of the most famous summer theaters in the area, the **John Drew Theater**, presents first-rate productions that draw actors from Broadway as well as California. The drive from New York takes you past miles of beaches, little fishing ports, and fabulous estates right out of the "The Great Gatsby." For driving instructions and visitor information, write ahead to the **Long Island Tourism and Convention Commission**, *213 Carlton Ave., Central Islip, NY 11722.*

"Great news! Our helipad is finished, so we'll be year-rounders now."

Drawing by D. Reilly; ©1995, The New Yorker Magazine, Inc.

New Jersey

Atlantic City

Las Vegas with salt water taffy. Who amongst us is strong enough to withstand the temptation of ocean views, a boardwalk, miles of good beaches, endless slot machines, and the place where Miss America is crowned? That's what the casino operators said before they decided to resuscitate a down-in-the-dumps seaside resort by making it the legalized gambling capital of the East Coast.

The easiest and most accessible way to travel is by bus from the **Port Authority Bus Terminal** *(42nd Street and Eighth Avenue;* ☎ *564-8484).* The trip takes about 2-1/2 hours. If you're going by car, begin at the **Lincoln Tunnel**, get on the **New Jersey Turnpike** until it leads into the Garden State Parkway. Get off at exit 38 and follow the Atlantic City Expressway into town.

Secaucus

New York's not-so-secret place for discount shopping. Unlike the usual shopping mall, Secaucus has a series of factory outlets and warehouses with discounted clothes, housewares, china, and even gourmet foods.

Designers like Calvin Klein, Donna Karen and many more are crammed into places that look like airplane hangers. Since everything is so spread out, having a car is the most convenient way of getting around. Take the **Lincoln Tunnel** to New Jersey and pick up Route #3 to the Meadowlands Parkway. There will be signs directing you from there. If you don't want to drive, there are shoppers buses that leave from the **Port Authority Bus Terminal** (*42nd Street and Eighth Avenue,* ☎ *564-8484*).

NEW YORK
AGENDA

The ferry to Liberty Island from Battery Park includes a stirring view of Lady Liberty and the city skyline.

One Day Agenda for New York

The following is elemental New York, a taste of the city to include my three top sights and just a whiff of the heady scent of "power." If you have only one day here, this is the best way to spend it.

Start off with a "power breakfast" in the **Edwardian Room** at the Plaza Hotel. It costs a fortune, but the room is gorgeous, the people are gorgeous, the view is gorgeous and even the corn flakes look better than they do in your Little Orphan Annie bowl back home.

Next, if you're a stranger in a strange land, a half-day bus tour (see "Tours") is strongly recommended as the most painless form of orientation. Put on some casual clothes, abolish the word "elitist" from your vocabulary, at least for the morning, and book yourself onto a bus tour. It's worth every penny to ensure that your first view of the city is hassle-free.

After taking a mobile look at the city it's time to start coping with it. Your next move is The Subway! Take the RR train downtown to Whitehall, get off and ask to be pointed in the direction of **Battery Park**. Take the ferry to the **Statue of Liberty**. You can be out and back in about two hours.

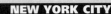

NEW YORK CITY

OFF THE BEATEN PATH LANDMARKS

Some of Manhattan's most fascinating landmark buildings are found in neighborhoods that are slightly off the normal tourist route.

Cathedral of St. John the Divine

Amsterdam Avenue at 112 Street.
Begun in 1892 and estimated to be under construction for another 50 years, this is destined to be the world's largest cathedral. The architecture features Romanesque, Gothic and medieval elements.

Flatiron Building

175 5th Avenue.
Once known as the Fuller Building, it was the tallest building in the world upon its completion in 1902. It was one of the first skyscrapers to use a steel frame and was severely criticized for its triangular shape

Jefferson Market Courthouse

425 6th Avenue.
Once named one of the 10 most beautiful buildings in the country and saved from the wrecking ball by preservationists in the 1950s, it has served as a courthouse, market and branch of the New York Public Library.

Trinity Church

Wall and Broad Streets.
Even though it now stands in the shadow of skyscrapers, this Gothic church still has a commanding presence. Many famous early New Yorkers are buried in the churchyard.

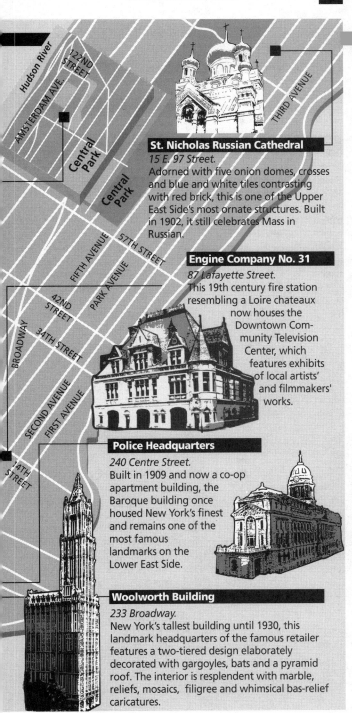

St. Nicholas Russian Cathedral

15 E. 97 Street.
Adorned with five onion domes, crosses and blue and white tiles contrasting with red brick, this is one of the Upper East Side's most ornate structures. Built in 1902, it still celebrates Mass in Russian.

Engine Company No. 31

87 Lafayette Street.
This 19th century fire station resembling a Loire chateaux now houses the Downtown Community Television Center, which features exhibits of local artists' and filmmakers' works.

Police Headquarters

240 Centre Street.
Built in 1909 and now a co-op apartment building, the Baroque building once housed New York's finest and remains one of the most famous landmarks on the Lower East Side.

Woolworth Building

233 Broadway.
New York's tallest building until 1930, this landmark headquarters of the famous retailer features a two-tiered design elaborately decorated with gargoyles, bats and a pyramid roof. The interior is resplendent with marble, reliefs, mosaics, filigree and whimsical bas-relief caricatures.

After your sea voyage, it's time to go uptown again and get a look at New York from the top of the **Empire State** building. You may not see Tom Hanks or Meg Ryan, but you will see the city at its best.

Back on terra-firma, it's time for a stroll up Fifth Avenue. While the most exciting part of Fifth is further uptown, your walk will give you a feel for the pace of the city, and bring you cheek to cheek with the literary lions (their names are Patience and Fortitude) in front of the **New York Public Library** on 42nd Street.

Walk north on Fifth Avenue till you come to 50th Street. You'll see **Saks Fifth Avenue** on the East side and on the West side of 50th Street, the **Chanel Gardens**, which will lead you to the spectacular **RCA Building** (re-named the **G.E. Building** when it was bought by them. The only people who call it that are the GE people!) It's been hailed as the greatest urban complex of the 20th century. Walk down to the sunken plaza for a good look at **Prometheus** and then perhaps a bit of refreshment at the **Sea Grill** or **American Festival Cafe**. Go into the lobby of the **RCA building** to see the glorious murals, and then save a couple of minutes to walk down the street for a glance into **Radio City Music Hall**. Once back on Fifth, you're directly across the street from **Saks Fifth Avenue**, and **St. Patrick's Cathedral**. Walk uptown one block to 630 Fifth Avenue, the **International Building**, with its famous statue of **Atlas** in front. And then, for heaven's sake, go into one of the Fifth Avenue stores between 50th and 59th and buy yourself a present. Have it gift-wrapped and do not open it until you get home.

After a pit stop back at your hotel to pick up the ticket your concierge got you for a Broadway show, you're now ready for a night on the town. Dress casually, i.e., a comfortable dress, or jacket and tie but a sports jacket is fine. You're going to the **Rainbow Room** (see page 189) to wet your whistle at the bar on the 65th floor where the view, and the hors d'oeuvres (pricey), are equally delicious. Don't be afraid of spoiling your appetite: that is dinner. You're going to be very "New York" tonight and "graze" instead of dine. Alternatively, you could dash in for a trendy pre-theater dinner.

By the time the curtain comes down, you're ready to put your money where your mouth is. Here is the city at its most seductive. You can choose **The Four Seasons** (see page 182) for an after-theater supper, the **Carnegie Deli** (see page 180) (remember *Broadway Danny Rose*?) for after-theater heartburn, or go to **Greenwich Village** and hang out at **John's Pizzeria** (see page 118) or **Sweet Basil** (see page 230). And of course, there are comedy clubs, tapas bars, discos, and coffee houses. Whatever you choose may it be tinged with a touch of the bittersweet. You will always wonder, as you review the glories of the evening, "Well, maybe I should have gone to xxx instead?"

Agenda for the 2nd Day of a Two-Day Tour

Now that you've gotten the "superstar" sights under control it's time to branch out and see some of the other wonders that led what's-his-name to "start spreadin' the news."

Begin with breakfast downtown today. If you're feeling really adventurous, a Chinese dim sum breakfast is your best introduction to **Chinatown** (see page 140) or you can get sweet crullers and congee (Chinese oatmeal) from a vendor as you stroll through the winding streets.

Next, it's time to go fight City Hall, right next to Chinatown. This whole area teems with city government and clothing discount stores (see page 139) which for some reason go hand-in-hand.

Wall Street and the **Stock Exchange** (see page 15) are just a hot tip away and walking through the streets where New York began, gives you a lesson in urban development you're not likely to forget.

Plan to have an informal lunch at the **South Street Seaport** while you're experiencing the Piers and museum, and of course gazing at the beauty of the **Brooklyn Bridge**. Then, head for the open sea. Take a boat ride. The **Circle Line** has a three-hour sightseeing cruise around Manhattan. (See Tours.) Or, if time is a problem, a twenty-minute ride on the **Staten Island Ferry** offers a postcard perfect view of the skyline as well as of the **Statue of Liberty**.

Hopefully, it's dusk by now. Time to visit the Observation Deck atop the **World Trade Center** (page 17) for thrilling views of New York as it takes on a rosy glow.

The rest of the late afternoon should be spent enriching your soul back uptown on Fifth Avenue at the **Metropolitan Museum of Art** (see page 212) Don't even think about trying to see all of it. That would take weeks, but you can hit the highlights (The temple of Dendur, Rockefeller collection of Oceanic art, etc.) and when you think a chair is truly the most exciting attraction around, you can cross the street to the **Stanhope Hotel** and revive yourself with one of the best tea's in town.

Okay. Now it's time to pamper yourself. Hop into a cab and head back to your hotel. Dress for dinner. You'll already have made a reservation (because you read *Before You Go*) and this is the night to zero in on the best restaurant you can afford. (see page 177.) It's time to go for the glitz! Give yourself one truly posh nosh before you become cranky about the dirty streets and the deafening traffic.

After dinner, stroll over to 59th and Fifth and take a carriage ride through the park. Stop in for a nightcap at the **Plaza** and then you'll have completed all the requirements for a dazzling second day.

Agenda for the 3rd Day of a 3 Day Trip

Your third day may be your last (in the city, that is). The most popular length of stay here seems to average three days. So, this may be do-or-die until you return to see all the hot spots you've mapped out for your next triumphant tour.

Breakfast at the **Guggenheim Museum** (see page 13) would be a good place to start. They have a wonderful cafe run by Dean and DeLuca where you can get a continental breakfast that won't slow you down as you make your way around the Museum's spiral ramp.

Then you're only a block from Madison Avenue and more shopping treasures than Ali Baba ever dreamed of. I've listed the most exciting ones (see page 65) to exercise your charge cards. If there's time, the **Whitney Museum** (see page 214) is right in the middle of the shopping action at 75th and Madison.

Ease on down the road till you reach **Barney's** (see page 66) and you should be ready for a chic, sophisticated lunch at Mad 61 in the basement.

After, walk back to Fifth Avenue and continue window or wanton shopping till you reach **Saks** at 50th Street. You've just seen some of the most glamorous merchandise in any city in the world, now it's time to check out a few more neighborhoods.

Take a cab to Spring Street and West Broadway. Voila, you're right in the middle of **SoHo**. It's up to you to explore in and out, up and down, because shops and restaurants are spread out. If you happen to finish around tea time (for us anytime is tea time) drop in at **T**, in the basement of the SoHo Guggenheim (see page 211). Green Street will take you down to **TriBeCa** on foot, or if your imminent collapse is just around the corner, cab it. TriBeCa is even trendier than SoHo because it still has a bit of grit around its edges.

Dinner should be in the **Lincoln Center** area (see page 100) so that you can arrive in time to see Mimi fall in love with Rudolfo.

My best apres opera treat is a snack at **Cafe des Artiste's Parlor** (see page 201) for smoked salmon or some devastating dessert that could have changed Mimi's whole life.

The Statue of Liberty weighs 225 tons, each eye is two feet, six inches wide, and the tip of the torch is 395 ft. above sea level.

Children's Agenda

New York is a kid's paradise. Unlike London or Paris, no one expects them to behave or show off their manners or look like something out of Dickens. Since this is a place where the adults aren't polite, have questionable manners and sometimes look like contestants from "Let's Make a Deal," kids fit right into the main stream of the New York "attitude."

The following is an Agenda in no particular order (since kids have unpredictable needs) that can be used to make up an exciting day for the biggest small fry:

American Museum of Natural History, The
See page 208.

Central Park Zoo, The
See page 48.

Central Park Carousel, The

Canoeing on the Central Park Lake

Children's Museum of Manhattan, The
See page 251.

Statue of Liberty, The
See page 6.

Chelsea Sports Complex
See page 110.

Intrepid Sea-Air-Space Museum
See page 251.

Adventure Playgrounds
Central Park.

Serendipity
See page 190.

F.A.O. Schwarz
See page 49.

Rumpelmayers' Cafe
50 Central Park South

Music Hall, The

Wollman Rink
Central Park.

Rockefeller Center Ice Rink
See page 239.

Forbidden Planet
See page 172.

Big City Kite Co., Inc.
See page 79.

Chinatown

Hard Rock Cafe
See page 60.

Planet Hollywood
See page 61.

Mickey Mantle's Restaurant
  42 Central Park South.

Peppermint Park
  1225 First Avenue, 66th Street.

Royal Canadian Pancake House
  1004 2nd Avenue, 53rd Street.

Harley Davidson Cafe
  1370 6th Avenue (56th Street).

Bronx Zoo, The
  Bronx River Pkway at Fordham Road; ☎ *(718) 367-1010.*

Tavern on the Green
  See page 195.

New York Skyride/Empire State Building
  See page 7.

Sony Plaza Wonder Lab
  Madison Avenue; 55th/56th Street; 833-8100.

Christmas Agenda

The Christmas season is "Magic Time" in New York. The whole city seems to smile and dress itself in a million twinkling lights. The weather is just cold enough for hot chocolate after shopping, but not bitter enough to keep everyone from standing in front of the fairytales that miraculously come to life in Department store windows. Pity the poor souls around the country who celebrate Christmas at the side of their pools.

This agenda should be spread over your time here so that you can enjoy the city without the pressure of having to do everything in one day.

Breakfasts should be eaten at a department store, so that Christmas shopping doesn't take up the whole day. **Bloomingdale's** has a simple cafeteria, but **Saks** has an elegant room that overlooks Fifth Avenue, **Rockefeller Center** and **St. Patrick's Cathedral**. That has to be the top choice for holiday scenery.

The department store windows can be accomplished as you shop, but don't be surprised at having to join a line. **Lord and Taylor** has the most extravagant displays, usually Victorian city scenes that revolve. The best Santa in the city holds court at **Macy's** *(34th Street & Herald Square)*.

In New York, we're always dreaming of a white Christmas so if there is snow or even the remains of snow in Central Park, a carriage ride will take you right back to the turn of the century. When you return you can go over to Rockefeller Center to watch the skaters and the lights on the giant tree, glitter over the ice. Sometimes they even have carolers in the evening. Would this make Tiny Tim cry or what? The most breathtaking indoor tree can be seen at the **Metropolitan Museum of Art** (see page 212). It lights up the **Medieval Sculpture Hall**.

Down at the **Public Library** at 42nd and Fifth, the very literary lions in front, sport huge wreaths between their paws. The shop inside the Library has wonderful cards and gifts for the reader on your list. If you're still looking for that special star to go on the top of the tree, wholesale ornaments can be bought once a year, three weeks prior to Christmas from the wholesale collection of **Kurt Adler's Santa's World**, *1107 Broadway;* ☎ *924-0900.*

If you've planned ahead, you probably have center orchestra seats for the Nutcracker Ballet at the **New York Ballet** (Lincoln Center), but if you've forgotten, then the **Radio City Music Hall** has a dynamite Christmas pageant and Rockette review that will really ring your jingle-bells.

Some of the hotels have a Nutcracker Tea or holiday menu to match the smashing decorations in their lobbies.

The churches give special musical offerings in the late afternoon and evening, and nothing is as exciting as hearing the Hallelujah Chorus live on Christmas Eve.

Peace on Earth, even in New York, no less.

Drawing by Mankoff; ©1984, The New Yorker Magazine, Inc.

AGENDA TOURS
OF NEW YORK

The bronze statue of a bull, symbol of Wall Street, is near the post office and Federal Hall National Monument.

Adventures on a Shoestring

300 W 53rd Street; ☎ *265-2663.*

All manner of wonderful excursions to see offbeat New York. Very inexpensive and very delightful. Call for info and price.

Art Tours of Manhattan

Princeton, NJ: ☎ *(609) 921-2647.*

East Village, SoHo and Madison Avenue galleries are included as well as visits to artist's studios. Since tours are customized for the individual or small groups, prices vary. They start at $35 and go to $75 depending upon time and admission costs. Some include lunch.

Big Onion Walking Tours

☎ *439-1090.*

Columbia University graduate students will uncover the wonders of New York layer by layer, peeling the onion to its very historic heart. Call for hours and price.

Circle Line Around Manhattan

Pier 83 at West 43rd Street; ☎ *563-3200.*

Three-hour look at Manhattan from the rivers that surround it. A guide points out the sights. Mar. thru Nov. Daily sailings, call for hours and price.

Gray Line Tours

900 Eighth Avenue; ☎ *397-2600.*

A wide range to choose from, including day tours around the city, harbor cruises, shorter harbor tours, birds-eye views of the city from a helicopter. Also foreign language tours. Call for hours and price.

Museum of the City of New York Walking Tours, The

☎ *534-1672, ext. 206.*

An overview of NYC's past. Walks have covered two centuries on the Lower East Side, the financial district, the East and West Village, etc. Tours last about four hours. Sat and Sun. Call for information and price.

Doorway to Design

1441 Broadway; ☎ *221-1111.*

Custom tours of New York's art, antiques, fashion, and theater worlds. An expert in each takes you on an in-depth tour behind the scenes to see professionals at work. Call for information and price.

Big Apple Greeter

☎ *669-2896.*

New Yorkers from varied backgrounds share with you this favorite New York experience. The greeters are all volunteers so this service is free of charge. Best of all they match the Greeter and visitor by language spoken and interests.

Harlem Your Way

Tours Unlimited, ☎ *690-1687.*

A two-and-a-half to three hour walking tour of Central Harlem that includes the Schomberg Center, Abyssinian Baptist Church, Strivers; Row, and the Apollo Theater. Daily from 1:30 p.m., $25.

Lower East Side Tenement Museum

Museum Walking Tours, ☎ *431-0233.*

One to two hour walks that take one back to the days of immigrants' struggles to carve out an existence in the New World. Hope, dreams, and the overflowing pickle barrels of this amazing area of New York are re-created.

Shortline Tours

166 W 46th Street; ☎ *397-2620.*

Offers a series of city tours as well as excursions to Atlantic City and Niagara Falls. Price range from $15 (two hours) to $267 (full day including flight to and from Niagara Falls.)

Sidewalks of New York

☎ *517-0201.*

Sam Stafford conducts theme tours of New York. His "Hollywood on the Hudson" is one of the most popular; he leads his group to apartment buildings and town houses (outside only); of stars living in Manhattan. Two hours (no reservations) $10.

HARLEM GOSPEL TOURS

AGENDA FOR
TRAVEL
ARRANGEMENTS

Times Square at 42nd St. is famous for its traffic-stopping signs.

Having a successful trip requires as much planning and imagination as a successful marriage. Because travel is an equally maddening combination of pleasures and pitfalls, what you do *before you go* is your best insurance.

The first travel arrangement you have to make is in your head. Take a few minutes to decide what you want to do and see in New York. Make your own agenda for the most important things, not just "shopping" or "theater" but which shops and what shows. Same thing with restaurants. *Do not* leave all of these choices to be made once you arrive. Why spend precious Manhattan minutes planning instead of experiencing? You can access all the information needed to make a decision before you go.

Once your travel reservations are confirmed, get a copy of the Sunday *New York Times*, *The New Yorker*, and/or *New York Magazine*. Go to the library and find out what articles have appeared recently on New York. Contact the **New York Convention & Visitors Bureau**, *2 Columbus Circle, New York, NY 10019*, ☎ *(212) 397-8200* for brochures. We promise that your advance planning efforts will pay off by allowing you to arrive in town with reservations at Lutece and tickets to "Rent."

New York Weather

The only thing predictable about New York's weather is its unpredictability. With the exception of a very short spring and an invigorating fall, this city may well have one of the worst climates on the planet. It is somehow always too hot or too cold. New York weather, like New York traffic, is a blight to be endured. The good news is that practically nothing you want to do as a visitor is dependent upon climate. Except, you need one clear day in order to see forever from the **Empire State Building** or **World Trade Center**, and that's about it.

Probably the very best times to be in New York, if you have any choice in the matter, are October and May. The former has crispy, brisk days and the latter offers the full pleasures of spring. The next best time, despite the incredible crowds, is between Thanksgiving and New Year's. New York puts on quite a show: the buildings on Fifth Avenue are decorated, shop windows are filled with marvelous displays and somehow the crosstown traffic is no longer a major topic of conversation. If you have no other choice but to come during summer, don't let the weather stop you, but be forewarned: the combination of heat and humidity in New York can dampen the most ardent spirits.

Average Monthly Temperatures °F

Jan	Feb	Mar	Apr	May	Jun	Jul	Aug	Sep	Oct	Nov	Dec
38	40	48	61	71	80	85	84	77	67	54	42

Dress Code

Some New Yorkers like to dress up, others like to dress down. You'll go to the theater and see people in formal attire sitting next to a couple in jeans. Frankly, that's okay for New Yorkers who don't think twice about such things, but you, as a visitor, might not feel at ease with either extreme. Remember, New York is the fashion capital of the country. Upscale restaurants are filled with beautifully dressed "beautiful people."

There's a wonderful new phrase, "designer casual" and it applies to many New York situations. From October through April you'll need sweaters, parkas, or topcoats depending upon the weather. Even in summer, because everything is air-conditioned (except the taxis), you'll want a shawl or sweater. Otherwise, summer is a time for your lightest clothes. Unlike many other cities, New York doesn't cool down considerably at night.

Since walking is often the preferred method of locomotion around the city, it's imperative that your shoes be comfortable.

Notes for Visitors from Abroad

If New York is your port of entry into the U.S., you'll need a valid passport and visa. Check with your local travel agent, airline, or closest U.S.

Embassy. Vaccination certificates are not required. You should also check on customs regulations since they are quite specific.

If you have currency other than U.S. dollars, do *not* expect it to be accepted anywhere except a bank. Plan to convert enough money so that you will arrive in New York with US$100. This amount should see you through all entry situations and well into your first day so that you're not pressed to exchange money immediately.

Hotel exchange rates are never as good as those at a bank. However, New York banks are open generally only Mon.–Fri, 9 a.m.–3 p.m. Even worse, most banks are not equipped to handle foreign currency transactions. In addition to banks, exchange facilities are offered by **Thomas Cook** *(29 Broadway;* ☎ *635-0540, 41 East 42nd Street;* ☎ *883-0400, 630 Fifth Avenue;* ☎ *757-6915),* But the best place for currency exchange is **Checque Point USA** *(551 Madison Avenue at 55th Street,* ☎ *980-6443)* because it's open seven days a week: Mon.–Fri., 8 a.m.–7 p.m.; Sat.–Sun., 10 a.m.–7.30 p.m., Sun. 10 a.m.–6 p.m. There are also several other branches around the city. Your hotel will have a complete list.

Money Manners

While most places accept credit cards and/or traveler's checks, be certain to inquire in advance. Policies change, shops may not accept the particular card you had in mind, etc. Increasingly, New York shops accept checks with proper identification. Before you swoop down to the Lower East Side on a Sunday morning when all the banks are closed, be sure you know how you're going to pay, and that you have a safe place to carry your money.

You never have to worry about tipping in a restaurant if you adopt the system used by many New Yorkers: simply, double the tax (.0875) and round it off. It works out to 17 1/2% which is perfectly fine if the service was up to par.

Cab drivers expect 15% to 20% of the fare. Porters and bellmen usually get $2 per bag. You may wish to be more generous if the bags are heavy or the distance far.

Note: For New York City directory assistance, dial 411. Even though Brooklyn and Queens are in a different area code, you can get directory assistance for the boroughs by dialing 411. For direct dial international calls, dial 011 plus the country code. For our visitors from other English-speaking countries, country codes are:

Australia, 61

Canada, 1

New Zealand, 64

Great Britain, 44

Use caution choosing a public phone on the street for long distance calls. Some of them belong to private companies who charge more expensive long distance rates than the normal street phones. It's difficult to tell them apart.

LIST OF ATTRACTIONS

LIST OF HOTELS

Hotel	Price	Rating	Pg.
Algonquin, The	$245–$425	★★	22
Beekman Tower	$119–$330		26
Dumont Plaza	$119–$330		26
Eastgate Tower	$119–$330		26
Essex House, The	$310–$500	★★★	23
Four Seasons, The	$490–$630	★★★	24
Franklin, The	$135–$145	★	24
Gorham, The	$175–$195	★	25
Hostelling International, N.Y.	$60–$90		35
Hotel Beverly	$149–$179	★	23
Hotel Elysee	$225–$825	★★★	23
Hotel Olcott	$95–$115	★	27
Hotel Plaza Athénéé	$285–$590	★★★	30
Hotel Wales	$165–$225	★★	33
Hotel Westbury	$285–$450	★★★	33
Larchmont Hotel	$70–$90	★	25
Lowell, The	$295–$495	★★★	25
Lyden Gardens	$119–$330		26
Lyden House	$119–$330		26
Manhattan East Suite Hotels	$119–$330	★★	26
Mark, The	$325–$500	★★	26
Morgans	$220–$475	★★	27
New York Palace, The	$275–$450	★★★	27
Paramount Hotel	$180–$380	★★	28
Peninsula, The	$340–$700	★★★	29
Pierre, The	$375–$595	★★★	29
Plaza Fifty	$119–$330		26
Plaza, The	$235–$650	★★★	29
Ritz-Carlton, The	$305–$600	★★★	30
Roger Smith Hotel, The	$195–$225	★	30
Royalton	$285–$400	★★	31
Shelburne Murray Hill	$119–$330		26
SoHo Grand Hotel	$199–$949	★★	32
Southgate Tower	$119–$330		26
St. Regis	$425–$650	★★★	31
Surrey Hotel	$119–$330		26
Waldorf-Astoria, The	$290–$600	★★★	33
Wyndham Hotel	$130–$210	★★★	34

LIST OF RESTAURANTS

Restaurant	Price	Rating	Pg.
"21"	$$$	★★	191
13 Barrow Street	$$		119
44	$$$	★★	204
44	$$$	★★	199
7th Regiment Armory	$$		77
A.B.C. Cafe; A.B.C. Carpet	$		108
Aja	$$$		109
Akbar	$$		77
America	$		109
American Festival Cafe			56
Anglers & Writers		★	201
Anglers & Writers	$$		120
Aquavit			55
Arcadia	$$$		75
Arizona 206	$$		81
Arqua	$$$		131
Au Manderin	$$$		148
B&H Dairy Restaurant	$		124
Baby Jake's	$$		122
Baci	$$		97
Barbetta	$$$	★★★	204
Barney Greengrass	$		98
Barolo	$$$		129
Becco	$$	★★	204
Benito I	$$		142
Bergdorf Goodman	$$		55
Big Wong	$		140
Blue Ribbon	$$$		131
Boathouse Cafe	$$	★★	193
Bolo	$$$		110
Bridge Cafe	$$		148
Bright Food Shop	$		114
Bryant Park Grill	$$	★★	179
Cafe Botanica		★★	202
Cafe Con Leche	$		97
Cafe Crocodile	$$		83
Cafe Des Artistes	$$$	★★★	179
Cafe Gitane	$		142
Cafe Pierre	$$$	★★	198
Cafe Tabac	$$$		124
Caffe Dante	$		119
Caffe Reggio	$		119

Restaurant	Price	Rating	Pg.
Caffe Roma	$$		143
Cals	$$		109
Campagna	$$$		109
Canton	$$		142
Capsuto Freres	$$$		134
Carlyle, The	$$$	★★	200
Carmine's	$$	★	204
Carnegie Delicatessen	$$	★	180
Chanterelle	$$$		132
Chat'N'Chew	$		58
Chelsea Central	$$		114
Chez Brigitte	$		118
China Fun	$		95
China Grill			56
Chumley's	$$		118
City Bakery	$		57
Claire	$$$		114
Coco Puzzo	$$$		75
Coffee Shop	$		108
Contrapunto	$$		81
Crab House, The	$$	★	193
Cupping Room Cafe, The	$$		130
Custard Beach			119
da Umberto	$$$		113
Dallas BBQ	$		94
Daniel	$$$$	★★★	180
Dawat	$$	★★	181
E. J.'s Luncheonette	$		81
Ecco	$$$		149
El Teddy's	$$		130
Elaine's	$$$		84
Elio's	$$$		84
Emack and Bolio's	$		97
Empire Diner	$$		114
Eureka Joe	$		57
Fantino	$$$	★	199
Ferrara's	$$		143
Fifty Seven Fifty Seven	$$$	★★★	197
Fiorello's Roman Cafe	$$		100
Follonico	$$		110
Four Seasons, The	$$$	★★★	200
Four Seasons, The	$$$	★★★	203
Four Seasons, The	$$$$	★★★	182
Fraunces Tavern Restaurant	$$$		149
Frico	$$	★★	204
Friend of a Farmer	$	★	203
Friend of a Farmer	$$		109

Restaurant	Price	Rating	Pg.
Gabriel's	$$$		100
Gascogne	$$$		114
Gino	$$		80
Godiva	$$		94
Golden Unicorn	$$$		141
Good Enough To Eat	$	★	202
Good Enough To Eat	$$		98
Gotham Bar & Grill, The	$$$	★★★	183
Gramercy Tavern	$$$		109
Great Shanghai	$		140
Grotto Azzura	$$		142
Harry Cipriani			55
Home	$$		119
Hotel Pierre	$$$	★★★	200
Hudson River Club, The	$$$	★★	194
Il Cortile	$$$		142
Il Mulino	$$$	★★★	185
Indochine			133
Isabella	$$		95
Jerry's	$		130
Jewel of India	$$	★★	204
Joe Allen	$$	★★	205
Joe's Shanghai	$		141
John's Pizzeria	$		118
Katz's	$		136
Kelly and Ping	$		130
Kiev Coffee Shop, The	$		123
Kokachin	$$$		198
L'Ecole	$$		133
La Luncheonette	$$$		113
La Metairie	$$$		119
La Tour D'Or	$$$		149
Layla	$$		130
Le Bernardin	$$$$	★★★	178
Le Bistro de Maxims	$$$		74
Le Madri	$$$		113
Le Regience	$$$	★	198
Le Relais	$$$		75
Lepinasse	$$$	★★★	199
Les Celebrites	$$$$		197
Les Halles	$$$		110
Lincoln Square Coffee Shop	$		101
Lipstick Cafe	$$		81
Lobster Club, The	$$		76
Lotfi's	$$	★	205
Lowell, The		★★	200
Lucky Strike	$$$		134

Restaurant	Price	Rating	Pg.
Luma	$$		114
Luna	$$		142
Lusardi's	$$		83
Lutece	$$$	★★★	183
Main Street	$$		95
Mandarin Court	$		140
March	$$$$	★★★	184
Marks	$$$	★	198
Matthew's	$$$		81
Mayrose	$	★★	202
McSorley's Old Ale House	$		123
Mesa Grill	$$$		58
Mingala West	$$		97
Miracle Grill, The	$$		123
Mitali	$		123
Mocca	$		84
Monkey Bar, The	$$$	★★	197
Monsoon	$		98
Montrachet	$$$		130
Moondog	$		118
Mortimer's	$$$		80
Mughlai	$$		95
Museum Cafe			95
Nector Coffee Shop			75
NHA Trang	$		142
Nobu	$$$$		134
Noodle Town	$		140
O'Neals	$$		101
Odeon, The	$$$		129
Old Devil Moon	$$		123
Ollie's Noodle Shop and Grill	$		102
Ollie's	$	★	205
One If By Land, Two If By Sea	$$$		119
Opera Espresso	$		101
Orso	$$	★★★	205
Osteria Del Circo	$$$	★★	186
Oyster Bar	$$$	★★	186
Palm	$$$	★★	187
Pamir	$$		83
Park Avenue Cafe	$$$		77
Park Bistro	$$$$		110
Parlor at Cafe des Artistes, The		★★	201
Patria	$$$	★★★	188
Peking Duck House	$$		141
Peninsula, The		★★★	202
Peppermint Park	$		87
Petaluma	$$$		87

Restaurant	Price	Rating	Pg.
Pete's Tavern	$$		108
Petrossian	$$$$	★★	188
Picholine	$$$		101
Pig Heaven	$$		83
Pink Teacup, The	$	★★	202
Pink Teacup, The	$$		118
Pipeline			148
Plaza, The		★★★	201
Plaza, The	$$$	★★★	200
Po's	$$		119
Pravda	$$$$		133
Provence	$$$		131
Quatorize Biz	$$		83
Rain	$$$		95
Rainbow Room, The	$$$	★★★	189
Ratner's			136
Red Tulip, The	$$		86
Regency Hotel, The		★	201
Regency Hotel, The		★★★	202
Republic	$		108
Restaurant Florent	$$		120
Rikyu	$$		94
River Cafe, The	$$$	★★	194
S. G. Mellon	$$		81
Saks Fifth Avenue			56
Sammy's Famous Romanian Jewish Steakhouse	$$		136
Sant Ambroeus	$$		75
Sarabeth's Kitchen	$$		97
Scaletta	$$		95
Screening Room, The			131
Sea Grill, The	$$$	★★★	194
Second Avenue Deli	$$		124
Serendipity 3	$$	★	190
Sette Mezzo	$$		80
Sfuzzi	$$		101
Shark Bar	$$		97
Sign of the Dove, The	$$$	★★	191
Silver Palace	$		141
Sistina			83
Sofia Fabulous Pizza	$$		75
SoHo Kitchen and Bar	$$		130
Soup Burg			75
Soup Kitchen International	$	★	206
Steak-Frites	$$		58
Sushisay	$$$		74
Sween 'N' Tart Cafe	$		140

Restaurant	Price	Rating	Pg.
Takashimaya		★★★	201
Tavern on the Green	$$$	★★	195
Tea & Sympathy		★★	201
Tea Box Cafe at Takashimaya, The			55
The Nice Restaurant	$$		140
The Saloon	$$		100
Three of Cups	$$		124
Tibet Shambala	$		98
TriBeCa Grill	$$$		131
Triple 8 Palace	$$$		141
Trois Jean	$$		80
Trump Tower	$		55
Typhoon Brewery	$$$		74
Ukrainian East Village Restaurant, The	$		123
Union Square Cafe	$$$	★★★	192
Veselka	$		123
Veselka	$	★	202
Viand Coffee Shop	$		74
Vinnie's Pizza	$		96
Virgil's Real Barbecue	$$	★★	205
Vong	$$$		80
Voulez Vous	$$		87
West 63rd Street Steakhouse	$$$		101
White Horse Tavern	$		120
Windows on the World	$$$	★★★	195
World Yacht Cruises		★	196
Yellowfingers	$		81
Yonah Schimmel	$		136
Zeppole	$$		131

INDEX

Order Your Guide to Travel and Adventure

Title	Price	Title	Price
Fielding's Alaska Cruises and the Inside Passage	$18.95	Fielding's Indiana Jones Adventure and Survival Guide™	$15.95
Fielding's America West	$19.95	Fielding's Italy	$18.95
Fielding's Asia's Top Dive Sites	$19.95	Fielding's Kenya's Best Hotels, Lodges and Homestays	$19.95
Fielding's Australia	$18.95	Fielding's Las Vegas Agenda	$16.95
Fielding's Bahamas	$16.95	Fielding's London Agenda	$14.95
Fielding's Baja California	$18.95	Fielding's Los Angeles	$16.95
Fielding's Bermuda	$16.95	Fielding's Mexico	$18.95
Fielding's Best and Worst	$19.95	Fielding's New Orleans Agenda	$16.95
Fielding's Birding Indonesia	$19.95	Fielding's New York Agenda	$16.95
Fielding's Borneo	$18.95	Fielding's New Zealand	$17.95
Fielding's Budget Europe	$18.95	Fielding's Paradors, Pousadas and Charming Villages	$18.95
Fielding's Caribbean	$19.95	Fielding's Paris Agenda	$14.95
Fielding's Caribbean Cruises	$18.95	Fielding's Portugal	$16.95
Fielding's Caribbean on a Budget	$18.95	Fielding's Rome Agenda	$16.95
Fielding's Diving Australia	$19.95	Fielding's San Diego Agenda	$14.95
Fielding's Diving Indonesia	$19.95	Fielding's Southeast Asia	$18.95
Fielding's Eastern Caribbean	$17.95	Fielding's Southern California Theme Parks	$18.95
Fielding's England including Ireland, Scotland and Wales	$18.95	Fielding's Southern Vietnam on Two Wheels	$15.95
Fielding's Europe	$19.95	Fielding's Spain	$18.95
Fielding's Europe 50th Anniversary	$24.95	Fielding's Surfing Australia	$19.95
Fielding's European Cruises	$18.95	Fielding's Surfing Indonesia	$19.95
Fielding's Far East	$18.95	Fielding's Sydney Agenda	$16.95
Fielding's France	$18.95	Fielding's Thailand, Cambodia, Laos and Myanmar	$18.95
Fielding's France: Loire Valley, Burgundy and the Best of French Culture	$16.95	Fielding's Travel Tools™	$15.95
Fielding's France: Normandy & Brittany	$16.95	Fielding's Vietnam including Cambodia and Laos	$19.95
Fielding's France: Provence and the Mediterranean	$16.95	Fielding's Walt Disney World and Orlando Area Theme Parks	$18.95
Fielding's Freewheelin' USA	$18.95	Fielding's Western Caribbean	$18.95
Fielding's Hawaii	$18.95	Fielding's The World's Most Dangerous Places™	$21.95
Fielding's Hot Spots: Travel in Harm's Way	$15.95	Fielding's Worldwide Cruises	$21.95

To place an order: call toll-free 1-800-FW-2-GUIDE
(VISA, MasterCard and American Express accepted)
or send your check or money order to:
Fielding Worldwide, Inc., 308 S. Catalina Avenue, Redondo Beach, CA 90277
http://www.fieldingtravel.com
Add $2.00 per book for shipping & handling (sorry, no COD's),
allow 2–6 weeks for delivery

International Conversions

TEMPERATURE

To convert °F to °C, subtract 32 and divide by 1.8. To convert °C to °F, multiply by 1.8 and add 32.

Fahrenheit	Centigrade	
230°	110°	
220°		
210°	100°	Water Boils
200°	90°	
190°		
180°	80°	
170°		
160°	70°	
150°		
140°	60°	
130°		
120°	50°	
110°		
100°	40°	
90°	30°	
80°		
70°	20°	
60°		
50°	10°	
40°		
30°	0°	Water Freezes
20°	-10°	
10°		
0°	-20°	
-10°		
-20°	-30°	
-30°		
-40°	-40°	

WEIGHTS & MEASURES

LENGTH

1 km	=	0.62 miles
1 mile	=	1.609 km
1 meter	=	1.0936 yards
1 meter	=	3.28 feet
1 yard	=	0.9144 meters
1 yard	=	3 feet
1 foot	=	30.48 centimeters
1 centimeter	=	0.39 inch
1 inch	=	2.54 centimeters

AREA

1 square km	=	0.3861 square miles
1 square mile	=	2.590 square km
1 hectare	=	2.47 acres
1 acre	=	0.405 hectare

VOLUME

1 cubic meter	=	1.307 cubic yards
1 cubic yard	=	0.765 cubic meter
1 cubic yard	=	27 cubic feet
1 cubic foot	=	0.028 cubic meter
1 cubic centimeter	=	0.061 cubic inch
1 cubic inch	=	16.387 cubic centimeters

CAPACITY

1 gallon	=	3.785 liters
1 quart	=	0.94635 liters
1 liter	=	1.057 quarts
1 pint	=	473 milliliters
1 fluid ounce	=	29.573 milliliters

MASS and WEIGHT

1 metric ton	=	1.102 short tons
1 metric ton	=	1000 kilograms
1 short ton	=	.90718 metric ton
1 long ton	=	1.016 metric tons
1 long ton	=	2240 pounds
1 pound	=	0.4536 kilograms
1 kilogram	=	2.2046 pounds
1 ounce	=	28.35 grams
1 gram	=	0.035 ounce
1 milligram	=	0.015 grain